Taking Our Time

Feminist Perspectives
on Temporality

the ATHENE series

General Editors

Gloria Bowles

Renate Klein

Janice Raymond

Consulting Editor

Dale Spender

The ATHENE SERIES assumes that all those who are concerned with formulating explanations of the way the world works need to know and appreciate the significance of basic feminist principles.

The growth of feminist research has challenged almost all aspects of social organization in our culture. The ATHENE SERIES focuses on the construction of knowledge and the exclusion of women from the process—both as theorists and subjects of study— and offers innovative studies that challenge established theories and research.

ON ATHENE—When Metis, goddess of wisdom who presided over all knowledge was pregnant with ATHENE, she was swallowed up by Zeus who then gave birth to ATHENE from his head. The original ATHENE is thus the parthenogenetic daughter of a strong mother and as the feminist myth goes, at the "third birth" of ATHENE she stops being Zeus' obedient mouthpiece and returns to her real source: the science and wisdom of womankind.

Pergamon Related Journals

(*Free sample copies available on request*)

Women's Studies International Forum

Reproductive and Genetic Engineering

Taking Our Time

Feminist Perspectives on Temporality

Edited by

FRIEDA JOHLES FORMAN

Ontario Institute for Studies in Education
Toronto, Canada

with

CAORAN SOWTON

PERGAMON PRESS

OXFORD · NEW YORK · BEIJING · FRANKFURT
SÃO PAULO · SYDNEY · TOKYO · TORONTO

U.K.	Pergamon Press plc, Headington Hill Hall, Oxford OX3 0BW, England
U.S.A.	Pergamon Press, Inc., Maxwell House, Fairview Park, Elmsford, New York 10523, U.S.A.
PEOPLE'S REPUBLIC OF CHINA	Pergamon Press, Room 4037, Qianmen Hotel, Beijing, People's Republic of China
FEDERAL REPUBLIC OF GERMANY	Pergamon Press GmbH, Hammerweg 6, D-6242 Kronberg, Federal Republic of Germany
BRAZIL	Pergamon Editora Ltda, Rua Eça de Queiros, 346, CEP 04011, Paraiso, São Paulo, Brazil
AUSTRALIA	Pergamon Press Australia Pty Ltd., P. O. Box 544, Potts Point, N.S.W. 2011, Australia
JAPAN	Pergamon Press, 5th Floor, Matsuoka Central Building, 1-7-1 Nishishinjuku, Shinjuku-ku, Tokyo 160, Japan
CANADA	Pergamon Press Canada Ltd., Suite No. 271, 253 College Street, Toronto, Ontario, Canada M5T 1R5

First edition 1989

Library of Congress Cataloging-in-Publication Data
Taking our time: feminist perspectives/edited by
Frieda Johles Forman, with Caoran Sowton—1st ed.
p. cm.—(The Athene series)
1. Women—Psychology.   2. Time—Social aspects.
3. Feminism.
I. Forman. Frieda Johles.   II. Sowton, Caoran.   III. Series.
HQ1206.T214   1988   305.4′2—dc19   88-22707

British Library Cataloguing in Publication Data
Taking our time: feminist perspectives.
1. Time. Perception by man. Sex differences.
I. Forman, Frieda Johles.   II. Sowton, Caoran.
153.7′53

ISNB 0-08-036478-0 Hardcover
ISBN 0-08-036477-2 Flexicover

Printed in Great Britain by A. Weaton & Co. Ltd., Exeter

To the memory of my parents,
MALKA and KASIEL JOHLES,
and to the future of my children,
GIDEON and JESSICA

Acknowledgments

Many friends and colleagues contributed to this book by their assurance that the time had indeed come for the exploration of this theme. In particular I would like to thank: Angela Miles for the years of feminist friendship and inspiration; Mary O'Brien, the mother of us all who are involved in feminist thought and practice: for her intellectually daring and spiritually enlivening work and for her very helpful suggestions; to Rusty Shteir, who on an almost daily basis kept alive for me the picture of the larger map; to Rachel Vigier, who came at the right moment with the right word and the right text; to Gail Geltner for the delight of her company; Peggy Bristow, my colleague at the Centre for Women's Studies, for her constant support; Renate Klein for her ability to integrate the generosity of sisterhood with the sharp skills of an editor; Gloria Bowles for introducing author to editor; Pat Mills for her cosmic laughter.

Contents

Introduction

More than a collection, the works in this volume resemble a fugue, in the musical rather than psychiatric sense (memory is very much present here—recalled and recoded): polyphony expressing many views on women's temporality but all committed to a feminist perspective. The contributing pieces come from across the world (Canada, US, Europe) and from varied settings—academic, literary, the arts, and a feminist workshop, a retreat where women went to discuss time, their time.

Temporality is a heavily laden concept from any perspective; but as women and feminists we need both an aerial and a telescopic perspective to reveal to us its multifaceted and multiform nature. A protean construct, temporality comprehends the quotidian experience, history in its many shapes and memory from the recent to the mythic.

"One cannot think intelligently about time within patriarchal history, with man-centered epistemologies." While we are still to a large degree living within patriarchal history, we do, nevertheless, have the beginnings of woman-centered epistemologies and that makes it possible for Mary O'Brien to cycle over patriarchal terrain with her giggling girlhood friends, stopping at the ruins of the past on her way to our own time of feminism. As we shall see throughout this book, linear time, "periods," whatever the frame, is inimical to cyclical time, the realm of nature and of women. Attempts, such as Hegel's, to interpret history dialectically leave patriarchy unchallenged: "Knowledge of these is knowledge of abstract time, time out of mind, not experienced time, not species time, not common time." Feminism, concludes Mary O'Brien in her "periods" piece, is the revolutionary process which empowers us to make of history a lifeline.

Linear time is not an abstract historical construct only: its manifestations are concrete and ubiquitous. Robbie Pfeuffer Kahn explores the reaches of linear time and its patriarchal values into pregnancy, birth, and lactation. "Where historical process gains ascendency over life process" we face an impoverishment of our lives and we lose the opportunity to build feminist theory based on women's life cycle. As feminists, urges Kahn, we must refuse to see our embodied connection to the world as either romantic or hedonistic and we must eschew the evolutionary approach which ties progress to greater freedom from our body and the natural world itself. "Uncorsetting our maternal bodies does not have to be incompatible with living in linear time, providing that this time move forward more slowly and with more digressions." Time is needed for "mixed zoning" of the public and private spheres.

For Elizabeth Deeds Ermarth, women's tie to nature, though more acceptable perhaps in this era of ecological consciousness than it was during the Romantic period, is still problematic in a world where binarism rules and "women are perpetual carriers of the depreciated half of the binarism, regardless of historical change." She asks whether any idea of time is now possible which is not phallogocentric. Pointing to Julia Kristeva's work (and to its problems with regard to a linguistic division of labor), Ermarth considers linking temporality with language and discourse as a way around conventional definition of time.

Eliot's Maggie Tulliver and Tolstoy's Anna Karenina exemplify the impossibility of women's acceptance as subjects in history: women's time as historical time is a contradiction, concludes Ermarth. Feminist emphasis on process offers some possibility however: women's self-awareness has inspired a search for new premises which may uncover new modes of liveable time.

Cheryl Walker presents the work of the poet H. D. as a paradigm for the changed relationship to history women have undergone during the modern period: H. D.'s early period is characterized by an avoidance of chronological time which she recognized as the "father's signature" and which did not include her; words, art are the mother's sign. Timelessness is her response to patriarchal temporality—"it will be myth; mythopoeic mind (mine) will disprove science and biological-mathematical definition." (H. D. 1927)

H. D.'s analysis with Freud during the 1930s represents her return to historical time, to the struggle with the world of fathers. In Nazi-dominated Vienna of that period, H. D.'s fear of the father's realm, historical time, became acute. The final phase of her work is agency: assuming responsibility to work for social change, her vision united history and metaphysics. H. D.'s quest found its reward in meaningful work perhaps, says Walker, because she lived in the twentieth century—history does matter. In the tradition of the male Modernists, the mythic meant to H. D. an explanation of the past in today's imagery, merging the distant future with the most distant antiquity.

"Women's consciousness raising, a process of re-forming female identity and social life, is motivated in its critique of women's domination by traces of memory;" so argues Patricia J. Mills. This memory is a temporal continuity, a function of reason and imagination in which woman's past is recaptured in the present. Here, the relation between myth and memory becomes significant: myths elucidate aspects of civilization and of ourselves which would otherwise remain unexplained.

The dominant myths of western civilization are those of man marching through time on a mythic journey in search of self, while woman remains outside historical time; they are myths of women's domination and self-alienation. Missing is the tale of the creation of a female self, through and with other women. What is required from a feminist perspective is not only a critique exposing patriarchal myths as male rather than universal, but a weaving and re-weaving of tales of creation of the self which focus on female mythic figures such as Antigone, Circe and Medea.

Mills focuses on the Oedipus myth, showing why it cannot explain female self-development and then points to Antigone as a precursor of contemporary feminists who proclaim the personal as political. Medea, the female counter-part to Odysseus, stands for woman's desire before its taming and for women's solidarity with women.

Women's relation to more recent patriarchal myth and history is the subject of Marie-Luise Gaettens' essay, "The Hard Work of Remembering", on German women's re-examination of Nazism. And it is indeed hard to recall a history which in relation to the dominant culture is one of exclusion and participation—while repressed also complicit. By focusing on the works of the two writers, Ruth Rehmann and Christa Wolf, who were profoundly shaped by Nazi ideology, Gaettens makes us explore what it means to say "I" when that "I" is connected to the ego through which the norms and values of such a society were internalized. History is not outside the subject but constitutes and shapes it. In making their experience public, these women unearth the repressed aspect of history: women's lives in patriarchal society.

For Christa Wolf the past continues to live within us—it is not a closed entity—yet a split exists and there is for her no unified subject who transcends the disruption of time. Rehmann engages in the arduous work of remembering in order to understand her own formation by history—a prerequisite for breaking the hegemony of the past. Active intervention is required to get beyond the memory of conformism which reinforces our accommodation into the patriarchal order.

Memory has the potential for resistance, for subversion: interrogating the past leads to questions about the present where women are still not subjects. Wolf's memory of her mother leads her to women's specific relation to history. While this is an undercutting of Nazi genealogy with its paterfamilias at the center, it also exposes the mother's integration into Nazi society and her complicity. Women must attend to their own memory, says Christa Wolf; through it they will encounter the repressed aspect of history and the silenced stories of women's lives—a source for a non-patriarchal future. Moral consciousness can only be developed with the help of memory.

Hélène Parmelin, the prolific French writer who is the subject of Maïr Verthuy's work, also encounters the history of nations and memory. A long time political activist in the cause of human rights, Parmelin reflects that reality in her work but allows it to unfold in a mode we've come to name women's writing: the hallmarks include a concern with the relationship between exterior and interior time, with the elasticity of time, with circularity and simultaneity.

Maïr Verthuy situates her subject in the world of New Physics where time is the fourth dimension and is perceived according to the speed at which the observer is moving: we have left the mechanical, linear, fixed world and have entered a unitary, holistic world which unites observer and observed. Hélène Parmelin, among others, has been influenced by these new ideas about the fluidity of time and space and the generic fit has not escaped Verthuy's notice: "the correspondence between the language of New Physics and the lives of most women seems nigh on perfect—women have perhaps never believed the world could be reduced to the individual, to the atomic—never known the universe other than through living continuity." Parmelin's "texts in time" embody this female temporal sensibility by their use of repetition, circularity, continuity in the lived experience of her characters and their intersecting and overlapping circles of reality.

In "Urania—Time and Space of the Stars," Heide Göttner Abendroth traces the transformations in the conception of temporality from the matriarchal Cosmos to the galactic world view of modern physics. Matrilineal societies with the moon goddess center of the goddess cult, conceived of time as a spiralling process based on their concrete observations of the movement of the stars in space—the sites of earliest astronomical observations still exist: Stonehenge and Avebury, among others.

The bodily processes of fertility in woman, for which she was so revered in matriarchies, ran synchronously with the clocks of the heavenly bodies; the mythic year had so much to do with women (menstruation with moon, pregnancy with the nine month period from vernal equinox to winter solstice) that time itself was considered female.

This concept of time slid seamlessly into matriarchal societies' concept of history which gradually also took on a spiral form. This concept of history as a non-linear, non-cyclical dynamic process is the earliest form of dialectics.

With the dismantling of matriarchal mythology the spiralling concept of time which was determined by the movement of the stars and women's fertility cycles was destroyed and replaced by an aggressively linear time conception. Linearity also ended the idea of rebirth so characteristic of matriarchal religions; death as definitive end was now the human lot. With the advent of Christianity, life was extended beyond death by way of a single resurrection in the hereafter and historical time received its extension in eschatology. These transformations and devaluations of the natural world were accompanied by the subordination of women in their association with the cyclical and supernatural.

With the rapid growth of mathematical science, and at its heels the industrial revolution, quantitative, metricized time establishes itself more broadly: time clocks, assembly lines, piece rates, etc. It is only with Einstein that time loses its progressive linearity and the mathematical imagination is seen to fail. Modern physics dissolves linear conception: galactic time surrounds us in rings and reaches us on a crooked path. "Is this not spiral time?" asks Heide Göttner Abendroth.

The insatiable urge of scientists and their technologists to quantify and impose linearity on the life cycle is nowhere more vividly seen than in male-dominated obstetrics. Meg Fox documents the way obstetrical staff reduce birth from an archetypal and eternally recurring act to a mechanized and time-bound process. (Reproductive technology has some roots here.) The woman in labor leaves behind her the measured time which rushes past her attendants: the rhythm of contractions takes over, submerging clock time in the eternity of body time. But hospital procedures are based on the assembly line model with its priorities of efficiency and time saving measures. Acceleration of labor is connected with alienation of labor. To view labor as if it were a pre-set goal which ought to adhere to routine and a protocol is to force a clash between two very different and incommensurate kinds of time: phallocentrically structured, forward moving time and gynocentric, recurrent time. For the laboring woman, points out Meg Fox, time stands still; past and future are not separate behind and before her.

Recollection of experience is an essential activity of consciousness, of identity, and to objectify labor and repudiate the inner experience is to encroach on the inner ground of female subjectivity. Restoring birth to its unimpeded, unique temporality would allow another source, body time, to emerge.

Masculinist hegemony of the life cycle is ubiquitous, spanning the archetypal experience of birth and the construction of theories on adult development and aging. Based on her work with mature women returning to college, Jerilyn Fisher examines such concepts as "transition," "maturity," "middle age," and "aging." In a feminist-centered context her women students re-evaluate their past, and once they no longer measure it against male standards for adult achievement they express optimism rather than regret about time to come. They find that male-defined adult development theory is incompatible with their lives and incomplete if it doesn't include values of interrelatedness and commitment.

New definitions emerge in the course of evaluating the tenuous connection between chronological age and life transitions: age is seen as a social construct rather than chronological; "maturity" is based on interdependence rather than separation. Fisher speculates that feminist research based on women's experience will provide the necessary revisions to life cycle theories: for example, women living with women, rather than men, would establish a distinct rhythm over the life span.

In their writings women indicate a mistrust of linear time and seek to subvert its power over them by creating rhythms which are their own and reflect their temporal experience. Not one work studied in Irma Garcia's "Femalear Explorations" gives a positive image of time; only childhood leaves a taste of freedom. The creation of interior time set against the clock is the response to the hostility of linear time. Through close textual analysis of selections from the works of Colette, Nin, Duras, Woolf, Stein and others, Garcia explores the literary forms of expression that bear the mark of a purely feminine time. The quest for origins and identity represents the struggle which defines all female experience: the return to sources enables women to undo the temporal chain. Memory plays a dominant role in women's writing by dislocating the linear train of thought: circularity and repetition are the modes which draw the reader into the text, inviting us to return to an inner temporal dimension. Memory is a labor of reappropriation, a remodelling of time; the writing of turning back and of resonance is women's.

There is a time in women's narratives when silence is allowed its place: these are *hors-temps*, times outside time, moments where nothing happens. These are moments of great peace and serenity, when the writer creates fluently and abundantly in a manner that enables her to become aware of her inner world. These *hors-temps* are essential to gaining insight into women's texts and their temporal experience. "This neutralization of temporality and the amalgamation of the temporal linear chain are approaches which bring about the explosion and valorization of the present," representing the total independence of woman in the face of temporal constraints—at least at the level of the written word.

The Agape Feminist Workshop held in Italy in 1984 is, to my knowledge, the only event of this sort to focus entirely on women's time. The "proceedings" of the workshop, the reports of meetings and plenaries are the only record we have of these discussions and reflections. They were very graciously given to us as a contribution to this volume on women and time. It is particularly fascinating, then, to see how resonant these explorations are with the more formal pieces, in terms of analysis, concerns, hopes and fantasies.

There is no embracing here, of one shape of time over another; both linear and cyclical time are viewed with skepticism. (The give and take of a lively workshop is apparent in the many voices and views expressed, confirmed and contradicted.) Women who seek refuge by inventing a different time which is elastic, should acknowledge that nature too has deadlines such as eating, sleeping, pregnancy. History is depicted as a particularly powerful myth—in which a "time fantasy" has been thrown over the facts. We imbue all time, cyclical or linear, with imagination. Memories, say the participants, bear fruit in the realms of speculation, in critical modes of considering one's life and also history.

A question arises: is maturity, a.k.a. autonomy, possible without separation—must we grow away from our mothers? Is it possible to have difference without separation?

Aversion to "deadlines," the heavy hand of temporality, is universal but was expressed here with a twist: women do not refuse the deadlines imposed on them by others but refuse to set them for themselves. A reconciliation must occur between internal and external time. Daily time shows traces of our capacity to give ourselves meaning in the present and it is friend or enemy, depending on how we succeed in self-signification.

A fantasy: time without limits.

DEDICATIONS TO "BASHERT"**★

Irena Klepfisz

These words are dedicated to those who died

These words are dedicated to those who died
because they had no love and felt alone in the world
because they were afraid to be alone and tried to stick it out
because they could not ask
because they were shunned
because they were sick and their bodies could not resist the disease
because they played it safe
because they had no connections
because they had no faith
because they felt they did not belong and wanted to die

These words are dedicated to those who died
because they were loners and liked it
because they acquired friends and drew others to them
because they took risks
because they were stubborn and refused to give up
because they asked for too much

These words are dedicated to those who died
because a card was lost and a number was skipped
because a bed was denied
because a place was filled and no other place was left

These words are dedicated to those who died
because someone did not follow through
because someone was overworked and forgot
because someone left everything to God
because someone was late
because someone did not arrive at all
because someone told them to wait and they just couldn't any longer

These words are dedicated to those who died
because death is a punishment
because death is a reward
because death is the final rest
because death is eternal rage

These words are dedicated to those who died

Bashert

*ba-shert (Yiddish): inevitable, (pre)destined.

★ From *Keeper of Accounts,* Montpelier, VT.: Sinister Wisdom Books, 1983, pp. 74-76

These words are dedicated to those who survived

These words are dedicated to those who survived
because their second grade teacher gave them books
because they did not draw attention to themselves and got lost
in the shuffle
because they knew someone who knew someone else who could
help them and bumped into them on a corner on a Thursday
afternoon
because they played it safe
because they were lucky

These words are dedicated to those who survived
because they knew how to cut corners
because they drew attention to themselves and always got picked
because they took risks
because they had no principles and were hard

These words are dedicated to those who survived
because they refused to give up and defied statistics
because they had faith and trusted in God
because they expected the worst and were always prepared
because they were angry
because they could ask
because they mooched off others and saved their strength
because they endured humiliation
because they turned the other cheek
because they looked the other way

These words are dedicated to those who survived
because life is a wilderness and they were savage
because life is an awakening and they were alert
because life is a flowering and they blossomed
because life is a struggle and they struggled
because life is a gift and they were free to accept it

These words are dedicated to those who survived

Bashert

1

Feminizing Time: An Introduction

Frieda Johles Forman

When women say, as we so frequently do, "I have no time," we know whereof we speak, as individuals and as a collective. From the humblest considerations of time to the most ethereal reflections, women as subjects have been profoundly absent. When we do appear, in those categories provided for us by the social sciences, the picture that emerges in terms of time spent in hours of paid and unpaid work makes us long for exclusion from that temporal realm.

My own interest in (and eventual obsession with) the subject of women and time did not come about, however, through scholarly involvement but rather through observation, informed by a feminist sensibility and a cultural predisposition to suffering; for to speak of women and time is to speak of the ultimate theft.

"Haunted by time" is no hyperbolic phrase when used to express women's experience of this most human of dimensions. As we become aware of the power of language when words fail us, when the word we need doesn't come, so too we become conscious of time when it is missing, when it flies away, when we are waiting. While it is true that availability of time differs from class to class, nevertheless, to be female is to have an uneasy relationship to time; and even the more privileged among us experience the anguish that accompanies that relationship. Would it be too extreme to say that time is an enemy, albeit domesticated and familiar? Certainly, common expressions suggest such a perception: "rushing against time," "juggling time," "deadlines," (literal meaning: a line around a military prison which no prisoner can cross without the liability or penalty of being shot).

Regardless of circumstance, women are strangers in the world of male-defined time and as such are never at home there. At best, they are like guests eager to prove helpful; at worst they are refugees, living on borrowed time. Whatever their status in that realm, time is there to fulfill duties and obligations, some of which are voluntary and undertaken in a spirit of love and service to others. In this capacity, time becomes a commodity and, once again, how brisk the trading is will depend on class; but we may be sure that it will remain a commodity and not a vehicle towards freedom. Time is not freedom for women (though some of us may have some free time now and then).

In *Silences*, Tillie Olsen quotes from a letter by the poet Louise Bogan to May Sarton describing Edmund Wilson's household:

> You would have loved the Wilson menage. Elena has really effected a tremendous change in Edmund's way of living. She really *loves* him, moreover! The little girl, Helen, is delightful; I must send her an Orlando book. The house couldn't be more attractive; and Elena has evidently put real elbow grease into decorating it; scraping floors and walls and making curtains. There is a "parlor" with a good deal of Federal mahogany (E's mother's) upholstered in yellow; a dining room with more mahogany against blue walls, plus lovely blue Staffordshire and silver; a "middle room" with more blue walls and blue chintz and linen; and Ed's magnificent study, with a bathroom attached, and a stairway to an attic, filled with overflow books. For the first time poor E. has attention, space and effectively arranged paraphenalia of all kinds—Mary never really helped in the more practical ways; and E. has had a very scrappy kind of life down the years. Now all moves smoothly: tea on a tray for his "elevenses"; absolute silence in his working hours, and good meals at appropriate intervals. Elena was very hospitable, and fed me enormous luncheons (one of lobster), with highballs at tea-time. … They have a tiny suntrap of a garden by the side door, and Elena has a little vegetable garden, v. European with lettuces and beans mixed with herbs and the zinnias.[1]

How remarkable that Louise Bogan (in Olsen's view, a consummate and peerless poet) could take such obvious pleasure in Wilson's domestic bliss while she herself had a daughter to raise, alone, and none of the benefits of a devoted wife.

Could any sociological study have given us such an elegant and comprehensive litany of women's work in the home! From the start, we are told that love is the matrix for this comfortable household where no detail has been spared to provide the aesthetic and material conditions conducive to Wilson's creative work: all that traditional mahogany and blue, good meals, balanced, one hopes, with fresh vegetables from the little garden; but more critical, for a writer certainly, "absolute silence in his working hours." If we were to consider the time spent and so well hidden in this epistolary ode, would not some of the lustre disappear: the time in caring for that "delightful" child, especially if absolute silence is to prevail; time to polish the silver and mahogany, wash the chintz and linen, clean the bathroom adjoining the magnificent study, dust the books, (occasionally, even the overflow in the attic); to prepare the meals (at appropriate intervals), planning all the while so that she can be home for his "elevenses" and should he need attention at other odd hours. From what one gathers, Elena was also an attentive and generous hostess: more time. Could Mary McCarthy who "never really helped in the more practical ways" have survived as a writer were *she* to have made all move smoothly?

Temporality is a problematic and pain-riddled area for us: whether in the everyday world, in mythic and iconographic expression, or in religious tradition and ritual. I'll offer a junior encyclopedic view of these topics then move to philosophy, especially that of Heidegger, and conclude in a speculative direction.

Housework, or as it is sometimes called, domestic labor, has been voluminously documented by feminists and other social scientists and therefore only the briefest indications are needed here.[2]

Despite technological changes in the home, unemployed women today spend as much time at housework as did their grandmothers (figures range from fifty-five to seventy hours a week) and in some specific areas, such as laundry and shopping, they spend more time.[3] Childcare, which is more complex today, assuming many psychological and educational dimensions, has added immeasurable hours to a woman's domestic work day. The drudgery of old-fashioned labor has given way to more diffuse and time-consuming activities. For mothers of lower income families, the amount of time spent on housework would rise above the fifty-five to seventy hours a week to include extra time spent on careful shopping and preparation of "budget-wise" meals, on sewing and mending clothing, and above all on childcare where there are no means to pay others for that service.[4] In developing countries, a woman's lot continues to be one of unspeakable toil.

In advanced Western society, where the leisure industry looms so large, one is quite right to ask how women are affected by this relatively new introduction of free time. In his Vancouver-based study, "Sexual division of labor and inequality: labor and leisure," Martin Meissner asks: "How meaningful is it to speak of married women's leisure? To begin with, time-budget hours of women's leisure are undoubtedly overestimated. Women's time spent in visiting, parties, outings, or watching television, is certain to contain some obvious work, in preparing, serving, and putting away dishes, . . . much of this "free time" is also *work* , in less obvious form perhaps, in attention to husbands' and children's emotional and physical needs." He concludes that ". . . leisure may well be completely incompatable with being a wife or a mother. In the conventions of sociology, the rôle of housewife is 'diffuse,' which means practically that she is 'legitimately' on call at any time and for any demands or requests. In the language of a labor contract, that state of affairs would make for a twenty-four hours a day, seven days a week require-ment to be available for work."[5]

When women work outside the home, as we do in increasing numbers, we need not fear that we will lose our hold on the domestic reins. That sphere is ours regardless of other demands. Studies have shown, only too clearly, that when a woman assumes the added obligation of a paid job, thereby increasing her work load by up to forty hours a week, her male partner's contribution to the organization of the household remains that of a reluctant "helper." We know only too well that women's employment earns us sixty percent of men's. Accordingly, in a world where time is money, and where money can mean time, women have little of either.

As for "quality of working life," there too women's time is undervalued and dehumanized. Particularly in industry, but not exclusively there, women's work is the most segmented, repetitive and constraining. Madeleine Guilbert, in her detailed study of women's work in French industry found that women were given jobs, often refused by men, because they required "a great deal of resistance to monotony."[6] The forms of resistance by the women were social: involvement in each others' lives, exchange of life experiences, gifts to celebrate birthdays and attention to co-workers' personal needs—dehumanizing work perhaps, but not dehumanized women.

Male dominion over time has been expressed in the mythology and iconography of Western civilization with a virulence that has permeated all subsequent thinking on temporality. In ancient Greek myth, Cronus, son of mother earth and father heaven, who devours his own children, is identified with Chronos, the personification of time: thus our chronology. During the Medieval and Renaissance periods, the allegorical linking of time and death becomes common iconography. The cannibalistic image of Father Time gives way in the sixteenth century to a more benign and paradoxical version: time is the ravager, as well as the revealer of truth, and that through a familial relation: "Veritas filia temporis" (Truth the daughter of time). As late as in the nineteenth century, however, we still find the identification of time with death, Goya's painting of "Cronus Devouring His Children," ranking as one of the most horrific works in art history.

As we know, technological innovation does not necessarily bring with it advantages to women, and thus when iconography in the seventeenth century reflects a new era of time-keeping, "God the watchmaker" is still very much male. Whatever else may be said about this iconography, it must be given its due for its generic consistency: right through to the eighteenth century, a pitiable "Father Time" serves as a reminder of our human fate.[7]

In William Blake, the visionary, we are able to see misogyny expressed visually and poetically. His essay, "A Vision of the Last Judgment," was written as a description for a large painting estimated to have contained a thousand figures and although it no longer exists, the iconographic detail which remains is elaborate and articulate:

> The Greeks represent Chronos or Time as a very Aged Man; this is Fable, but the Real Vision of Time is in Eternal Youth. I have, however, somewhat accommodated my Figure of Time to the common opinion, as I myself am also infected with it and my Visions also infected, and I see Time Aged, also, too much so.[8]
>
> Allegories are things that Relate to Moral Virtues. Moral Virtues do not Exist; they are Allegories and dissimulations. But Time and Space are Real Beings, a Male and a Female. Time is a Man, Space is a Woman, and her masculine Portion is Death.[9]

Predictably, Blake is conscious of the contaminating influence of common perception as it touches upon the portrayal of Time's age, but not Time's gender. (Androgyny is death to women, it appears.)

The masculinity of Time through the ages, and with it the metaphors of devastation and death, have fundamentally shaped Christianity. In her book *His Religion and Hers: A Study of the Faith of our Fathers and the Work of our Mothers*, Charlotte Perkins Gilman reflects upon the question of whether birth or death is to be the basis of religion. She speculates in this way:

> Had the religions of the world developed through her mind, they would have shown one deep, essential difference, the difference between birth and death. The man was interested in one

end of life, she in the other. He was moved to faith, fear, and hope for the future; she to love and labor in the present.

To the death-based religion the main question is, 'what is going to happen to me after I am dead?'—a posthumous egotism.

To the birth-based religion the main question is 'what must be done for the child who is born?'—an immediate altruism.[10]

Judaism, more earth-bound than Christianity and less preoccupied with an afterlife, is among the most time-conscious religions; and it is the element of time which deprives women of full status and participation in Jewish life. In traditional Jewish law as established in the Talmud, women, along with children and slaves, are exempt from all positive ("thou shalt") commandments which occur within time limits, i.e., which are timebound. The most significant of these are the three daily services: prayers said morning, afternoon, and evening, throughout the year. To be excluded from these is to be effectively barred from public religious life, that life which takes place in the synagogue. Women also cannot be counted as a member in the "Minyan," the most basic Jewish communal unit, the religious counterpart to a quorum, without which public prayer cannot begin.

Whereas male children and slaves, can, in time, acquire full legal membership in the Jewish community, the child at the age of thirteen and the slave when he is freed, time has no such transforming potential for woman: she remains forever outside.

The centrality of daily prayer for the observant Jewish male cannot be overstated: it is the ritual which binds him to the past, and to his history. As such, it is a continuous affirmation of the holy for him, providing a constant reminder of a spiritual covenant with God. From this spiritual identity the Jewish woman is absent, and indeed in Jewish thought she is consigned to the category of physicality while he is entrusted to spirituality.[11]

Continuity in Jewish tradition is inextricably tied to learning and teaching the holy text, the Torah, the Bible, which is the source of all Jewish belief and referred to as "a Tree of Life to them that hold fast to it." Jewish women have had little access, over the centuries, to this arboreal connection and are thus not allowed to fulfill the commandment of teaching one's children.

The more benign explanations given to account for women's exclusion from these fundamental religious obligations, public prayer and study, have focussed on her domestic rôle with its ideology of separate but equal. More acute critics have seen this as another instance of the private sphere for her, the public realm for him.[12] My own interpretation is, I'm afraid, more sinister: the exclusion from timebound commandments was a profound reflection of the reality that only free men can undertake to give their time while women (and slaves) don't have it to give.

In Jewish life, where the notion of generational continuity is so fundamentally a lived reality, one would expect that childbirth, the realization of that continuity, would provide women with a religious moment which is uniquely theirs. This expectation, based on grounds of historical consciousness, is heightened when one considers that blessings and prayers accompany the observant Jew's every act and are so exquisitely precise as to embrace the entire sweep of human activity: from the ordinary to the sublime, from the quotidian to the unforeseen event. For all these, the creator is blessed and the act consecrated. But—there is no specific prayer which a Jewish woman can say upon giving birth.

In philosophy, where reason comes to bear on time and where one would anticipate an articulation of the subject which is comprehensive and universal, once again, it isn't us they're talking about. The reflections which follow focus mainly on nineteenth- and twentieth-century Phenomenology and Existentialism, but one can go back to St. Augustine's contemplations on time, in the fourth century, and discern the absence of women. More than with any other philosophical category, there is no entry point for women in the discourse on time and temporality. In my view, there are two major explanations for this absence. First, awareness of death is a crucial component of masculine time consciousness, which becomes the essence of being-in-the-world in the work of Heidegger. Secondly, human time unfolds in history, but history, as a fusion of conception and action is a category from which we are largely absent.

In Martin Heidegger's major work, *Sein und Zeit* (*Being and Time*), awareness of one's own death is the ground for an authentic ("eigentlich" "own")[13] existence, an existence that questions what it means to be; "the meaning of Being," is centrally related to what it means *not* to be. Authentic Dasein, ("Being-there," man's (sic) special way of being) is revealed through the phenomenon of death, through an awareness that it is possible not to be. Inauthentic Dasein, conversely, is characterized by avoiding thinking of one's own death, through absorption in the everyday world with its trivial distractions, the world of the "they."

It is important, even in this extremely brief exposition, to show how Heidegger derives the temporal analysis of Dasein from the characterization of authentic existence. How is an awareness of one's own death, in Heidegger's view so necessary for a total perspective on life, to be realized as an existential? The answer lies in Heidegger's concept of the "not-yet," the future. Dasein already is its "not-yet" because it is "ahead of itself." "Anticipation" is the view of "not-yet," the view which offers us possibility, the possibility of death. The possibility of death, "Being-towards death," is anticipation: looking forward to something as a possible way. "Anticipatory resoluteness" is Being-towards one's possibilities and this is possible because there is a future towards which we can go. To be, therefore, is always to be in time. Time is the Being of Dasein. To the fundamental question, what does it mean to be in time: it is to be in the future. This awareness of the future, if it is authentic, is aware that one is not-going-to-be; "Being-toward" death is future.[14]

The Heideggerian disclosure of temporality, however seductive and compelling in places, cannot serve to illuminate women's experience and sense of time, principally because of its inextricable connection of death with futurity.

The notion of a death of one's own, as the condition expressed in the Heideggerian formula for authentic existence, is inconceivable for women if it is not rendered dialectically with birth, because for us the future as generative is as much a determinant in our lives as is our mortality. But more fundamentally: our very awareness of death, given the existentials of our lives as women, cannot be viewed from the same perspective which for men makes death the ultimate source of courage and freedom. As a collective, women do not only live *in* time (from birth to death), they also *give* time and that act makes a radical difference to Being-in-the-World. Heidegger speaks of an existence from which we are absent, and is silent on the subject of our temporality: women's time consciousness.

If we were to extend Dasein's Being to comprehend the rich and complex give-and-take which characterizes woman's time, would death not be dislodged as the final arbiter of authentic existence? We might in the process even begin to question the concept of authenticity itself, which is so central to Heidegger's work, not with the purpose of dismissing it but rather with the intention of radically exposing it.

If we acknowledge that for women, the giving of time, i.e., birth, is prior to and takes both ontological and temporal priority over the taking away of time, i.e., death, then we must re-examine this notion of authenticity which relies so heavily on death and not at all on birth. It must be said at this point, that among existentialists it is not Heidegger alone who is guilty of viewing birthing as ontologically insignificant: for Simone de Beauvoir, as Mary O'Brien indicates in *The Politics of Reproduction*, "Authenticity remains an individual affair, as does freedom: to each her own. The notion of a real female collective consciousness, transformed by objective change in its reproductive base, is excluded by the ahistorical and abstract dogma of immanence."[15]

"Authentic" is the accepted translation for the German "eigentlich" which Heidegger uses; it is derived from "eigen," "own," in both senses of the word: possession and relation; thus, authentic existence is "my *own*," and one that "*I* own." Is it meaningful for us, as women redefining authenticity, to speak in the language of ownership and singularity in describing our existence? And, moreover, do we want to? Of course, Heidegger would not deny that Dasein's Being-in-the-world is alongside that of others. In his phenomenology, the origin of a word, its root, gives us, however, an intimation of its meaning which no amount of qualifying can obscure.

If we were to ask, in Heideggerian fashion, what does it mean for a female Dasein to be, we would have to say that for us "Care" (Sorge), that existential which unifies the future, past and present, is grounded in Being-toward-birth and life. And if the shift from a death-determined future to a birth-determined one, with attending metaphoric changes in temporality, is conceivable, are we not feminizing time? And isn't it about time that we do?

Since the entire discussion of reproduction, nature, and feminization is so fraught with the possibilities of misunderstandings, I feel obliged to articulate at least what I do not mean by feminization of time. I do not regard it as a return to lunar consciousness, nor a celebration of women's natural cycle. Although I have misgivings about these revived traditions, I fully appreciate both the scholarship and passion which feminists have invested in that realm. As feminists, while not disowning our very real bond to the natural world, we must continue to resist the definition of women as nature: that is, we must live in the world as subjects whose transcendence is grounded in a generative temporality.

Male temporal consciousness has excluded women from its domain by denying ontological significance to birth, as event and as consciousness; male historical consciousness has written us out of its chronology by demeaning and ignoring our contribution, thus robbing us of our collective memory as women. In her fundamental work *The Politics of Reproduction*, Mary O'Brien addresses de Beauvoir's interpretation of Hegel's master-slave relation which de Beauvoir has applied to the male-female encounter:

> The life-risking confrontation of master and slave is, for Hegel, the beginning of history; a journey towards the universal union of the rational with the real. ... Yet Hegel's scenario remains a recognition and a struggle for recognition between two adult males. Master and slave are inaugurating human history and the transcendence of nature in conditions under which the institution of patriarchy is already established for all time, and from time out of mind. ... Hegel's parable is very significant in the class struggle model of history, as Marx was able to see, but it said little about the history of generic struggle.[16]

That women are missing in the account of history's emergence, at least according to Hegel and de Beauvoir, is no mere abstraction which can be bracketed while we go on with the task of living our lives: that unrecorded past is always with us and its absence strikes at odd, unsuspecting moments. While it may be true that we share with men a national or cultural history, our share is a mere shadow of the full heritage which is theirs, and to say that we inhabit different worlds is no overstatement. If we belong (in the uncritical sense of the word) to an oppressed minority, such as Jews and Blacks, we find it easier to see ourselves in that history, since its history is one of oppression with which we so readily identify; and, of course, as it is a recorded history, however prejudicial such recording may be.

Time is occasionally on our side: the intellectual and spiritual conditions exist now, not only for women's history but for feminist historiography: for women making history and for feminists recording it. We have cause for exhilaration when we reflect upon the enormous creativity of feminist historians whose work encompasses the reclamation of our foremothers' lives, the recording of our history making, and the redefinition of history from a revolutionary perspective, that of feminism. Hegel was quite right in his belief that without historical records there can be no political development; historians therefore make that development possible.[17]

Feminists must begin to see women's time, or more often the lack of it, as a political issue, placing it center-stage in our struggle. It is not enough to acknowledge fleetingly that a problem exists and to move on to more pressing points. To deny its centrality is to disregard a fundamental truth about women and to make invisible an aspect of our reality which is not only philosophically "authentic" but is critical to our political activity.

NOTES

1. Tillie Olsen, *Silences* (Seymour Lawrence: Delaconte Press, 1978), p. 220.
2. Some books on housework:
   Bonnie Fox, (ed.) *Hidden in the Household* (Toronto: Women's Press, 1980).
   Penney Kome, *Somebody Has To Do It* (Toronto: McClelland and Stewart, 1982).
   Meg Luxton, *More than a Labour of Love: Three Generations of Women's Work in the Home* (Toronto: Women's Press, 1980).
   Ellen Malos, *The Politics of Housework* (London: Allison & Busby, 1980).
   Ann Oakley, *Sociology of Housework* (Martin Robinson, 1974).
   Monique Proulx, "Five Million Women: A Study of the Canadian Housewife" (Canadian Advisory Council on the Status of Women, June 1978).
   Natalie Sokoloff, *Between Money and Love: The Dialectics of Women's Home and Market Work* (New York: Praeger, 1980).
3. Joanne Vanek, "Time Spent in Housework," *Scientific American*, November 1974.
4. Betsy Warrior, "Slavery or a Labor of Love," in *Houseworkers' Handbook* (Cambridge, Mass.: Women's Center).
5. Martin Meissner, "Sexual Division of Labour and Inequality: Labour and Leisure," in Marylee Stephenson (ed.) *Women in Canada* (General Publishing Co. Limited: Ontario, 1977), p. 173.
6. Ibid., p.
7. S. Macey, "The Changing Iconography of Father Time," *The Study of Time*, Vol. III (Springer Verlag, 1976).
8. William Blake, "A Vision of the Last Judgment," from the Note-Book, *Blake: Complete Writings* (Oxford University Press, 1966), pp. 604, 614.
9. Ibid., p. 614.
10. Charlotte Perkins Gilman, *His Religion and Hers: A Study of the Faith of our Fathers and the Work of our Mothers.* (Hyperian Press, Inc., Con.: original 1923 reprint 1976).
11. Rachel Adler, "The Jew Who Wasn't There: Halacha and the Jewish Women," in *Response*, Summer 1978, no. 18 (The Jewish Woman).
12. Rabbi Joan Friedman expressed this view to me over a hurried lunch.
13. Martin Heidegger, *Being and Time*, trans. John Macqverrie and Edward Robinson (N.Y.: Harper & Row, 1962).
14. Michael Gelven, *A Commentary on Heidegger's Being and Time* (Harper & Row, 1970).
15. Mary O'Brien, *The Politics of Reproduction* (Boston, London and Henley: Routledge & Kegan Paul, 1981), p. 73.
16. Ibid., pp. 69-71.
17. J. N. Findlay, *Hegel: A Re-Examination* (London: George Allen & Unwin Ltd., 1958), p. 329.

WITCHCRAFT WAS HUNG, IN HISTORY

Emily Dickinson

Witchcraft was hung, in History,
But History and I
Find all the Witchcraft that we need
Around us, every Day—

2

Periods

Mary O'Brien

I remember that when I was at school in the 1930s I was much perplexed by the notion of periods. Our school day was divided into periods: math period, sewing period (I hated that) and history period. In history period we learned about historical periods, generally associated with kings or poets: The Augustan, Caroline, Romantic, Jacobean periods. While the words "age" and "era" have become more popular, periods persist in the time sense and with continuing ambiguity. To learn about them as temporal phenomena, stretching from forty minutes to a thousand years was bad enough, but there were other resonances at work. There was grammar, where period meant full stop and had apparently nothing to do with time. There were "period pieces," the childish sobriquet for any female teacher over thirty. We were being introduced to something called a periodic table, which certainly granted no elemental legitimacy to time. This opacity in the notion of periods, however, paled in the significance of our pre-pubescent anticipation of our "first periods," which, unlike the elements, had heavy temporal connotations: "that time of the month," "a woman's time." But historical periods were tidily continuous and linear, while the monthly sort, we were told, might have a tendency to irregularity. As we had never been offered information about alternative modes of time consciousness, the contradictions of linear and cyclical modes were puzzling and irregularity seemed faintly pathological. In those days, too, we had to cope with families impoverished by "short time" or "idle time" in an industrial depression: (nice capitalist ambiguity in this proletarian usage which identified unemployed workers as "idle:" wasting time?) We also had a school-mate, a sort of awesome kid, who walked proudly because her brother was "doing time" for a bit of "petty" larceny. He *was* idle, of course. A grander larceny might have brought hard labor.

Fortunately, I hadn't yet met time out of mind, in the poetic sense, or time as mind in the philosophic sense: these would come—at a later period.

There is still some slight tendency to refer to early modes of social organization in terms of periods: Lower and Middle Pleistocene periods for example. The words "age" and "era" are kept for *homo sapiens* in a more recognizable form—obsessed with technology and prepossessed with male power. Stone Age "man" despite some limitations, had managed to define the species as male in terms of its capacity to record its history, however obliquely. It may well be that the ridiculous word "prehistoric" actually means prepatriarchal, consigning societies which might have been either matriarchal or simply egalitarian to the murky caverns of ahistoricity.[1] In modern terms, "ages"— political, literary, economic—have widely supplanted "periods" in historical description. An interesting exception is the "Romantic Period," which resists definition as an age or an era. This may well be due to the preoccupation of the romantic imagination with the ambiguities of nature and images of eternal return, with a good dose of elegant misogyny thrown in. There is perhaps something profoundly unmanly in the effort to reconcile cyclical time, which destroys the very possibility of the triumph of Reason, with historical time which leaves us all groping in a night in which all cows are black and there are no male progeny of Minerva's owl left to see in the dark the glint of wisdom. Yet Hegel himself was determined to produce a system of philosophy which would abolish the triviality and divisiveness of periods for the splendors of transfigurative processes. It is clear from the closing pages of the *Phenomenology* that women disrupt man's reconciliation with time and with god: "Just as the individual divine man (Hegel means Jesus C.) has an implied (essential, *an sich*) father and only an actual mother, in like manner the universal divine man (i.e., patriarchy), the spiritual (ideological) communion has as its father its own proper action and knowledge, while its mother is eternal love (no periods, we note) which it merely *feels*, but does not behold in its consciousness as an actual immediate object."[2] For these reasons, the world awaits transfiguration, but Hegel had not identified *patriarchy* as a period awaiting transcendence. Had he done so, he could then have envisaged a human future rather than snatched in melancholy desperation at the abstract trouser legs of absolute spirit.

Hegel's system is important because it is the most ambitious European attempt to "master" time: time-consciousness is an eternal battle which Hegel tries to endow with "periods" which are neither circular nor cyclical nor linear. He conceives(!) a history mothered by negativity and fathered by transcendence— body by mind, nature by history, intuition by reason. The Romantic failing was to think that body, nature and intuition ought to be taken seriously, a dangerously unmanning procedure. "Periodicity" was historicized in the positing of a creative antithesis—dialectical process— in which man's self-consciousness was eventually to be subsumed in his spirituality, and reborn as universal Reason. Unfortunately, Hegel's notion of negation as the plant food of historical process has moved steadily from men's theorizing to men's practice: we know now that negation as the motor of time does not clear the path for rational spirit but clears the earth of the life that gives mind any reason at all for contemplating human history. In any case, all this clever reconstruction of time within mind silenced the romantics or drove them mad, leaving the way clear for the men of the scientific age who never did read Hegel's luminous critique of their intellectual deficiencies. They had no time for philosophy, finding the future of "empty" space more interesting than faulty memories of past history.

It did not silence women, for they had not spoken to Hegel, although he had this quite romantic notion about our capacity for feeling, playing dizzily, dangerously and ignorantly with the dialectic of power/reason. Hegel's women whispered furtively and chaotically with ancient household gods, who lived in domestic inglenooks more murky than the pastures of invisible cows. These were the days when women were spoken "for," a social process of the negation of rights in the dialectic of patriarchy and the conjugal family. Hegel's *Philosophy of Right* is, for women, the transfer of their rights from father to brother to husband, a "Right" grounded in female incapacity for transcendence of domestic labor and the cycle of regeneration of the species, "periods" of mindless dumb necessity, a massive philosophical yawn supervised by big brothers. Hegel thought the loving and sacrificial relation of brother and sister to be the earthly manifestation of the highest peak that the phenomenology of female minds might aspire to: hence his admiration for Antigone for love of her brother, dead before she bred.

We are no longer silent, some of us: of what, when we speak, do we speak? Doubtless, the patriarchate would like to think of a feminist "period," another historical outburst of collective nagging, due to stop—full stop— part of a repetitive cycle of uppityness, a climacteric of some kind, women's trouble, troublesome women whose activities are historically cyclical. A little period of insubordination, after all, acts as a safety valve for the sustenance of the sex/gender system. A few concessions: let them emerge from the private realm and test themselves against all reason: they will go back to their natural sphere, worn out by the effort to simulate reason in their naturalistic way.

But let me cycle back to those youthful covens in which the essence of periods was distilled in womanhood/sisterhood, in continuity: when the ageless wisdoms of menstruation struggled with the historical trivialization of femininity. Much giggling, one remembers: nervous, anticipatory, puzzled, awed. Menstruation was constructed by adolescent patriarchs in the debased language of the dirty joke, the rag, the curse, the cunt. For us, periods were shared secret things, runes of linguistic cyphers and magical powers, badges of inferiority-through-vulnerability, strength-through-sisterhood. Given this confusion, it was not odd that the prime mode of communication of these mysteries was the giggle. The language of women's experience was gone, as our Parisian sisters keep telling us so eloquently. Did we know where the vulnerability really lay? Did we guess at the envy? Perhaps not. But we certainly did not suffer from the sense of a separation of fecundity and sexuality which afflicted our brothers. We assured each other that we would never have sex with a man we did not love, we exchanged misinformation about "safe periods," we decided how many children we would have (two) and the qualities of acceptable fathers for them. We hinted at arcane knowledge about masturbation, single and mutual, about abortion and contraception: falling off the table after drinking a bottle of gin was considered the sophisticated methodology of the former and virginity ambivalently perceived as the only effective strategy for the latter. But of our sexual experience: of importunate fathers and experimenting brothers; of gropes and fumbles; of rape; of these we never spoke. It was a new romantic period, spawned by industrial stagnation and Hollywood fantasy, the motionless "cycle" of the economy dulled by celluloid trivia. Yet we knew sisterhood in the perplexities of burgeoning womanhood. We did not giggle because we were silly but because, in some feminized version of Sysyphus we knew that we were happy—for a period. The curse would come upon us somehow as a time of change, as maturity, as fulfillment. We were strong in our covens, even though we had been taught the evil of witchcraft.

"There is a kind of magic in recollection" de Beauvoir says, "a magic one feels at every age."[3] She goes on to argue that the past was lived in the "for-itself mode" yet becomes an "in-itself" with aging. One's youthful past, she claims, is the remembrance of "guilt, shame and anxiety."[4] No doubt she would, in 1970, have regarded what I have written above as evasive sentimentalism, an inauthentic defence of Sartre's "practico-inert," the processes by which we objectify ourselves in the world. For existentialism, we are captives of our past, of periods congealed in an experience we cannot recover as we face the inevitability of our deaths. Yet de Beauvoir's strictures on the winding-down weariness of old age are perhaps less convincing when one thinks of the vitality of her own late involvement in feminist politics. We shall miss her, for the book of her youth and the politics of her agedness. In between? A different period. A period of that fixation with finitude which is, I believe, specifically masculine: the preoccupation with death, the despair; the new romanticism which sees eternal return as the no-longer-courageous, now merely pointless cycle of the natural world; a mindless on-spinning continuum of triviality that takes its meaning from an intellectualized subjectivity that cannot stay here, that dies too soon, too inevitably, that waits out life in the doomed ante-rooms of mortality, the condemnation of self by self's immersion in finitude, in abrupted linearity, in the momentous moment of one's death.

One cannot think intelligently about time within patriarchal history, with man-centered epistemologies. If indeed mankind is engaged in a continuous linear or even dialectical process of making history—a process understood only by philosophers and therefore qualifying as more real than reality—somewhere a line must be drawn. Where this line is to be drawn, by whom, its erasures, amendments, breaks, recapitulations; its lies and secrets, its crippled language, its ethical unconcern, its empty elegance; where it is to be drawn is precisely the lie of male supremacy and the truth of masculine inadequacy. History tumbles outside of drawn lines and selective dialectic. For example, the dialectic of nature and history, of season and clock, of individual and generation, of fecundity and decay. Knowledge of these is knowlege of abstract time, time out of mind, not experienced time, not species time, not common time. Men have used mind for the sorts of understanding of reality embedded in the history of the conquest of time, men's history. Women "mind" the children. The obvious thing that is wrong with this is the failure to realize that the first is destructive of history, a quest for Nirvana, the periodization of abstract heroes arrogantly symbolized in the cyclically insignificant death of the deified individual: the second—coping all the time—is the absolute condition of a human existence in time. Human history has meaning only in species time, a reality dimly recalled by "remembering" our individual birthdays while forgetting the cyclical integrity of species life.

Yet we cannot simply assert the "brute" presence of the natural world as "necessary," though it is clearly so in economic terms. Our relations of production, however, have become relations of destruction, and the task of feminism is much larger than transforming existing structures of political domination. Human freedom cannot be understood as license to destroy the natural world. A dim awareness of this is evident in patriarchy's space and nuclear "energy" programmes, in which the need to find other planets to exploit creates a destructive obsession which explodes the wealth of nations in "incidents," "accidents," blow-outs, blow-ups and mounting martial hysteria about "races against time." This phrase crystallizes the limitations of linearity: one does not race against a cycle; horrors of treadmills, circular thinking and square rings notwithstanding. A cycle is not a circle, not an eternal return, not just a pseudonym for the inadequacies of capitalist production, not a temporary malfunction in linear history. Patriarchy, particularly capitalist patriarchy, is very sulky about recycling: conservation is bad for business. Patriarchy examines space, sees it is an environment in which circular objects abound, but chooses to "penetrate" it with phallic rockets. Patriarchy sees regeneration itself as a "line," and works out the racial, ethnic and class "lines" which cannot be "crossed."

We were of course wrong, we little girls in speaking of our "periods." The cycle of regeneration is not subject to full stops. The older word, "courses," makes more sense. Collectively, there is no moment in history when menses are not flowing, the promise of fertility and regeneration, a nuisance on occasion but hardly a curse, unless fertility itself is a curse or life itself unworthy of renewal. In human terms, in female experience, our "periods" cannot grammatize our fecundity: they are reminders that we have chosen not to reproduce at *this* time, not by "controlling nature" but by self-discipline, by intention, by preference: by that practical rationality which does not abstract from reality but learns to live with it. There are periods in which the interplay of rational/ethical decision-making, personal responsibilities and species continuity are apprehended in temporal consciousness. To do or not to do, *that* is the question which must be posed when we act in life rather than indulge in macabre fantasies of power over death.

That is also the question which faces contemporary feminism as modern Hamlets play out their depressed ontologies of the end of the line: jumbling dialectic with juxtaposition, subject/object obscuring the truth of subject/species while they reach out to touch the face of imagined god-the-fathers. (Hands on holsters in case it turns out to be the other fellow's god.) The birth of a child is the cord which links and breaks and reconstitutes the integrity of history and nature, of linear time and cyclical time. These are not two different time modes but the dialectic vitality of human existence, the linear/cyclical entwinement whose promises of universality threaten those who are indifferent to difference, cowed by the notion of death, careless of their reproductive power and exploitative of that power in "Others," the not-us.

The problem now is, of course, species death, the "end" of historical time, the expiration of mind which originally named time so that it might be straightened out. The "scientific" appropriation of women's reproductive powers is an essential part, perhaps the ultimate move in creating time as an unfrayed rope with which to hang our species. Reproductive technology gives to man in general the power to control both individual birth and with on-rushing genetic "engineering," species continuity. (Hand me that spanner buddy, I'm spanning time.) Reproductive technology also offers the dizzy vision of a world without women, the end of gender, but also the chaos of the disintegration of universal man at the end of his time. What happens when all that phallic imagery confronts the reality of masturbation into a dish in some institutional lavatory?

This scientific period, promising a final solution to the "reproductive problem," would be a depressing prospect if it were simply the latest phase in patriarchal history, another step in the control of women's fecundity. However, its totalitarian, universal dimensions historically create resistance. To be sure, reproductive control may seem like a dot on the line of history—until we remember that history is not a line and a dot is not a period. Feminism is a clear example of the power of cyclicality, not a romantic eternal return but a never-going-away. What we now have is the possibility of technological control of reproduction, of the total displacement of birth from culture to science. Feminism in this sense has no longer to look to abstract concepts of man's justice and ethics to know that women are near the beginning of their time because men have betrayed their historicity, have lost the dialectic of nature and history in the "transcendence" of birth. Reproductive technology exposes the fallacy of scientific enterprise, which attempts to negate women without noticing that in so doing it negates the historical, social, sexual, born subject.

This desperate fling at reproductive imperialism won't work, partly because it destroys the very fortresses which patriarchy has built to contain "its" women, the most notable of these being the varied set of social relations known as "the family," of private life as opposed to public life. The feminist revolution astonishes all those men who write snide, bewildered letters asking editors what women want so that it can be arranged that we don't get it: whatever it is. In practice, feminism has redefined revolution in a way that creates problems for martial modes of consciousness. Revolutionary "periods" abound in men's history, periods of spilled blood and sudden death, black magic breaking the linearity of time, of magic male moments strung together with the sticky glue of seminal white magic. Revolution has been understood as progressive violence in the public realm, that changing from one period of history to a better one. Feminism has created a new kind of revolution, a non-violent revolution in the private realm. This is not monolithic of course. The only constant factors in modern family forms are patriarchy and hierarchy, and the variations in different societies and time-frames affect the pace of development and frequently create tensions in the movement itself as international conferences and interpersonal struggles often show. These divisions among women cannot be simply dismissed as the "legacy" (linear) of patriarchy. Though they are that, enormous efforts have to be made to mediate injustices while conserving the vitality of female difference with the yeast of feminist respect. Despite this, the patriarchal family is in a state of dissolution by the contradictory forces of feminist politics on one hand and the male project to control women's fecundity on the other. Clearly, the former is the way to go and the latter must be resisted. Nonetheless, it would be naive not to notice that this revolution has already had far-ranging effects, not necessarily experienced by individual women as triumphs of any kind, but transforming gender and sexual relations in quite clear ways related to work, education, child-raising, income distribution and, where they exist, to civil rights. Further, the developing consortium of peace and environmental groups are welcome retinues in women's struggle for human dignity. The revolution of the private realm is difficult and painful, but it is an event in time in which transformed feminist consciousness is the essential creativity. The impact is, of course, obscured by masculinist perceptions of righteousness in *their* "liberation" of women, an ideological liberation from the struggles of dual work loads, single parenting, cheap labor moderated by trendy sexuality and the benign hand of the state. But other gains are real: for lesbian women, in education, independence but above all in the rising revolutionary potential of the movement itself.

But is there time? Not only time to dismantle patriarchy, but to heal the divisions which separate women from each other? If we are to continue to think of temporality as linear, to set an hour, a date, for the Feminist Period, all we do is saddle ourselves with the apparatus of what are appropriately called "deadlines." If we are to conceptualize history as a lifeline, we not only have to challenge male power, but to destroy the myth of men's time and produce a regenerative time consciousness. This cannot be done by changing the meanings of words in an arbitrary way, but then, it need not be a process of abstraction—of meaning, of significance, of power, of time. There is an ancient base for a new knowledge of the world in the concrete, non-objectified female experience of the unity of continuity in the practical act of birth, the experience of species persistence as accomplishment rather than fate, of life rather than death, of practicality rather than ideology, of wisdom rather than power. These are the premises of feminism, which cannot be decontextualized because their context is us and our experience.

There are three very young women walking in the shopping centre. They

are beautiful, these bosom friends. Their heads are close. They are giggling.
All is well; on and on. ...

NOTES

1. Marilyn French's recent historical encyclopedia has a strong sense of this kind of process,
    as well as an impressive summary of what men have chosen to know and chosen to forget.
    See, *Beyond Power: on Women, Men and Morals* (N.Y.: Summit Books, 1985), pp. 43-112.
2. G. W. F. Hegel, *The Phenomenology of Spirit*, translated by J. B. Bailie (N.Y. and Evanston:
    Harper Torchbooks, 1967), p. 184. The emphases are textual, the bracketed interpolations
    mine.
3. Simone de Beauvoir, *Old Age*, trans. Patrick O. Brian (Harmondsworth: Penguin, 1977),
    p. 402.
4. Ibid., p. 413.

I do not like 'foot-noting' women: reminds me of 'foot-binding.' But I must acknowledge the
debts which come as much from informal talking as formal writing. So to Somer Brodribb, Frieda
Forman, Madeleine Grumet, Sandra Harding, Nancy Hartsock, Angela Miles, Dale Spender and
many others: salutations.

FROM WINE FROM THESE GRAPES*

Edna St. Vincent Millay

Time, that renews the tissues of this frame,
That built the child and hardened the soft bone,
Taught him to wail, to blink, to walk alone,
Stare, question, wonder, give the world a name,
Forget the watery darkness whence he came,
Attends no less the boy to manhood grown,
Brings him new raiment, strips him of his own;
All skins are shed at length, remorse, even shame.
Such hope is mine, if this indeed be true,
I dread no more the first white in my hair,
Or even age itself, the easy shoe,
The cane, the wrinkled hands, the special chair:
Time, doing this to me, may alter too
My sorrow, into something I can bear.

3

Women and Time in Childbirth and During Lactation

Robbie Pfeufer Kahn

The kind of time we are most familiar with is historical or clock time, a life sequence which moves relentlessly forward. In the West we have lived in this kind of time for so long it almost seems impossible for things to be otherwise. From the time of Homer, the Western tradition has pitched itself toward the future like the trajectory of a spear. Above all else, the Homeric heroes, Hector and Achilles, longed to transcend the cycle of life through brave acts—to be remembered by those in times to come.[1] From the moment of creation in the Bible, men and women entered history, a time sequence which increasingly distanced them from source; indeed over time God became less and less accessible to humans.[2] With the arrival of Jesus, while close contact with the source is re-established, it becomes imperative to transcend the body and all things that change—to be "born from above," in order to enter an eternal domain.[3]

Hannah Arendt notes a destructive impulse in this striving for what is outside and beyond the time of life process. She recalls the words of a Russian scientist twenty years before Sputnik was launched (1957): "Mankind will not remain bound to the earth forever," and in a sharp criticism says:

> Should the emancipation and secularization of the modern age, which began with a turning-away, not necessarily from God, but from a god who was the father of men in heaven, end with an even more fateful repudiation of an Earth who was the Mother of all living creatures under the sky?[4]

However much Arendt criticizes the wish to transcend Mother Earth, she belongs firmly to the Western tradition in her valuation of linear or historical time. To Arendt, "man's" ability to make durable objects, things which endure over time and demonstrate the exercise of human invention over nature—the killing of a tree for the wood to make a chair—is one of our most distinctive human traits, in her mind far superior to activities which tie us to the cycle of life.[5] As a young girl growing up surrounded by the granite walls of New York City, then learning the Western tradition in college, afterward as a graphic designer preparing books in time to printers' schedules—books which would endure over time—like Arendt I lived, not necessarily happily, but more or less unquestioningly in linear time.

This linearity pitched toward the future differs radically from living within the cycle of one's own body, the organic cycle of life. Perhaps because of my experience with the printing process I have come to think of linear time as *industrial time*, time organized around a productivity which has nothing to do with the generative activity of nature; the organization of time in the industrial process even erases the differences between night and day since assembly lines operate continuously. In contrast to industrial time there is the organic cycle of life or what I want to call *agricultural time*, meaning time which is cyclical like the seasons, or the gyre-like motion of the generations.

Although I enjoyed each returning spring while growing up, I never became aware that two kinds of time govern our lives, much less their relative value until I had a child. Here is how these two senses of time were recorded in my journal some years after I experienced them:

> I thought I never wanted to have a baby. The mess, the clutter, the personal untidiness, the boredom. But it didn't turn out the way I had feared. I had just come home from the hospital the day the milk came in; it was high summer. I sat out on our porch, admiring the nasturtiums, morning glories, and marigolds which had grown noticeably in my absence. Like my body, everything seemed to be in full bloom. I watched a sea gull glide on an air current, a row of poplar trees lean away from a breeze in the yard next to ours, and at the same time I became aware of the surge of milk in my breasts. These different currents—of milk, of air, of the sap in the trees and water columns in the flowers—seemed to me to flow into one another, so that I became part of them and they part of me. I returned to my old job to work part-time, and put my son in a parent-cooperative day care center (which we had founded) when he was two months old for four hours every weekday morning.
>
> One of my favorite times of day was when I came home from work at one o'clock. I would lie down to nurse him for a nap. After being at work, with deadlines, schedules and meetings, everything marked off by the clock, I would float with him into a different kind of time. It was more cyclical, like the seasons, the tides, like the milk which kept its own appointment with him without my planning it out. I lived during those years in two kinds of time—agricultural and industrial. I loved the two of them side by side. I often thought that if our social structure was different, if it permitted many women to spend early motherhood this way, we would all approach motherhood with more optimism about how it would be after the baby came.

It is agricultural time, or the organic cycle of life which the states of pregnancy, birth, and lactation make available to women living in industrial society. While I say "women," I recognize that men also can enter agricultural time and, indeed, in many ways women in industrialized society, despite being pregnant, may find agricultural time hard to enter. For example, in Nancy Shaw's early sociological study of maternity care for clinic patients called *Forced Labor* (a title she took from Marx's description of the nature of working-class labor), she shows that the conditions of labor for a woman giving birth may not be that different from an assembly line, governed by industrial time.[6] As far back as the 1950s, when the hospital became the common place for birth, women themselves began to compare hospital birth to the industrial process and the link is not merely metaphorical.[7] Obstetrical texts refer "scientifically" to labor as a mechanical process, thus making the metaphor real through their management of birth.[8] A key feature of the industrialized management of birth is the imposition of industrial or clock time upon the process of birth. If the woman does not follow a prescribed sequence of labor events (called "Friedman's curve," a graph of the curve of labor which her body must match, and indeed her labor progression is plotted on the graph paper in relation to Friedman's curve) the hospital will intervene in her labor to make it follow the "correct" progression.[9] For example, if a woman during the expulsive stage of labor does not push her baby out within one and a half hours she will be "aided" by the use of forceps, or by a caesarean delivery. As Barbara Katz Rothman has shown, women giving birth at home show great variation in the course of their labors and may push for many hours.[10] When birth is not measured off by the clock, it is observed as a continuous flow of activity, rather than as discrete units of action which can be plotted against a norm. An industrialized birth, which I call *impeded birth*, governed by the practice of "obstructrics," may make it hard for a woman to experience agricultural time as a normal feature of the experience of childbirth. And this obstructed birth experience may have consequences for the management of lactation.[11]

Industrial time may be brought to bear not only upon childbirth but upon the conduct of the feeding relationship. In Tillie Olsen's story "I Stand Here Ironing," the organic cycle of life is interrupted by a rigid nursing schedule.[12] Emily's mother—who narrates (silently at the ironing board) the story of her daughter's life, trying to figure out why it has been so difficult—chose to nurse at a time when it wasn't popular. "They think it's important nowadays," she says looking back on Emily's infancy, showing her preference for the organic cycle of life over the rationalization of life.[13] But the mother's youth and inexperience compel her to pay deference to cultural dictates. Between Emily and her mother comes an advice book, a cultural voice, which tells her to nurse by the clock. Both she and Emily suffer from the disruption of a more organic state of nurture. Emily's cries "battered me to trembling and my breasts ached with swollenness," but she "waited until the clock decreed."[14] The constraints of clock time or linear time are a palpable historical reality which interferes with the baby's embeddedness in organic or cyclical time, which knows nothing of clocks.

"Why do I put that first?" the mother asks about the nursing of Emily, "I do not even know if it matters, or if it explains anything."[15] The mother puts it first because, properly speaking, it belongs first. Emily's mother has chosen to favor what Niles Newton—a psychologist who has studied the infant/mother dyad in the feeding relationship—calls "token breast feeding," where access to the mother is more or less severely curtailed. "Unrestricted breast feeding" on the other hand, is a condition where the mother is available to the baby more or less "on demand."[16] Token breast feeding can be said to place industrial time first, and unrestricted breast feeding to favor agricultural time. Depending upon the parents and siblings and the practical realities of a family's economic circumstances, one or another form of feeding will be chosen, as we see with Emily's mother.

Like the industrial conduct of birth, the restricted feeding of infants is similar to the organization of factory life, with its time clock and the severe limits placed upon the worker's opportunities to eat, sit, go to the bathroom, or get a drink of water; indeed, along with grammar school rigors, restricted feeding may be a preparation for the factory tempo.[17] However unpleasant historical or linear time may be, this organization of time favors the upper classes, who are not so much its victim as its perpetrator. A black mother who migrated to the north in the 1940s describes the organic cycle of life as the only kind of time in which, as a person outside the "haves" of society, she feels a sense of progress:

> To me, having a baby inside me is the only time I'm really alive. I know I can make something, do something, no matter what color my skin is, and what names people call me. When the baby gets born I see him, and he's full of life, or she is; and I think to myself that it doesn't make any difference what happens later, at least now we've got a chance, or the baby does. You can see the little one grow and get larger and start doing things, and you feel there must be some hope, some chance that things will get better; because there it is, right before you, a real, live, growing baby. The children and their father feel it, too, just like I do. They feel the baby is a good sign, or at least he's *some* sign. If we didn't have that, what would be the difference from death?[18]

To those from a less favored class, linear, industrial, or clock time is merely a reminder that they must sell their labor to live. For this mother's family, only agricultural time offers the possibility of progress.

Thus far, I have spoken about the antipodes, agricultural and industrial time, and how the occasion of pregnancy, birth, and lactation makes agricultural time available to the modern person, to men and to women, but to women in particular. Three other kinds of time become accessible under the dispensation of childbirth, once one has departed from historical or industrial time. These are—generic time, mythic time, and maialogical time. What is meant by each of these? I see *generic time* as distinct from *genderic time*, the latter being historical or linear time, which has been made by men throughout recorded history. Generic time signifies the time of all things of the earth and universe; from this point of view agricultural time is part of generic time. To give birth generically is to enter the "great streams of the universe"[19]—not to leave Mother Earth as Arendt fears, but to participate in her cycle which is part of the longer cycles of the life process of the universe itself.

From the point of view of generic time children and parents are like two planets that touch. Children come into orbit from inside the woman's body; as each child is born the orbital arrangements alter. If you have ever lent a hand to a family you can feel the sphere of influence each member has; you can feel your own critical mass in that context as lesser in comparison to theirs. In time the orbit widens to include the wider world; finally the parents fall away, and new children may enter the orbit of the once child. Given our temporality, it becomes a deprivation to live all of one's life within linear time which lacks the capaciousness of these other experiences of time. Although limited, time stretches to a fullness while remaining *within* the cycle of life; indeed remaining within the cycle of life is the condition for fullness. It cannot be otherwise because we are not otherwise. As Marge Piercy writes:

> Nothing living moves in straight lines
> but in arcs, in epicycles, in spirals, in gyres.
> Nothing living grows in cubes or cones or rhomboids
> but we take a little here and give a little here
> and we change
> and the wind blows right through us and knocks the
> apples
> from the trees and hangs a red kit suddenly there
> and a fox comes to bite the apples curiously
> and we change
> or die
> and then change.
> It is many as drops
> it is one as rain
> and we are in it, in it, of it.
> We eat it and it eats us
> and fullness is never and now.[20]

From the very beginning Western tradition has tried to overreach the cycle of life in a search for permanence: we observe this in the desire of the Homeric heroes to become immortal through song, or of Plato's Socrates to die and be free of the body.[21] The Western tendency to move out of the cycle of life intensifies in the Biblical tradition. Northrop Frye points out that the Biblical God who, significantly, is male, stands outside of nature altogether:

> The maleness of God seems to be connected with the Bible's resistance to the notion of a containing cycle of fate or inevitability as the highest category that our minds can conceive. All such cycles are suggested by nature, and are contained within nature—which is why it is so easy to think of nature as Mother Nature. But as long as we remain within her cycle we are *unborn embryos*. (emphasis added)[22]

Likening our connection with the life cycle to an embryonic state, Frye clearly values a trajectory of time which takes us outside the life cycle. Although he acknowledges that "every human and animal form is born from a female body," the product of female generativity in the Western conception of things becomes that which is unborn.[23] To be awake or truly "born" is to go beyond the cycle of life. Associating linear time with the male, Mary O'Brien, the feminist social theorist, observes: "Men have always sought principles of continuity outside of natural continuity;" in her view a pursuit springing from men's separation from the generative continuity of life which belongs to women.[24]

Female earth goddesses antedate male gods—sky-gods like Zeus in the Olympian pantheon—and were associated with the organic cycle of life. Carol Downing speculates that these "vegetal goddesses" actually were based upon the female body itself. She says:

> That goddesses identified with vegetal fertility should also be associated with human fertility seems inevitable. Women were linked with food not only because they cultivated and prepared it but also because their own bodies were a source of food and life. ...
> What provoked goddess veneration was the recognition of feminine energy as transformative

energy. The food associated with the feminine is food as mystery, food as transformed substance. Through cultivation and cooking, grass becomes bread. Women perform this transformation and incarnate this transformative power in their capacity to make milk out of blood and to give birth out of their own bodies to an utterly other creature: a male, a son. Yet these transformations are never absolute spiritualizations; the corporeal realm is never wholly abandoned. The various extensions of the goddess's province always retain a connection to her essential identification with physical sustenance, with the material realm. From the goddess-worshipping perspective, the necessarily more alienated and intellectualized creative capacity of men is but a pallid imitation of women's natural procreative capacity.[25]

We first receive life into our bodies by the umbilical cord, and later by nursing; and these essential ties to the mother's body as surface and sustenance palpably recreate the presence of Mother Earth, who in turn may have been derived from the reality of pregnant and lactating women. That the relationship between earth and life forms is more than a metaphor is demonstrated in recent research which suggests that life began in the clay of the earth.[26] When women are identified with nature as childbearers, it is Mother Earth, not Demeter who most readily comes to mind. As Carol Downing indicates, in her wonderful discussion of the Greek goddesses' relationship to her own life, Demeter is a more appropriate figure for the parent/child relationship during childrearing, and the slow but irreversible loss of the child to time, culture, and ultimately, death.[27] It can be difficult to accept that although our children will outlive us—at least that may be our greatest hope—we cannot protect them from death. Their life course, which carries them into the next generation, nevertheless follows the same curve as ours: they, as we, will die. The knowledge of these losses we see represented by the grieving Demeter.

If linear time were not the dominant experience of time in the Western context—an organization of time which is at odds with the life cycle events of pregnancy, birth, and lactation—such conceptualizations as Frye's or Arendt's would pose no problem. But where historical process gains ascendancy over life process something is lost, despite historical "progress." By "historical process" I mean organizations or representations of life which subordinate life process to more "significant" things. For example, in the Bible where humans move further and further away from the moment of creation, the solution to the problem of historical time and distancing from source comes in the Gospels—but at the expense of life process. Life on earth becomes merely a preparation for everlasting life. When Jesus disavows knowing his mother in the Gospel according to St. Matthew,[28] he repudiates what could be called "birth from below," or birth into the cycle of life and death in favor of "birth from above," as it is called in the Gospel according to St. John,[29] a spiritual birth which is a necessary condition for joining the "Father" in everlasting life. Turning from representations to organisations of life, the efforts of middle-class women to build careers which might entail the sacrifice of life process events is another example of choosing birth from above over birth from below. Here it is not the kingdom of heaven which is desired but the domain of social recognition and achievement. For example, one professor suffers a nightly conflict over whether to lie down with her three-year-old daughter to get her off to sleep, or whether to attend to her writing, an "offspring" which will live in the public domain of the written word.

If Western men and women would benefit from living under a different organization of time, what would it be? Generic time is one such organization; mythic time is another. Very probably women have known about both from the beginning of the Western tradition (and of course even before) but their understanding has not been conserved in the written record. As it happened I had to learn these kinds of time from the experience of giving birth itself.

By *mythic time*, I mean a return to origins; this kind of time sense belongs to the foundations of any culture, as can be seen by the universality of creation myths. But what would mythic time mean in relation to pregnancy, birth, and lactation? The birth of every child is a return to origins, and both male and female writers acknowledge this. In the Greek creation story Mother Earth brings forth all life, even her husband;[30] when the medieval writer Dante approaches the source of the whole universe (to him a God of love) he compares himself to an infant at its mother's breast, and he is almost unable to utter in words what he sees; and what he sees—a radiant circle with our own likeness in the center—is nothing if not a birth image.[31] For at the moment of birth (if allowed to give birth by her own powers) the mother's body forms a perfect circle around the crowning head of the baby—the circle long having been a symbol of wholeness and unity.[32] Adrienne Rich speaks with ardor of the return to the source of origins, the mother, when she says:

> Remind me how we loved our mother's body
> our mouths drawing the first
> thin sweetness from her nipples
>
> our faces dreaming hour on hour
> in the salt smell of her lap   Remind me
> how her touch melted childgrief ...[33]

What is the offering of Jesus to eat and drink of his body if not the placental and then lacteal relation of mother to baby?[34] Much of Jesus's appeal may be due to his connection to the vegetal goddesses who are a source of life. Mythic time is felt most dramatically perhaps during pregnancy, birth, and lactation, but is also present in any moment of love and healing throughout life which re-establishes the connection to origins. The women's spirituality movement finds a transformative power in the recovery of origins, which they call finding the "goddess within."[35] By this phrase they mean reconnecting with the transformative energy of the woman as Downing describes it, which lies outside (or before) historical time and its phallic trajectory. A women healer, Susan Weed, explains that healing can take place by finding the goddess within:

> All who heal through the power of the loving, nourishing, passionate woman-self, whether in male or female bodies, are healing in the Wise Woman tradition. Mothers, lay midwives, death counselors, "yarb women," and many nurses instinctively heal in the Wise Woman

way. But allopathic doctors, surgeons, chiropractors, all types of practitioners may also work in the Wise Woman way, which is not so much a body of techniques as a belief system.[36]

Mythic time can be entered over and over, although its most intense expression, the formative expression, may come at the moment of birth—both for the one giving birth (insofar as you find the mother in yourself) and for the one being born—and in the nursing relationship which might continue for a number of years. Mythic time nourishes day to day life; it does not lift us out of the cycle of life. The two kinds of time, generic and mythic, illustrate the difference between a *metaphysic* and what could be called a *metafact*—that is, a fact that is larger than a fact. Although the term "metaphysic" is based upon the Greek word "phyein", which means "to bring forth, to make grow," conventionally the term has come to mean abstract thinking divorced from ordinary life, if not superior to it, insofar as it posits something beyond the ordinary facts of existence.[37] For example, when Marx is accused of making a "labor metaphysic" out of the working class what the critic means is that Marx has made an abstraction out of a certain class of society, endowing them with ontological significance.[38] Although the root of "metafact" is the Latin word "facere," which means "to do," the term suggests a kind of conceptualization which does not transcend life, but takes its meaning from the facts or doings of the world.[39] We are part of the universe but tend to perceive ourselves as distinct from it, and impressively so. In the Bible, God creates man apart from nature, and dominant over it (and over woman, his helpmate).[40] Pregnancy, birth, and lactation give us entrance into larger realities grounded in life rather than abstracted from it, as is the case with metaphysical notions. Childbearing allows us to participate in the metafact of mythic time.

Having spoken about generic and mythic time, I want to discuss *maialogical time*, by which I mean a time of mutuality, or interrelatedness. Many feminists advance the idea that like time, our whole language system (having been developed by men) is a genderic, rather than a generic construction.[41] In the spirit of neologisms I want to use the word *maialogical* to stand for that period of the woman's life when she bears children, and lactates. The Greek word "maia," which means mother or nurse, comes from the Indo-European root "ma²," which has come into language by way of infants. This root is imitative, deriving from the child's cry for the breast, as *The American Heritage Dictionary* explains, and is a linguistic universal found in many of the world's languages.[42] Because its origins are both free from male construction, and include the infant "as a speaking voice," the word maialogical might be useful. From a maialogical perspective childbirth becomes the founding moment of the relation of self to other, grounded in the body, since both the *one being born* and the *one giving birth* are taken into account.

Maialogical time is interactive or reciprocal, unlike the time inhabited by individuated Western man who follows the linear trajectory of history, a trajectory considered to be healthy. Historical time, too, is social but it is a sociability based upon the collective activity of "autonomous" individuals frequently in competition with one another, or working for the benefit of someone else at the expense of the self.

In the *Iliad*, Hector and other warriors speak of winning fame from someone else, or giving it to him: one life at the expense of another.[43] Of course, maialogical time is not reciprocal in the ordinary sense, since for obvious reasons infants and young children cannot care for us as we care for them. Indeed, mothers may feel that they are working for the benefit of someone else at the expense of the self, as Adrienne Rich describes in *Of Woman Born*.[44] But the experience of children as a burden surely has a great deal to do, as she points out, with what she calls the *institution* of motherhood, that is, motherhood under a social system dominated by linear time which is extremely inhospitable to the slower tempo of children, and which offers little support to women who are still asked to put in most of the "time" in the care of the young.

By nature, infants live in maialogical time, showing us that fundamentally we are social beings from birth. If labor and birth progress in an *unimpeded* fashion the baby often takes an active, indeed interactive, rôle as soon as it is born. After passing down and out of the mother the baby often will make its way up and over the mother's belly to her breast. Sheila Kitzinger, anthropologist and childbirth educator who has written widely on birth, describes these movements in one of her children's births.[45] The newborn brings about the separation from the mother itself, for its sucking at the breast stimulates contractions of the uterus which expel the placenta. Thus birth becomes not so much a separation of mother and baby as a realignment of self and other. Maialogical time adds another critical perspective on the Western notion of selfhood achieved through individuation and separation. As Carol Gilligan, Jean Baker Miller and Jan Surrey have shown, the separation model of development is anything but universal even in our own culture, since women seem to maintain a connection to others throughout the life cycle.[46] To the model of the "relational self," as Surrey and Miller call it, a maialogical birth offers as an observable fact a self essentially related to others in mind *and* body.

Because it includes the infant as a speaking voice, maialogical time is also slow. Small things count if they are noticed; for babies are social beings at birth, and make social gestures through their bodies. It is odd that in a culture which may define the fetus as a person the newborn is not thought of as a person, as capable of taking an active part immediately in the culture it is born into, an active part which might include its own sense of time.[47] For example, babies are natural semiologists (as Brazelton and others have shown); they speak to us through signs.[48] In Leboyer's film (the doctor who made the important discovery that birth ought to be conducted without violence, but who to his discredit included the mother as one of the twin causes of the violence—the other being medical practice), as he is busy rescuing a baby from what he believes to be the "trauma" of birth, the baby is trying to suck on its fist in the bath, a real sign that for the baby it is time (and indeed high time) to be at the breast.[49] Signs, like words, can be ignored, since Leboyer continues with the saving bath. When infants are allowed to take actions on their own, their fundamental sociability shows them to be cultural beings right from the start, with a sense of time which we might call agricultural or maialogical, signifying their integration *into* the organic cycle of life. Women potentially have privileged access to these states of time which differ from historical, clock, or industrial time. Although the dominant time form of our society militates against it, women can recover something of life-cycle time through the experiences of pregnancy, birth, and lactation.

However, a problem is introduced. For if the infant has not been a speaking voice, she or he certainly has been *spoken for* in exceedingly conservative tones by those who wish to call women back to the task of childrearing. Bowlby and others make a plea for the mother's continual presence in childrearing.[50] And medicine has been assuming more and more control of the birth process purportedly "on behalf of" the baby, even obtaining a court order to make a woman give birth in the hospital.[51] Feminist critics of the "in defense of motherhood" writers, such as Dorothy Dinnerstein and Nancy Chodorow, argue that both women and men not only *can* mother but *have* to, since the development of boys and girls is damaged by the fact that only women mother.[52] By saying this, both women mean not only that the absence of the father is harmful to the child, but that the exclusivity of the mother's rôle is as well. As can be seen, these women make the noun "mother" into a verb, an action, which either sex can perform. Diane Ehrensaft writing in *Socialist Review*, puts in footnote form that the time of breast feeding is problematic with respect to fifty:fifty parenting.[53] But by shrinking breast feeding to seven point type Ehrensaft does not dispense with the problem. That is, most couples, in favor of co-parenting, describe the time of breast feeding as one where the mother is the focus of the baby's attention. Whether being raised solely by women damages children is highly debatable. A recent article in *The Boston Globe* reported research which shows the good effects upon children of women-headed households.[54] The point here is not so much to argue the comparative merits of men and women mothering as to identify the co-parenting theory as one major direction of feminist thinking on childrearing. Most importantly, it is an idea which comes about in part from women wanting to be free to participate in linear historical time. At the other extreme are feminists like Adrienne Rich who feel that children should be raised in a female world where women help other women, a world apart from the linear time of men.[55]

Thus, feminist visions of the management of childrearing (childbearing is usually lumped into this) tend to project an androgynous world on the one hand where "men and women mother," or a female world on the other, where women, with the support of other women, could raise their children, and would be able to pursue a work life. Neither vision makes the necessary separation between childbearing and childrearing, for childbearing and lactation are things only women can do, and hence constitute the only natural division of labor; nor do they take account of the life cycle. For the female life cycle is crucial to theory building about women's lives. Including the life cycle in a discussion of what we might call "birth time" permits the development of a special perspective on that period of a women's life when she gives birth and lactates, a period which in the West may be short compared to other cultures and historical times. Acknowledging maialogical time places childbearing in the context of the female life cycle, rather than regarding a woman's relationship to time as the same over the whole course of her life. Middle-class women may fear being locked into a life*time* of caring for children, because until very recently (even with bottlefeeding) the knot between childbearing and childrearing was tied very tight; and so these women may shy away from claiming a special role in the immediate childbearing period. The meaning of "immediate" would depend upon how long a woman chooses to, or can, nurse, given work and other constraints. (As was seen in the quote of the black mother, this fear of maialogical time is not shared by all women in society.) Another concern is voiced by the partner who may fear being excluded from the mother/infant dyad. But if a child's life cycle is taken into account, that is her or his existence in time, it will be seen that the child has many opportunities for closeness to others at different points along the way. Strict fifty:fifty divisions at every moment are perhaps unrealistic, and make for too much imposition of clock time over the organic cycle of life.

To recover the organic life cycle, presuming that were possible, and the kinds of time appropriate to it would not mean to regress into an endless childhood on the one hand, nor to become a full time earth mother on the other. What it would mean is refusing to see our embodied connection to the world as either a romantic or hedonistic notion—that is as a reaction to the industrial revolution, or as an outgrowth of the notorious sixties. With respect to the former, human history does *not* begin with the invention of the cotton gin. Recognition of our embodied relation to the world, and its value, antedates the Indo-European invasions of around 3000-2000 BC—thought by some scholars to be the time when matrifocal societies were overcome by patrifocal invaders bringing with them their male gods.[56]

First, then, we would recognize that we are connected to nature and furthermore that women have a special relation to the time of nature because of their childbearing capabilities. Second, in order to enter agricultural time we would shrug off the "evolutionary" approach to history, a product of linear thinking where the development of human life over the millenia is seen as moving toward, among other things, greater and greater freedom from the body and even, as Arendt points out, freedom from Mother Earth herself.[57] From a psychological perspective the evolutionary approach views early matrifocal societies as belonging to the infancy of humanity, as Monica Sjöo and Barbara Mor point out in their critique of Jungian and anthropological thought about matriarchy:

> Using without question the nineteenth-century developmental models of inevitable and linear "progress," Jungians theorize that Mother Goddess religions—*if* they existed—existed only near the temporal origins of human culture. Therefore they must express only the "infancy" of the race, or of the individual psyche. Psychoanalytical arrogance corresponds to the Christian theology's view of all pagan religions as "spiritually underdeveloped" by positing Mother Goddess archetypes as "infantile," or as "inchoate subconscious material."[58]

To the evolutionists, patrifocal spiritual systems are an inevitable and necessary step in the maturation of humanity. Leaving evolutionary thinking behind, we would begin to enter maialogical time by recasting our spiritual beliefs, as feminist theologians are doing; by working for the reorganization of work structures; by realizing that we do not have to be just like men in order to have social value, and that as women we have much to offer both in the realm of thought and action coming from our distinctive relationship to agricultural, generic, mythic, and maialogical time.

Above all, living in maialogical time would mean recognizing that the vegetal goddess is our own bodies. Far from corseting our bodies into the one-sex (read male) shape which is the twentieth century fashion (is this physical confinement any better than the stylized women's shapes of the nineteenth century?) we would allow ourselves to understand that what we share with other lactating mammals—bringing forth and suckling our young—is perfectly compatible with being human, indeed is part and parcel of it. Why should we avidly explore our sexuality all the while ignoring our embodied nature as mothers?[59] As it happens, breast feeding even relies upon the same hormonal system as sexuality: the hormone which releases the milk is the same hormone which triggers orgasm. Uncorseting our maternal bodies does not have to be incompatible with living in linear time, providing that this time move forward more slowly and with more digressions. Thus, there would be time out for children. There would be what could be called "mixed zoning" of the private and public spheres. For example, students in a women's studies course, observing a mother nurse her two-and-a-half-year-old daughter as she talked about mothering, went on to write papers about how, during the lecture, the mother lived in the "historical" and "natural" worlds simultaneously (terms which they took from Mary O'Brien, whom they had read) because the woman responded to the child through her body at the same time as she conceptualized about her life as a mother.[60] Perhaps the time will come when both productive and reproductive labor will be honored equally. Not the tokenism of Mother's Day, but an appreciation expressed through the reorganization of work structures to accommodate the uncorseted maternal body. Then, women (in particular middle-class women) might not any longer fear what has been called "the mother knot."

In the *Iliad*—one of the earliest stories of our tradition, with which this paper begins—Hector's mother tries to recall him from a confrontation with the greater warrior Achilles, an encounter which will bring Hector certain death. She bares her breast to remind him of his connection to her as a source of life and comfort and says: "Hector, my child, be moved by this,/ and pity me, if ever I unbound/ a quieting breast for you."[61] Despite her plea, Hector chooses to fight and die for fame and honor, chooses, that is, to comply with the severe imperatives of patriarchal culture rather than to heed the woman's message. Hecuba's attempt to call Hector back to the organic cycle of life from the vanishing point of linear time into which he disappears is an act of recall which we as women and mothers need to invoke again after 2,750 years—not only on behalf of men but on behalf of ourselves as well. We, too, have become attracted to the rewards of living in linear time. We begin, as she did, with our bodies. Perhaps this time we will succeed.

NOTES

1. Homer, *The Iliad*, trans. Robert Fitzgerald (Garden City: Anchor/Doubleday, 1975).
2. In Genesis, God interacts frequently with humanity in the creation story, the Abraham story, and the flood story, for example. *The Jerusalem Bible*, Reader's Edition (New York: Doubleday, 1968).
3. I will discuss the meaning of "birth from above" later. The words come from The Gospel according to St. John, when Jesus says to Nicodemus: "I tell you most solemnly, /unless a man is born from above,/ he cannot see the Kingdom of God." (John 3:3). *The Jerusalem Bible*, Reader's Edition (New York: Doubleday, 1968).
4. Hannah Arendt, *The Human Condition* (University of Chicago, 1958), pp. 1-2.
5. Ibid., p. 139.
6. Nancy Shaw makes the point that the treatment of poor women in the hospital (clinic patients) is reduced to an assembly line process even more than for middle-class women (private patients). Nancy Stoller Shaw, *Forced Labor: Maternity Care in the United States* (New York: Pergamon Press Inc., 1974), p. 110.
7. Richard W. Wertz and Dorothy C. Wertz, *Lying In: A History of Childbirth in America* (New York: Schocken Books, 1979), p. 172.
8. The most recent edition of *Williams Obstetrics*, a text which is used as a standard of care in a court of law, meaning that the norms it sets are accepted as definitions of the reality of childbirth, states: "Labor is work, and work mechanically is the generation of motion against resistance." Jack A. Pritchard and Paul C. MacDonald, *Williams Obstetrics* (Norwalk, CT: Appleton-Century-Crofts, 17th edition, 1985), p. 311. Over the last fifteen years the text has deleted all metaphors comparing birth to the process of nature. (See 14th edition, 1971, p. 349.)
9. Beginning with the 16th edition of *Williams Obstetrics*, Friedman's curve is moved from a section of the text dealing with dystocia—when labor goes amiss—to the section on normal birth, to establish protocols for all labor and delivery. *Williams Obstetrics*, 16th edition, 1980, p. 385.
10. Barbara Katz Rothman, "Midwives in Transition: The Structure of a Clinical Revolution," *Social Problems,* Vol. 30 (Feb. 1983), p. 266.
11. The Boston Women's Health Book Collective, *Ourselves and Our Children: A Book by and For Parents* (New York: Random House, 1978), p. 216.
12. Tillie Olsen, "I Stand Here Ironing," *Tell Me A Riddle* (New York: Dell Publishing Co., Inc., 1961), pp. 9-21.
13. Ibid., p. 10.
14. Ibid., p. 10.

15. Ibid., p. 10.

16. Niles Newton, "Psychological Differences Between Breast and Bottle Feeding," *The American Journal of Clinical Nutrition*, Vol. 24 (Aug. 1971), pp. 993-1004.

17. Harry Braverman discusses the application of time-motion studies to the work force, and refers to the limitations placed upon satisfactions of the body on the job. Harry Braverman, *Labor and Monopoly Capital: The Degradation of Work in the Twentieth Century* (New York: Monthly Review Press, 1974), p. 178.

18. A Black woman who came to Boston from Georgia in the mid 1960s, from Robert Coles, *Children of Crisis*, in Nancy Caldwell Sorel, *Ever Since Eve: Personal Reflections on Childbirth* (New York and Oxford: Oxford University Press, 1984), pp. 28-29.

19. Montaigne, "Of Repentance," *Selections from the Essays*, ed. & trans. Donald M. Frame (Arlington Heights: AHM Publ. Corp., 1973), p. 88.

20. Marge Piercy, "I Saw Her Dancing," *Women of Power: A Magazine of Feminism, Spirituality and Politics* (Winter 1987), p. 76.

21. Plato, "Phaedo," *The Last Days of Socrates* (Harmondsworth: Penguin Books, 1984), pp. 112-13.

22. Northrop Frye, *The Great Code: The Bible and Literature* (San Diego: Harcourt, Brace, Jovanovich, 1982), p. 107.

23. Ibid., p. 107.

24. Mary O'Brien, *The Politics of Reproduction* (Boston: Routledge & Kegan Paul, 1983), p. 33.

25. Carl Downing, *The Goddess: Mythological Images of the Feminine* (New York: Crossroads, 1981), pp. 11-12.

26. John Noble Wilford, "New Finding Backs Idea That Life Started in Clay Rather Than Sea," *The New York Times* (3 Apr. 1985), 18(N), C2(L), Col. 1.

27. Downing, op. cit., p. 133.

28. The text reads: "He was still speaking to the crowds when his mother and his brothers appeared; they were standing outside and were anxious to have a word with him. But to the man who told him this Jesus replied, "Who is my mother? Who are my brothers?" And stretching out his hands towards his disciples he said: "Here are my mother and my brothers. Anyone who does the will of my Father in heaven, he is my brother and sister and mother." (Matt. 12:46-50). The Gospel according to St. Matthew, *The Jerusalem Bible*, Reader's Edition (Garden City: Doubleday, 1968).

29. See endnote 3. It is uncanny that in the very same language as the Gospels, obstetricians speak about caesarean section as taking the baby "from above," hence the female generative act, having been taken over by the physician, becomes male-identified. Vaginal birth is called taking the baby "from below."

30. Hesiod, *Theogony*, trans. Norman O. Brown (Indianapolis: Bobbs Merrill, 1984), pp. 56-57.

31. Dante Alighieri, *Paradiso, The Divine Comedy*, trans. John D. Sinclair (New York: Oxford University Press, 1979), Canto 33: 109-145.

32. See Aniela Jaffee, "Symbolism in the Visual Arts," in *Man and His Symbols*, ed. Carl Jung (New York: Dell, 1968), pp. 266-85.

33. Adrienne Rich, "Sibling Mysteries," *The Dream of a Common Language: Poems 1974-1977* (New York: W. W. Norton, 1978), p. 48.

34. John 6:53-56, *The Jerusalem Bible*, Reader's Edition (Garden City: Doubleday, 1968). For a discussion of maternal imagery associated with Jesus during the Middle Ages, see Caroline Walker Bynum, *Jesus As Mother: Studies in the Spirituality of the High Middle Ages* (Berkeley: University of California Press, 1982), pp. 110-69.

35. See the growing number of books on women's spirituality. The idea of the goddess within is discussed in all of them. A short bibliography includes: Carol Christ, *Diving Deep and Surfacing: Women Writers on Spiritual Quest* (Boston: Beacon Press, 1980); Anne Cameron, *Daughters of Copper Woman* (Vancouver: Press Gang Publishers, 1985); Charlene Spretnak, ed., *The Politics of Women's Spirituality: Essays on the Rise of Spiritual Power Within the Feminist Movement* (Garden City: Anchor/Doubleday, 1982); Starhawk, *Dreaming the Dark: Magic, Sex and Politics* (Boston: Beacon Press, 1982); Jean Shinoda Bolen, *Goddesses in Everywoman: A New Psychology of Women* (San

Francisco: Harper and Row, 1984); Marija Gimbutas, *The Goddesses and Gods of Old Europe: 6500-3500 BC Myth and Cult Images* (Berkeley: University of California Press, 1982); Monica Sjöo and Barbara Mor, *The Great Cosmic Mother: Rediscovering The Religion of the Earth* (San Francisco: Harper and Row, 1987).

36. Susan Weed, "The Wise Woman Tradition," *Woman of Power: A Magazine of Feminism, Spirituality and Politics* (Winter, 1987), pp. 70-72.

37. William Morris, ed., *The American Heritage Dictionary of the English Language* (Boston: Houghton Mifflin, 1973), p. 989.

38. Ralph Miliband, *Marxism and Politics* (Oxford: Oxford University Press, 1977), p. 41.

39. Morris, op. cit., p. 469.

40. Genesis 2: 18-23, *The Jerusalem Bible, Reader's Edition* (Garden City. Doubleday, 1968).

41. Dale Spender, "Defining Reality: A Powerful Tool," *Language and Power*, eds Cheris Kramarae et al., (Beverly Hills: Sage, 1984).

42. Morris, op. cit., p. 1527.

43. Homer, *The Iliad*, trans. Robert Fitzgerald (Garden City: Anchor/Doubleday, 1975).

44. Adrienne Rich, *Of Woman Born: Motherhood as Experience and Institution* (New York: W. W. Norton, 1976).

45. Sheila Kitzinger, "Antenatal Teaching Workshop," Boston Association for Childbirth Education, Boston, Mar. 1976. See also her books *The Experience of Childbirth* (New York: Taplinger, 1972); *Birth at Home* (Harmondsworth: Penguin, 1979); *The Experience of Breastfeeding* (Harmondsworth: Penguin, 1979).

46. Jean Baker Miller, *Toward a New Psychology of Women* (Boston: Beacon, 1977); Carol Gilligan, *In a Different Voice: Psychological Theory and Women's Development* (Boston: Harvard UP, 1983); Jan Surrey, "Psychoanalysis and Women" (Women in Culture and Society, Women's Studies Program, Brandeis U., Waltham, MA, 6 Oct. 1983).

47. Marshall H. Klaus and John H. Kennell, *Parent-Infant Bonding* (St. Louis: CV Mosby, 1982); Marshall H. Klaus and P. H. Klaus, *The Amazing Newborn* (Reading: Addison Wesley, 1985).

48. W. S. Condon and L. W. Sander, "Neonate Movement is Synchronized with Adult Speech: Interactional participation and language development," *Science*, Vol. 183 (1974), pp. 99-101; T. B. Brazelton, M.Z. School and J. S. Robey, "Visual Responses in the Newborn," *Pediatrics,* Vol. 37 (1966), pp. 284-90; A. MacFarlane, D. M. Smith and D. H. Garrow, "The Relationship Between Mother and Neonate," in Sheila Kitzinger, and J. A. Davis, eds. *The Place of Birth* (New York: Alfred Knopf, 1975).

49. "A Gentle Birth," Frederick Leboyer, film shown at Harvard Medical School, 29 Sept. 1976; See also Frederick Leboyer, *Birth Without Violence* (New York: Alfred Knopf, 1975).

50. John Bowlby, *Attachment and Loss*, Vol. 1 (New York: Basic Books, 1969).

51. See V. Kolder, J. Gallagher and M. Parsons, "Court-Ordered Obstetrical Intervention," *New England Journal of Medicine,* Vol. 36 (1987), pp. 1192-96. All the mothers in this national survey were poor: 21 court orders were described from the previous 5 years, 18 of which were granted, 15 were for caesarian sections.

52. Nancy Chodorow, *The Reproduction of Mothering: Psychoanalysis and the Sociology of Gender* (Berkeley: University of California Press, 1978); Dorothy Dinnerstein, *The Mermaid and the Minotaur: Sexual Arrangements and Human Malaise* (New York: Harper and Row, 1977). Both writers place responsibility on the social institution of women mothering for problems in the mother-infant relationship, but in the end they see exclusive women's mothering as harmful. Chodorow focuses upon the harm more than Dinnerstein when she says:

> That women turn to children to complete a relational triangle, or to recreate a mother-child unity, means that mothering is invested with a mother's often conflictual, ambivalent, yet powerful need for her own mother. That women turn to children to fulfill emotional and even erotic desires unmet by men or other women means that a mother expects from infants what only another adult should be expected to give.(212)

Dinnerstein is more circumspect when she says: "It is true, and by now widely understood, that woman's limited opportunity to develop her own self does in fact often make her batten on, and sabotage, the autonomy of others.(112) Rather than excoriating mothers,

Dinnerstein focuses more upon the ways in which the all-powerful mother of childhood makes men turn on women and nature later in life, which isn't saying that women *do* harmful things to children, as Chodorow suggests.

For a woman-centered critique of Nancy Chodorow's book see Pauline Bart, "Review of Chodorow's The Reproduction of Mothering," *Mothering: Essays in Feminist Theory*, ed. Joyce Trebilcot (Totowa: Rowan and Allenheld, 1983), pp. 147-52 (originally published in *Off Our Backs* 11 (Jan. 1981)). For example, Bart asks why two such books as Dinnerstein's and Chodorow's, which do not follow "patriarchal academic conventions," as she puts it, should be so admired by the establishment. She says:

> one has to ask the sociology of knowledge question *cui bono*—in whose interest are these books? The answer is not difficult to find. Radical feminist approaches to motherhood such as Adrienne Rich's *Of Woman Born* and Judith Arcana's *Our Mother's Daughters* suggest women bonding as a solution to the oppressive nature of motherhood as an institution. But Chodorow and Dinnerstein claim that most of our difficulties are caused by socialization by mothers; thus, they maintain, most of the problems we face will wither away like the state after the revolution if men, whom they have previously described as inadequate to the task because they were socialized by their mothers, are brought into childrearing. It is clear which solution is less threatening to the status quo.(149)

53. Diane Ehrensaft, "When Women and Men Mother," *Socialist Review,* Vol. 49, Jan.-Feb. 1980, pp. 37-73.

54. Pamela Reynolds, "Men, They Grew Up Happy in a Female-Headed Family," *The Boston Globe* (24 Aug. 1986), B 25.

55. In *Of Woman Born*, Rich recommends that men should share in the care of children but she believes that even boys should remain "in the deepest sense, the 'sons of the mother.'"(210)

56. Marija Gimbutas, *The Goddesses and Gods of Old Europe: 6500-3500 BC Myths and Cult Images* (Berkeley: University of California Press, 1982), p. 238.

57. Arendt, op. cit., p. 2. If detachment from the body is harmful for Westerners it may do even greater harm in countries which are not "modernized." For instance, the bottle feeding of third world babies, promoted by Nestle's advertising, offers mothers freedom from their embodied attachment to their infants at the expense of the baby's health, and in many cases, its life. The Nestle boycott of 1984 has been resumed by Action for Corporate Accountability (ACA) ACA, 3255 Hennepin Ave. S., Suite 255, Minneapolis, MN 55408.

58. Monica Sjöo and Barbara Mor, *The Great Cosmic Mother: Rediscovering the Religions of the Earth* (San Francisco: Harper and Row, 1987), p. 29.

59. The recent feminist book, *Powers of Desire: The Politics of Sexuality,* eds. Ann Snitow, et al. (New York: Monthly Review Press, 1984), neglects to include any essay which has to do with the sexuality of maternity.

60. Myla Kabat-Zinn and her three-year-old daughter, Serena, speaking about birth and mothering, Women and Work, Sociology Department, Brandeis University, Waltham, Spring 1984.

61. Priam, her husband also tries to bring Hector inside the walls of Troy, but his appeal focuses on glory, the claims of linear time. Homer, *The Iliad*, trans. Robert Fitzgerald (Garden City: Anchor/Doubleday, 1975), XXII: 28-29, 84-86.

James Hannon says that men, too, must resist the old patriarchal imperatives, commands, for example, like the one which moved Abraham to be willing to sacrifice Isaac, his son. Hannon adds that respect for our children's lives must also extend to our "enemies." "Good fathers do not sacrifice their children—or the children of others. To save our sons from war we must save all from war. We are fathers of a new dispensation of parenthood, present at the birth of our children and truly present thereafter, free to love fiercely and protectively. As parents who truly know our children, we must challenge the power of the patriarchs. We will have to do without their blessings." (In "Fathers, Sons, and War: Refusing to Sacrifice our Children," *The Heart and Wings Journal* (Sept./Oct. 1987), p. 26.

While I am critical of an androgynous approach to parenthood, I do feel that alone we women cannot win against the imperatives of generic time—not only the claims of the work world but also of the nation state. Women *and* men must cooperate to fore-ground the organic cycle of life in the structuration of the state and society. It is a good thing that fathers are moving from Priam's to Hecuba's side, with the added feature of refusing to accept the idea of an "enemy."

For a fine discussion of "maternal thinking" and pacifism, see Sara Ruddick's, "Preservative Love and Military Destruction: Some Reflections on Mothering and Peace," *Mothering: Essays in Feminist Theory*, ed. Joyce Trebilcot (Totowa: Rowan and Allenheld, 1984), pp. 213-30.

4

The Solitude of Women and Social Time

Elizabeth Deeds Ermarth

I begin with the hypothesis that the phrase "women's time" is a contradiction in terms. If, as I believe, our conventional definitions of it are rooted in patriarchy, then women's time *qua* time does not exist at all: except as an exile or an absence of time as it is conceived in patriarchal conventions, that is, as what Julia Kristeva calls "linear time, the time of project and history."[1] Opposition to those temporal conventions only feeds them, and it is as yet unclear whether there can be a viable conception of temporality that is separate but equal.

If, as Hélène Cixous suggests, women are the repressed of culture, then in order for them to have a rôle in culture at all they must volunteer as sacrifices to the system so that the system, and thus their oppositional rôle in it, may survive. We see endless reiterations of this sacrificial plot in detective television where the police or problem solvers are usually men and the victims usually women for whom the threat of rape or death is the logical outcome of their magnified vulnerability; he is the power that unfolds truth while she is the (justified) sacrifice. It is possible to show that the discourse of historical time exists in the first place by means of the crucial exclusion or repression of women. To participate in that discourse, then, would engage women in a discourse of violence against themselves, and to engage them at the deepest roots of this discourse. Historical time and its project is a time to which women have personal, professional, and cultural attachment; yet this same time, as it has existed in Western cultural conventions through several centuries, consistently defines them as absence, as Other, so that the hand sustaining them is the automatic hand of suppression.

This logic leads to some searching questions. Does the use of terms like "women's time" or "female tradition," or "feminine point of view" merely re-inscribe a binary definition that divides without equalizing? Is there *any* idea of time possible now that is *not* phallogocentric? Such questions have been made possible by a large body of feminist work still in process; they are not easily answered, if they can be answered in the 1980s at all. One plausible way around conventional definitions of time is to link temporality with

37

language and hence with discourse. This strikes me as a fruitful course, but one still plagued with familiar difficulties.

Julia Kristeva, for example, deals with a division of labor in language that locates various binarisms (symbolic *vs* semiotic, law *vs* poetry) and then *genders* them. She distinguishes between two separate but equal powers of language: on the one hand, the *symbolic* or thetic power for logical and conclusive formulation; on the other hand, the *semiotic* or multivalent power for playful and deconstructive activity. "As social practice," she writes, language "necessarily presupposes these two dispositions." The two powers should function together; alone each is crippled. She seeks in a reunion of these dual powers a recourse beyond the "constraints of a civilization dominated by transcendent rationality" and basically—that is, symbolically—"bored to death." The "ideological stakes" of breaking the linguistic order are very high, as is testified by the current signs of "symbolic and social unrest" (she cites youth, drugs, women). In her recourse to language, Kristeva favors a mode of knowledge bound to process rather than product and freed from static conceptions of structure. Rather than searching language "for the coherence or identity of either *one* or a *multiplicity* of structures," we must search instead "for the *crisis* or the *unsettling process* of meaning and subject."[2] I will return to this unsettling process, but first I think it important to notice the more conservative elements of this formulation.

Even in Kristeva's entirely valuable discussion traditional difficulties creep in unexplained. She associates the symbolic and semiotic powers of language with paternal and maternal functions. Even though she insists that both are united in discourse and not specific to individual subjects, still the gendering of linguistic function associates gender with content—with some real or imagined substantial quality. The problem with this is that, though the qualities change, the gender difference retains its hierarchical order. For example, writing in the mid-twentieth century Kristeva would find digressiveness maternal whether it appeared in Vladimir Nobokov or in Virginia Woolf. But this catholicity nevertheless still retains the dichotomy that makes biology once more into destiny. Had she been writing in the mid-eleventh century, Kristeva might well have retained the dichotomies between semiotic and symbolic, and between maternal and paternal, but she would likely have reversed the equations between them, making the paternal mode the semiotic, the maternal the symbolic. Why? Because semiosis and parataxis were prevailing values in medieval writing and the prevailing values, when gendered, usually turn out to be masculine. Women are perpetually carriers of the depreciated half of the binarism, even though the qualities carried are completely reversed by the course of historical change. Even when the relative values change radically over time, women's position remains the same. Thus the association of particular values with gender prevents feminist theory from reaching the premises it seeks. Each succeeding gendered definition further encodes and validates the idea that biological difference is relevant to problems of meaning and signification, and in that persistent difference woman is always the Other, always the excluded, always the repressed of culture.

The perpetual re-inscription of women as Other has had especially virulent effect in the empiricist tradition which has associated women with "nature," thus naturalizing their repression. How common this association still is can be judged by listening for the metaphor "mother nature" routinely used by, among others, margarine advertisers and weather reporters. The association took a definitive turn in the late Enlightenment where, as Margaret Homans shows, Romantic poets confirmed the binarism that identifies women with nature and men (the poets) with the transcenders of and commentators on that nature.[3] Even the Sentimental idea that women, as natural beings, somehow were superior to the men who were inspired by them and who wrote about them from an estranged position, was an idea that reinforced the biologically based separation and excluded women from the activity of culture. In the era when Nature became a goddess, the identification of women with nature meant that women were formally and deliberately (even cheerfully) put on automatic: governed *by* forces, as nature is, but never, like the (male) poet, themselves doing the governing. In this role, of course, women are not only "like" nature they act as stand-ins for nature in the cultural schema and hence as forces to be governed. This is a convenient position for the middling bourgeois gentleman who does not maintain the discipline of the botanist or the astrophysicist but who nevertheless can maintain control or governance over nature through one of its female stand-ins (a group already economically and politically powerless). It is easier to interfere with a nature that has human consciousness than with a nature that looks—as it increasingly did in the Romantic period—red in tooth and claw and ever less sympathetic to human affairs.

What response may be most appropriate to this tradition remains an important question. In an era that seems increasingly to value ecological and more generally systemic considerations, it may be preferable to accept rather than deny the association of women with nature: preferable, that is, to valorizing the other half of the binarism with all its well-known repressions. Nature, after all, has its wisdom, its economy, and in many cases its intelligence. But most desirable, as the long history of women as depreciated Other seems to indicate, is the departure from binarism altogether and hence departure from emphasis on gendered binarism as well. As Evelyn Fox Keller has recently suggested, both nature and mind must be renamed if we are to escape endless vacillation between the opposition of passive object to active subject, of female nature to male mind.[4] This alternative gestures towards the massive redefinition of the human sciences and the associated epistemological critique now underway in so many disparate fields and, perhaps, coming together with the force of a spring flood. This redefinition amounts to a critique of Western discourse itself: its obsession with power, its ethic of winning, its quantifiable and objective knowledge and its association of knowledge with power, its preference of the symbolic and thetic function of language over the semiotic and ludic, its reliance on rationalist and categorical means of identification and exclusion, its belief in a linear and progressive history, its individual subject, and most powerfully its common media of exchange (time, space, money) which make possible certain ideas of political and social order (for example, ones favorable to democracy and to revolution). Whatever the eventual fate of gendered binarism in cultural discourse, one thing at least seems clear. So long as women are carriers of whatever is not privileged by the prevailing discourse—and this practice has been nearly universal—discussion of smaller issues only recodifies the problem that ostensibly is being addressed.

How this paradox works temporally for women is obvious in many novels of the nineteenth and twentieth centuries. Fictional women on the edge of time belong to a large company; it includes Marge Piercy's Connie Ramos, Flaubert's Madame Bovary, George Eliot's Maggie Tulliver, Hardy's Tess, Richardson's Clarissa, Kate Chopin's Edna Pontellier, Tolstoy's Anna Karenina, Charlotte Gilman's woman in *The Yellow Wallpaper,* Virginia Woolf's Rhoda, Heinrich Boll's Katarina Blum. The list could go on. I will select two of these who are as different as any fictional heroines could be in terms of circumstance and who yet both inhabit the same temporality and the same plot of female sacrifice. Both are pressed to extinction by remarkably similar forces; both die with remarkably similar words on their lips.

George Eliot's Maggie Tulliver, in order to maintain continuity in her experience, accepts conditions that require of her a kind of prolonged psychological suicide. Her long-sought reconciliation with her family, especially its male leader, eventually entails her drowning death and continued life only as an idea inspiring to others. The metaphor of consequence that dominates the novel, the flow of the river Floss, continually underscores the perception that the very conditions of existence, *at once temporal and social*, inexorably draw her toward death, and that this end is the only possible result of her quest for poisoned partnership.

Tolstoy's Anna Karenina replicates this plot almost uncannily. The description of Anna's final walk along the railway platform efficiently recapitulates the process of dissociation that has been entailed by the social invisibility forced upon her despite her notoriety and class privilege. In the final scene a series of distancing glances intensifies her despair, uncomprehending as they are, or envious, or depersonalizing, and idly cast her way in a public place. Maidservants and young men comment audibly on her magnificent dress or fix their eyes on her as a specular object until the effect is one of physical pain. They take her in without taking her in. She is a piece of woman-flesh, a consumer, a curiosity. The denial of recognition that began with her husband's refusals and that extended to those of Vronsky and her women friends here punctuates her last moment. Such denial—subtle, all-pervasive, impossible to confront—wears down her life and ends it. Anna's inward cry at the end is, "O God, where shall I go?" Seventeen years earlier at her end, Maggie Tulliver cried out in the dim loneliness, "O God, where am I? Which is the way home?"[5] Both heroines are outsiders in their societies; both vacillate painfully between longing and privation; both cripple themselves striving to get free; both die as a result of their own efforts and just at the moment when they fully realize their utter isolation. Most importantly, the very temporality from which they expect continuity and the possibility of change not to mention growth and development, turns out for both to be a medium of death.

The cental resource of their novels—the time of project and history—is contaminated by the hidden requirement that development transform them entirely into instruments of social arrangements—social arrangements that are sustained by their suppression. Both George Eliot and Tolstoy underscore the action of time by de-emphasizing events in favor of the reflexes to and from events, so that time itself only ripens and matures the solitary woman's tragedy. Increasingly uncoordinated with social time, the heroines private consciousness increasingly founders and finds no support apart from the roles of ornament and functionary. Initially each takes seriously the opportunities for change apparently offered within the temporal conventions of her novel; each initially mistakes her enemy for a single individual; but finally each learns her radical solitude in a social world that exists in the first place by means of her exclusion. Tom Tulliver is backed up variously by his family, public opinion, and the local minister; Alexey Karenin by the entire society that smiles on Oblonsky's betrayals of his wife and winks at the oppression of other less well-clad slaves. For these heroines history is a process of depletion; for them no reserves are developed to validate the great historical and social idea of time that is held out with such silent persuasiveness by the narratives in which they appear and in which readers can find hope in a future.

The logic of these instances suggests that so long as time means what our novelistic and social conventions generally have told us it means, women's acceptance or incorporation as autonomous subjects in the discourse of history is simply impossible. When either Maggie or Anna attempts to change her life the step brings a fatal break, not a development or an opportunity, and this break reveals to them in a lightening flash their unequivocal solitude; for each this revelation immediately precedes death. At least in these two representative, culturally central cases, there is time, and there are women, but there is no women's time.

These literary examples can be matched with many more historical examples of what is at stake personally in terms of living subjects. In the interest of space some brief but evocative texts will stand as reminders that the problems under consideration spread far beyond novels and survive the nineteenth century. The first text is from Elizabeth Janeway's essay on the history of women: "Like their personal lives, women's history is fragmented, inter-rupted; a shadow history of human beings whose existence has been shaped by the efforts and the demands of others." Is a shadow history the same thing as a real history? Do women have a history of their own? or a not-history of their own? This problem, put so clearly by Elizabeth Janeway, has a deeply personal import that comes home in the passionate description of longing and of solitude to be found in women's writing. None are more passionate than this one by Alice James: "Those ghastly days, when I was by myself in the little house in Mt. Vernon Street, how I longed to flee in to the firemen next door and escape the 'Alone, Alone!' that echoed through the house, rustled down the stairs, whispered from the walls, and confronted me, like a material presence, as I sat waiting, counting the moments as they turned themselves from today into tomorrow."[6] Does such intense experience as this count as history? The language of solitude and anguish suggest lack; the temporal arrest suggest a slow, fatal erosion as the moments independently turn *themselves* from today into tomorrow. History goes on by itself while Alice James sits apart counting the days from her solitary rack. What a contrast this is to the social environment implied by the profoundly inclusive and homogeneous temporal medium of nineteenth-century novels where even solitude must be grasped in terms of the common ground.

Although extended discussion of that common medium of historical time is a large subject, it is one with interesting links to patriarchal culture (feminists could profitably uncover more of those links). Even a brief discussion will suggest how paradoxical and difficult the subject of women's time can be. Linear time, then, the time of project and history, is something we take for granted. It is there, like Mont Blanc; it is a given; it is "natural." But such faith is a trick of perspective. Linear time is an artifice. It is, for better or worse, one of the massive achievements of Western culture, and as such is a profoundly collective construct: not only generally as an artifice with important historical and ideological boundaries, but also specifically as the collective construct that valorizes collective constructs.[7]

For present purposes we will assume that a single, public, common time—the homogeneous medium of "human" and of empirical events—is a construct of the past two or three hundred years and that it has served a particular cultural order. This time is a medium of development, progress, and pro-duction; a medium for accumulation of knowledge, power, and other forms of capital. This historical time, as we have collectively agreed that it should be, has these capabilities because it "is" a universally consistent, neutral, homogeneous medium. This is the view of time encoded by a series of great formulations, among them those by Newton, Kant, Adam Smith, Darwin, George Eliot, and Tolstoy. Given this idea of time it would be contradictory to speak of a development in solitude, the Romantic poets notwithstanding, because in this cultural discourse any change is by definition *ex*change. Solitude may be profitable for the soul going in providential circles (Richardson's

Pamela, for example), but solitude is not a medium for the self in its definitively social development. For our culture, at least until recently, the connectedness of past and future seemed automatically to involve every individual (male or female so the *premise* goes) in collective agreements that, like the medium, are universally consistent and neutral. These collective agreements are profoundly influential partly because they are relatively invisible and seem to involve "natural" truths; their self-evidence makes them far more subversive than the more practical and conscious contracts of daily living.

Both Alice James and Elizabeth Janeway allude to the convention of linear time, the time of project and history. For both, that time is always elsewhere. It is a medium of the kind of premeditated action and collectively validated event to which they are aliens; they inhabit a situation—one can hardly call it a medium—of fragmentation and paralysis that contrasts utterly with the medium of action and event. Alice James manages to communicate the sense of ontological disaster that comes with the radical solitude she describes. In such ontological disaster, as many nineteenth-century heroines discovered, the need for relief is urgent and immediate; and the need is not confined to nineteenth-century heroines. Writing of "Monroe according to Mailer," Ingrid Bengis says flatly: "Psychic starvation is a desperate business: one does not wait around for Baked Alaska."[8]

For women, historical time has been a resource that is radioactive. In historical time the paradoxes for women are maddening. On the one hand a consciousness, if it is not to run berserk, needs the validations that seep in continually from other persons in the daily round as we exchange reassuring clichés, take our marked exits, and make our entrances in a system guaranteed externally to our minds in the diverse languages of culture. On the other hand, validation of a woman's consciousness in our culture requires her exclusion and repression. Milton thought that exclusion from social exchange meant blessed shelter from chaos, and he left his Eve out of history. In the women's experience described by George Eliot and Tolstoy or by Janeway and James, however, such exclusion plainly means isolation from the ground of being and hence the doom of those marked for sacrifice. Whether a woman tries to join history or to find a place outside it, her experience is defined by similar formulations, ones fundamentally consistent with the empiricist definition of time as the medium of project and history.

Finding a truly new alternative means moving the struggle to a different site. According to Kristeva the first wave of contemporary feminism sought a place for women in patriarchal culture and became involved in "the logic of identification" that such ambition required. A second wave in the late 1960s sought to secede entirely from patriarchal culture in order "to give a language to the intra-subjective and corporeal experiences left mute by culture in the past." The search of identification with the symbolic and patriarchal function gave way to the valorization of the semiotic and maternal function: an effort quite remarkably new and one brilliantly dramatized in the essays of Luce Irigaray.

In making this move feminism participated in the radical rejection of empiricism that was already making headway in many other fields and gave to that general rejection a new theoretical perspective and vocabulary, not to mention a new energy and relevance. Feminism's rejection of patriarchal order has much in common with the anti-empiricist and anti-humanist writings of Michel Foucault, Roland Barthes, Alain Robbe-Grillet and others who have become eloquent concerning the heedless bankruptcy of the culture of progress and capital. Beneath all these new departures lies a similar critique of premise and a similar search for the deepest new departures in the linguistic and symbolic order of things. "History is linked to the *cogito*," writes Alice Jardine in her introduction to Kristeva's essay on time, "to the paternal function, representation, meaning, denotation, sign, syntax, narration, and so forth. At the forefront of this thinking is a rejection of what seem to be the strongest pillars of that history: anthropomorphism, humanism, and truth."[9] The fragmentation and paralysis evident in the passages from Alice James, *Anna Karenina* and the rest may be instances of a more general cultural dislocation underway since the late nineteenth centry, memorably captured by the modernist poets and by existential novelists, and pursued since by so many major writers. The challenge to this modernist and post-modernist movement is the challenge of moving beyond negative critique to positive process and it may be here that feminist theory may make its most important mark.

The third wave of feminism, according to Kristeva, is moving beyond the duality implied by both the preceding feminist positions, the effort to join patriarchy, and the effort to secede into a matriarchal order and to articulate a world heretofore mute. Both these "alternatives" preserved the same dichotomy between gendered functions. So for example, if patriarchal function entailed governance over natural forces, matriarchal function entailed evasion of that governance and gave priority to those forces even if that meant accepting identification with "nature." Whether the emphasis was on patriarchal or matriarchal function, the dichotomy with all its cultural baggage remained the operative premise. The third wave of feminism seeks to move beyond these dichotomies to the sociosymbolic contract itself. "The new generation of women is showing that its major social concern has become the sociosymbolic contract as a sacrificial contract."[10] Kristeva claims that this third wave is a "mixture" of the two attitudes formerly in opposition, the patriarchal that has been associated with linear time (the time of history and of project), and the matriarchal that has been associated with estrangement (voluntary or not) from the time of history and of project.

What this "mixture" implies for linear time and its associated values remains unclear; whether the new critique of culture can or will preserve those pillars of history and the *cogito*, "anthropomorphism, humanism, and truth," also remains unclear. The most promising step may be the difficult one that goes beyond structure to process, what Kristeva specifies as "the *crisis* of the *unsettling process* of meaning and subject." This alternative for women is also an alternative for an entire culture, or at least that is the hope. In recent years feminist criticism has proven its creative originality, its power to move beyond the particular agendas (winning the vote, seeking constitutional equality) upon which recent feminist affluence has been based. The project to change the sociosymbolic contract will call on the limits of that creative originality.

The linguistic order is a formidable opponent. If the feminist critique of culture is to break new ground, the interim conclusion must be that nothing can remain unexamined, *especially* the premises of any interpretive method because method is the process whereby the linguistic order is continually re-encoded and re-inscribed. A "mixture" of Kristeva's first two modes of feminism seems to me a course fraught with irresolution, although it is a logical consequence of using totalizing dualities like symbolic-and-semiotic or paternal-and-maternal that cover all the available possibilities; and, given such duality, some convention that privileges both alternatives rather than arranging them hierarchically has a logical appeal. But the problems of fundamentally radioactive definitions remain. The key new approach, it seems to me, is the one Kristeva announces as the unsettling process of meaning and subject, throwing the emphasis off what is finished, conclusive, static, identified and on to what is open, playful, mobile, relational. Such a process does not abandon the ideas of subject and meaning, but heightens their hypothetical status and their potential multivalence. Such a process may actually preserve history as a form of linguistic process and in so doing make fully explicit the radical potential available in the idea of history from the first. It might even be fun.

The emphasis on process, in short, may preserve linearity while controlling its deficiencies. For intellectuals in Western constitutional societies giving up the time of project and history is a move with massive implications for a way of life still valuable despite its liabilities; and a way of life that includes the educational institutions and intellectual traditions that have been the support of so much recent cultural deconstruction, including feminist theory. It may be, in the end, that these traditions are already bankrupt beyond recall but in that case the losses have only begun to be counted. The deliberate effort to disown them is a large and costly effort with as yet uncertain benefits. These cautions are especially true in Anglo-American culture where the linguistic order is itself so profoundly linear. The fact that the phrase "women's time" is currently such a contradiction can inspire feminist writing to move into really new avenues. What is most exciting is that women's self-awareness has inspired a search for new premises that may uncover new modes of liveable time and that may avoid mere re-inscription of paralysing old modes. The road is long and without glory. The prize is the articulation of women's life as discourse and not Other.

NOTES

1. Julia Kristeva, "Women's Time," trs. Alice Jardine and Harry Blake, *Signs*, Vol. 7, No. 1 (Autumn, 1981), p. 18.

2. Julia Kristeva, "From One Identity to Another," in her *Desire in Language: A Semiotic Approach to Literature and Art*, trs. Leon S. Roudiez, Thomas and Alice Jardine (New York: Columbia University Press, 1980), pp. 133-36; "Women's Time," p. 18; "From One Identity to Another," pp. 140, 125.

3. Margaret Homans, *Women Writers and Poetic Identity: Dorothy Wordsworth, Emily Brontë, and Emily Dickinson* (Princeton: Princeton University Press, 1980), especially Chapter 1, "The Masculine Tradition," pp. 12-40.

4. Evelyn Fox Keller, *Reflections on Gender and Science* (New Haven: Yale University Press, 1985).

5. Leo Tolstoy, *Anna Karenina,* tr. Aylmer Maude, ed. George Gibian (New York: W. W. Norton & Co., Ltd., 1970), p. 694; Part VII, Ch. 31. George Eliot, *The Mill on the Floss* (Boston: Houghton Mifflin Riverside Edition, 1961), p. 453; Book VII, Ch. 5.

6. Elizabeth Janeway, "Reflections on the History of Women," in *Women: Their Changing Roles* (New York: Arno Press for the New York Times, 1973), p. vii. Alice James, *The Diary of Alice James* (quoted passage written July 9, 1889, of the years 1883-84 when she was alone after her parents' deaths), ed. Leo Edel (New York: Dodd, Mead & Co., 1964), p. 45. First published in 1934 (infamously and tellingly enough) as *Alice James, Her Brothers, Her Journal.*

7. For discussion of historical time as a collective act of faith with historical and ideological boundaries in the Renaissance and modernism, see the first 100 pages of Elizabeth Ermarth, *Realism and Consensus in the English Novel* (Princeton: Princeton University Press, 1983).

8. Ingrid Bengis, *Ms Magazine*, October 1973.

9. See both Kristeva's essay, "Women's Time," and Alice Jardine's "Introduction" to the essay in *Signs*, Vol. 7, No. 1, pp. 19, 8. Also relevant in Michel Foucault's inaugural lecture, December 1970 at the Collège de France, "The Order of Discourse," tr. Ian Mcleod, in Robert Young, ed. *Untying the Text, A Post-structuralist Reader* (London, Henley, and Boston: Routledge and Kegan Paul, 1981), pp. 48-76.

10. Julia Kristeva, "Women's Time," p. 25.

I want to thank Andrea Dimino for her invitation to deliver a first version of this essay at her 1985 MLA panel on Women's Time.

5

H. D. and Time

Cheryl Walker

Much of recent H. D. criticism focuses on two parts of the poet's accomplishment: her recuperation of female and maternal meanings from cultures of the past and her contributions to the revision of her own culture through her extraordinary achievements in creating new female-centered myths.[1] There is no doubt that in her quest to find a voice and to gain legitimacy, H. D. both chafed against patriarchal strictures and sought to elevate the female to a position at least illustrious as that of her male counterparts. As she wrote in *HERmione*, "A lady will be set back in the sky. It will be no longer Arcturus and Vega but stray star-spume, star sprinkling from a wild river, it will be myth; mythopoeic mind (mine) will disprove science and biological-mathematical definition."[2] This 1927 statement represents one version of her quest.

However, in our desire to make H. D. "the mother of us all," we have perhaps overestimated her congruence with contemporary feminist patterns just as in our desire to reclaim Emily Dickinson, we have neglected to make room for Dickinson's nineteenth-century reservations. Like Dickinson, H. D. took fire from the spark created by her passion for and friction with powerful male figures. Like Dickinson again, H. D. took little delight in women as a group or in political struggles to liberate them. As Barbara Guest rather stringently puts it: "H. D.'s attitude toward women was either a reach for total possession, a need to overwhelm them, as in her struggle with (Elizabeth) Bowen, or she remained critically aloof; she regarded those women who did not interest her as mere members of the tribe."[3] For her part, Emily Dickinson is reported to have said to T. W. Higginson: "Women talk; men are silent: that is why I dread women."[4] Though we need not forget Dickinson's rhetorical strategies in her conversations with Higginson, this comment is quite within the parameters of what we know of her mind, as H. D.'s undervaluing of political activism and lack of engagement with women as a tribe are within what we know of hers.

However, it would be a mistake to conclude that these poets have nothing to teach us about the relationship between patriarchy and the female artist simply because their views were mediated by personal and historical conditions. Though at times out of patience with female behavior, both Dickinson and H. D. created probing analyses of patriarchy's effects on women. Both began with a distrust of history, feeling instinctively that history had been constructed as "his story" even as science had come to represent the triumph of his-story in the present age. In their meditations on time and timelessness, both women poets revise that story; Dickinson by her linguistic dislocations designed to dismantle patriarchal certainties, and H. D. by her decision to examine the flow of history, committing herself to a conscious attempt to alter it with her art.

The difference between the two strategies is instructive. Dickinson never set herself up to speak for the female principle, remained consciously ahistorical, and accepted with comparative ease the social limitations on her freedoms— even symbolically ridiculing them by choosing for herself a more restricted role than her times would have required. H.D., on the other hand, did set herself up to speak for the female principle, did become historical, and lived a thoroughly unconventional life which, if not particularly bohemian, mocked almost every standard dear to the Pennsylvania middle class from which she came.

My purpose in making this comparison is to remind us again that history does matter. What was possible for H. D. was not possible for Emily Dickinson even if she had desired to defy convention in the ways H. D. did. Furthermore, just as Dickinson and H. D. could not have lived one another's lives, so neither of them is quite the model for our own quests we sometimes wish her to be.

However, a closer look at one aspect of H. D.'s shaping of a woman's life in literature suggests a paradigm for the whole modern period linking Emily Dickinson's times to our own. That aspect is the woman poet's relationship to the problem of time and history. By recovering some of the structural properties of H. D.'s development, we can see come into focus the possibility of a change in women's relationship to history. H. D. began to write with an outsider's sense that time was a force she could not alter, which did not include her, and which threatened her movements so that only by discovering an evasive strategy for avoiding the temporal could she hope to establish a place for herself. The poppy dream is the form she gives this strategy in *Sea Garden*.

By the end of her life, H. D. has developed a very different sense of her relationship to time. She is no longer running away from history but has accepted both her place in it and her responsibility to work for change. Instead of the poppy-seed ecstasy of her early Imagism, she writes in *Hermetic Definition*: "I need no rosary/of sesame/only the days' trial,/reality."[5]

Though still a visionary poet, H. D.'s ability to imagine herself embedded in history and potent for change locates her as a twentieth-century woman and opens her texts to interpretation in terms of the stages Julia Kristeva describes in her essay, "Women's Time." I would like to initiate this exploration of H. D.'s temporal development by quoting a rather lengthy passage from that essay. Kristeva says:

As for time, female subjectivity would seem to provide a specific measure that essentially retains *repetition* and *eternity* from among the multiple modalities of time known through the history of civilizations. On the one hand, there are cycles, gestation, the eternal recurrence of a biological rhythm which conforms to that of nature and imposes a temporality whose stereotyping may shock, but whose regularity and unison with what is experienced as extra-subjective time, cosmic time, occasion vertiginous visions and unnameable *jouissance*. On the other hand, and perhaps as a consequence, there is the massive presence of a monumental temporality, without cleavage or escape, which has so little to do with linear time (which passes) that the very word "temporality" hardly fits: all-encompassing and infinite like imaginary space, this temporality reminds one of Kronos in Hesiod's mythology, the incestuous son whose massive presence covered all of Gea in order to separate her from Ouranos, the father.[6]

Though this is a complicated and even somewhat obscure description of two types of "women's time," it is strangely evocative of the early poetry of H. D. Here is H. D.'s voice in the second section of "Sea Gods":

> But we bring violets,
> great masses—single-sweet,
> wood-violets, stream-violets,
> violets from a wet marsh.
>
> Violets in clumps from hills,
> tufts with earth at the roots,
> violets tugged from rocks,
> blue violets, moss, cliff, river-violets.
>
> Yellow violets' gold,
> burnt with a rare tint—
> We bring deep-purple
> bird-foot violets.
>
> We bring the hyacinth-violet,
> sweet, bare, chill to the touch—
> and violets whiter than the in-rush
> of your own white surf.[7]

This is not an instantaneous perception captured in a moment of time, as Imagism demanded. Its effect is cumulative and deeply dependent on repetition. Yet the effect is one of speed. H. D.'s agility here sends the mind hurtling from repetition toward eternity. We are faced with "vertiginous visions," on the one hand, and the massive presence of something eternal, a landscape, on the other. The speaker also becomes the landscape with its precipitous cliffs, its thundering shores, its flowers of serenity; as though Gea were being separated by an act of will from Ouranos, the father.

But what of *jouissance*? Ecstasy there is but it is a poignantly erotic ecstasy, subject to loss, despair, and so subject to time. While furnishing us with an important part of H. D.'s early temporal orientation, Kristeva's description can only point to part of our experience of the early poems. The undertow is the recuperated presence of the father, the antagonist and the representative of another form of time. He is the presence who freezes the speaker and upon whose "frozen altars," as D. H. Lawrence called them, H. D. sometimes seems to pile her poems.

H. D. is certainly not the only writer to see in linear time the signature of the father. James Joyce wrote: "Father's time, mother's species." Adrienne Rich remarks sardonically: "Time is male/ and in his cups drinks to the fair." In *The Gift* the grandfather clock hovers over the action with the same haunting suggestion of impending doom we feel when Rafe's watch is mentioned in *Bid Me to Live*. Time, clock time, chronological time, is the property of the fathers whereas words and word games, art, belong to the women or to men like Lawrence, whom H. D. thought of as a feminine spirit. Mama in *The Gift* plays with anagrams. "It was a game, it was a way of making words out of words, but what it was was a way of spelling words, in fact it was a *spell*. The cuckoo clock would not strike; it could not because the world had stopped."[8] Mamalie's power also stops time and creates a palimpsest in which figures from different eras overlap.

Papa, on the other hand, merges with images of Bluebeard and nightmare, the witch who flies in the night. His schedule is formidable, inexorable: "everything revolved around him." He goes out in the night to look at the stars. In her child voice H. D. mulls it over: "He goes out to look at stars that have something to do with time flying, Mr. Evans said, that has something to do with winter and summer and the way the earth goes round the sun" (*G* 52). In *The Gift* various forms of time are gendered as the child persona slides between father and mother, between *kronos* and *kairos*. At one point she says: "Clock-time and out-of-time whirl round the lamppost" (*G* 66).

Part of the project of the later H. D. was to resolve the conflict between mother and father which raged for many years in the poet's psyche. *The Gift* could not be written until that peace was made and was not complete until the last years of World War II. By that time, H. D. had made her peace with both her father's and her mother's legacies. Her mother's legacy she would embody in the vision of womanhood implicit in *Helen in Egypt* which is dedicated to her mother, a vision which reconstructs masculinity through the force of love. But it had always been easier to find a positive force beyond time in the eternal maternal. At the point at which she could finish *The Gift*, H. D. could also accept her position in time with much greater ease than the young girl does in the novel. The girl will feel frozen for many years—"because to live I had to be frozen in myself"—but the adult narrator can say: "I seem to be sitting here motionless, not frozen in another dimension but here in time, in clock-time" (*G* 140). The return to clock-time was part of that psychological process of healing.

If H. D.'s early poetry illustrates her desire to escape the dead hand of the fathers with its temporal signature as history, it certainly makes a strong attempt to establish a realm of imaginative and creative life in which the poet's special group of partisans might redeem the compromised present. In "The Tribute," for instance, the narrator allies herself with a scattered remnant who inhabit "a city set fairer than this/ with column and porch." The "we" whose vision she represents seem to be mostly male. Though eclipsed by time and war, they are part of a prophecy of redemption.

We are veiled as the bud of the poppy
in the poppy-sheath
and our hearts will break from their bondage
and spread as the poppyleaf—
leaf by leaf, radiant and perfect
at last in the summer heat.

Beauty here, though a female presence, is timeless and immortal, for "could beauty be done to death,/ they had struck her dead/ in ages and ages past" (*CP* 59-68). Another way of reading this is to see in it a belief that the female, as subject to time, is lost, dismembered. Only in a timeless realm, in which female-male bonding occurs without conflict and almost without gender, is there a chance for a female poetic voice.

Perhaps this is an overly schematic example: the early H. D. appropriating a vatic voice to evade the problems of time and gender which left her frozen if not mute. However, I believe this instance is useful to consider as a limit or boundary, one toward which much of her early work moves again and again. Eventually, she would find it unsatisfying, and for some of the reasons that Kristeva outlines in "Women's Time."

After the passage describing the two types of time associated with female subjectivity that I quoted above, Kristeva goes on to caution: "Female subjectivity as it gives itself up to intuition becomes a problem with respect to a certain conception of time: time as project, teleology, linear and prospective time as departure, progression, and arrival—in other words, the time of history" (192).

From the mid-1920s through the 1930s, during what I call H. D.'s middle phase, this problem was one the poet began to feel more and more acutely. In the poetry she seems to be struggling with a sense of stultification. Time is stopped or predictable and repetitious but not with the repetitions of unnameable *jouissance*. There is no timeless serenity any longer. Her persona seems to be unravelling literally in the repetitious lines of the poems in *Red Roses for Bronze*. At the other extreme, she is a statue or a marble mask, as in "Trance." The voice is struggling against incoherence and half in love with easeful death. In the "Sea-Choros" from *Hecuba*, she writes:

I am dead
whether I
thread the shuttle for Pallas
or praise the huntress,
the flower of my days
is stricken,
is broken,
is gone

(*CP* 240-41)

I would submit that this is not only the character Hecuba speaking of her losses at the fall of Troy but H. D. herself bemoaning a loss of poetic power and centeredness.

In 1933 and 1934, H. D. underwent analysis with Sigmund Freud out of a need to move on in her life. She wrote: "I wanted to free myself of repetitive thoughts and experiences—my own and those of many of my contemporaries."[9] Freud made her write "history" and reactivated her struggle with her father, thus bringing her back to time.

Though a close examination of her *Tribute to Freud* cannot be undertaken in the limited space we have here, it should be said that H. D. employs in it the same metonymic style she uses in other late prose works like *The Gift*, *End to Torment*, and *Bid Me to Live*. On the one hand, we have a narrative, a progression of events, but on the other, we have a set of associations linking concepts and individuals synchronically in patterns that are frustratingly difficult to pin down in a logical sequence. Nevertheless, it is possible to recover these metonymies if we stare fixedly and for a long time into the semantic pool.

An important series of associations for the purpose of this argument is Freud-father-time-catastrophe-death. Her old fear of the realm of the fathers which was experienced often as a fear of time became particularly acute in the face of the possible catastrophes of civilization made manifest in Nazi-dominated Vienna of the 1930s. Furthermore, Freud himself as a surrogate father was moving nearer and nearer to his own death. H. D. remembers him saying to her dramatically, "Time gallops"—a phrase linked in her mind with the "time flies" she dilates upon in *The Gift*.

H. D. struggled against Freud in certain ways and remained immune to his influence in others. Yet he certainly helped her. In "The Master" she writes: "it was he himself, he who set me free/ to prophesy" (*CP* 458). Because Freud was committed to a maternal, nurturing function with his patients, H. D. seems to have experienced him as both male and female. Through her analysis, the poet was able to acknowledge the positive elements of both the male and the female legacy. She was able to achieve a degree of independence and flexibility she had not felt before.

The encounter with Freud is energetically depicted in "The Master" which contains H. D.'s self-proclamation of that independence from the father ("for she needs no man,/ herself/ is that dart and pulse of the male"— *CP* 456) as well as her tenderness and dedication to him. The strength of both sides of her ambivalence can be felt in the following lines:

> Let the old man lie in the earth,
> (he has troubled men's thought long enough)
> let the old man die,
> let the old man be of the earth,
> he is earth,
> Father,
> O beloved
> you are the earth,
> he is the earth, Saturn, wisdom,
> rock, (O his bones are hard, he is strong,
>   that old man)

(*CP* 457)

Here, in addition to the obvious ambivalence of the speaker's feelings, we find the association of the father with power, fear, rock, intellectual "wisdom," and death. We might also remember that the god Saturn was alternatively known as Kronos, the same as the Greek word for time. Though the father is associated with time, however, he is also earth. The violent dichotomy Kristeva describes in which Gea is wrenched from Ouranos, the father, seems to have given way here as the father merges with the mother, and becomes nurturing as well as terrifying, spatial as well as temporal, female as well as male.

Yet the vision of time in "The Master" is only briefly historical (in section VII where H. D. rightly predicts the contentiousness over Freud's legacy which followed his death). Most of the poem is rendered mythically in the Greek disguise of the journey to Miletus. In crucial ways H. D. still felt it necessary to avoid the ordinary as one can see by the fact that she adheres to a vision of change effected by two exceptional individuals, Freud and herself.

As the men squabble over Freud's legacy, she alone, a woman, finds the most potent application of his theories in the "turn from easy pleasure/ to hardship/ of the spirit" (*CP* 460). And Freud is the "only one, the old man,/ sacred to God" who is allowed to be spiritually present at the celebration of female mysteries with which the poem culminates in sections XI and XII. Both figures are able to transcend gender and lose their personal specificity at the end in a dilation which is far from clear on the idea that "woman is perfect." Though H. D. claims at the end that the prophesy that the Lord will become woman has already been fulfilled, this visionary moment is unconnected to actual historical time. We have no idea when or under what conditions it occurred. It simply allows her to leave behind the thorny problem of Freud as tyrant and of herself as a misguided disciple searching for "a neat answer."

Still, in terms of her orientation toward time, I feel that H. D.'s experience with Freud was crucial and that its effects can be traced in her late masterpieces *Trilogy, Helen in Egypt,* and *Hermetic Definition. Trilogy* is a re-encounter with history and time in poetry such as H. D. had never undertaken before. "This search for historical parallels"—as she names it in *The Walls Do Not Fall* (section 38)—produced some of her greatest poetry. Though she is Psyche, able to transcend the destructive effects of time brought home to roost in war, we should remember that her vision here is an epiphany experienced *in time*, a revelation she hopes to pass on to illuminate her readers, much as Mary opens the eyes of the ordinary servant Kaspar. Kaspar receives the gift. As H. D. describes his transformation, first he is lost in the experience of revelation, "out-of-time completely," but ultimately he is returned to his present-day existence: "or rather a *point* in time," to integrate what he has learned.

Helen in Egypt is H. D.'s most extended discussion of the relation between gender and time. The poem takes up many other issues as well—the role of psychology in re-membering, the relation between love and death, the role of an agape-like Love in redeeming history—but this poem too returns to a moment in time. L'Amour and La Mort "will always be centralized by a moment, 'undecided yet,'" as the poet says late in her poem.[10] Relationships of all sorts, parents and children, men and men, women and women, men and women, are confined within the repetitive patterns one discovers in history and yet they are protean too, always capable of breaking out of these forms into dimensions of expanded possibility. Thus, following Stesichorus, H. D. tells us that the Helen of Troy for whom the battle was fought was an illusion produced by the expectations of a narrow historical focus. Another Helen, more complex and more substantial, sat out the war in Egypt and struggles in the poem to take responsibility for the confusions of a history which she both shares and transcends.

In the first section of the poem where Helen and Achilles meet, Helen's task is to neutralize the anger of this figure representative of patriarchal history who holds a women responsible for historical mayhem. Using the symbols available to her in the temple, "Helen achieves the difficult task of translating a symbol in time, into time-less time or hieroglyph or ancient Egyptian time" (*HE* 13). Egyptian time is controlled by the Amen-script of the god which Helen understands intuitively rather than intellectually. In the symbolic realm of the Amen-script, Helen knows she is innocent of the guilt imputed to her by history but her greater integrity demands a confrontation with her avatar, the Helen of Troy whose experiences she also mysteriously shares.

In the first section of the poem, "Pallinode," she struggles against history in order to neutralize the anger of Achilles and make him accept the transcendental reality of a womanhood innocent of the destructiveness connected with women in human time. One can read *Helen in Egypt* as a kind of temporal autobiography in which this first phase corresponds to H. D.'s first approach to the problem of time through strategies of evasion or escape into a timeless realm.

"Leuke," the second section of *Helen in Egypt,* chronicles Helen's return to Greek time and to intellectual rather than intuitive knowledge. Like H. D.'s middle period of poetic creativity, "Leuke" takes as its central organizing event the encounter with Freud, here called Theseus. Theseus guides her, helps her unstrap the heavy burden of her past, and listens to her description of her dilemma. Should she return to Achilles and take on the challenge of patriarchal history with its hostility toward women or should she remain with Paris, who represents personal time and the triumph of the psyche over the debilitating aspects of the past? Paris's love constructs Helen as Eros and offers her the peace of "a small room," a heaven-haven illuminated by the light of Leuke, the white island, where male and female merge without anger in the spirit of life. During their first encounter, Theseus tells Helen:

> that only Love, the Immortal,
> brings back love to old-love,
> kindles a spark from the past; (*HE* 149)

His message means that "Helen must be re-born, that is her soul must return wholly to her body" (*HE* 162). The trance of Egypt with its transcendental mysteries must be broken.

Theseus counsels Helen to choose Paris in order not to give way to the death-cult seemingly represented by Achilles. Yet in the end she goes her own way. Like the H. D. who wishes to re-encounter her father and her own personal history through myth, Helen decides to measure "time-in-time (personal time)" but also "star-time (the eternal)" by returning to Achilles and "the writing" which is herself.

> I will encompass the infinite
> in time, in the crystal,
> in my thought here. (*HE* 201)

Though Theseus has been of great help in bringing her intellectual wisdom and reconciliation with her historical past, she knows that Achilles awaits her in Egypt where historical realities and transcendental meanings must be brought together, through the connection of Eros and Eris, love and death.

"Eidolon," the third section, begins with an acknowledgment of the centrality of time to Helen's quest. H. D. says: "Now after the reconciliation with time, Greek time, (through the council and guidance of Theseus), Helen is called back to Egypt" (*HE* 208). But why Egypt again? H. D. herself poses this question in Book Two of "Eidolon." It appears that Achilles also seeks in Helen a way into Love, not erotic love but rather mystical love under the sign of his mother, Thetis, whose eidolon—or avatar, or image—frees him from his anger against the historical Helen and reminds him of the larger vision of acceptance and wholeness represented by the sea, her element.

> She fought for the Greeks, they said,
> Achilles' mother, but Thetis mourned
> like Hecuba, for Hector dead. (*HE* 296)

In order to be fully human, H. D. seems to say, one must accept both the realm of personal love, of war and history, and the realm of transcendental Love, of Egyptian mysteries, and divine forgiveness. Refusing to choose one or the other, Helen seeks a third answer. So in returning to Egypt, "this third Helen, for the moment, rejects both the transcendental Helen and the intellectual or inspired Helen" (*HE* 258) of Theseus' Greek wisdom.

Most readers are convinced that in the end Helen finds a third way, resolving the contradiction represented by Paris-Achilles and situating herself in what Frank Kermode describes as the *aevum*. According to Kermode, "The concept of *aevum* provides a way of talking about this unusual variety of duration—neither temporal nor eternal, but, as Aquinas said, participating in both the temporal and the eternal. It does not abolish time or spatialize it; it coexists with time, and is a mode in which things can be perpetual without being eternal."[11] Albert Gelpi, responding to a similar model, also quotes Aquinas and sees Helen "between time and eternity and participating in both." He compares H. D.'s vision with T. S. Eliot's "still point of the turning world" and Ezra Pound's "SPLENDOUR,/ IT ALL COHERES." As Gelpi, and other readers read the poem, "everything (is) caught up in the resolution."[12]

Despite its neatness and persuasiveness, I would like to dissent from this widely-held view concerning H. D.'s temporal resolution at the end of *Helen in Egypt*. If all we had were the lines before the coda, we would certainly have to conclude that the poem ends in triumph and synthesis:

> there is no before and no after,
> there is one finite moment
> that no infinite joy can disperse
>
> or thought of past happiness
> tempt from or dissipate
> now I know the best and the worst;
>
> the seasons revolve around
> a pause in the infinite rhythm
> of the heart and of heaven.

> (*HE* 303-04)

But after this lovely moment in which "the Wheel is still," the poem goes on, into the coda, "Eidolon." After the pause, the rhythm of the heart resumes and Helen asks in her "wholly human" guise, "But what could Paris know of the sea?" Having resolved the issues raised by Paris by telling us that the dart of Love is the dart of Death, the poet turns again to Achilles. Achilles represents a timeless dimension which "spells a charm" like Mama's anagrams in *The Gift*. He has broken with the patriarchal Command—with Father Time—in favor of previously repressed allegiances which are even more potent.

> only Achilles could break his heart
> and the world for a token
> a memory forgotten.

> (*HE* 304)

Thetis/Helen are together the "memory forgotten" and they represent the power of the eternal/maternal as against the power of paternal time, even erotic time. Achilles represents not the *aevum* but H. D.'s old love, *kairos*, the fullness of synchronicity outside of linear temporality.

My argument, then, is that H. D. does not resolve the conflict between these two temporal dimensions in *Helen in Egypt* but instead leaves open the dialectic for further development in *Hermetic Definition*. As she says in Book II of this last section: "Perhaps it is the very force of opposition that creates the dynamic intensity of 'the high-altar, (Helen's) couch here'" (*HE* 225).

In choosing for Achilles at the end, she does not simply resurrect the transcendentalism of her first anti-historical vision in Egypt. Yet she does diminish the importance of historical time in favor of those images of eternal return, the sea and the sand, "the infinite loneliness" of a quest for other shores than those upon which one is born mortal and mundane.

Hermetic Definition is the most personal and least transcendental, in the old sense, of all H. D.'s volumes. Its temporal code, rather than *Helen in Egypt*'s, shows the real integration of body and spirit, time and timelessness, as the poet acknowledges her imminent death and joys in the persistence of her work as an artist. Perhaps the most poignant aspect of this sequence's treatment of time is the fact that in it the poet does allow a resolution, suggesting her surrender of life construed as ongoing dialectic. There is "the sense of an ending" here, a sadness we don't feel in H. D.'s earlier work.

In "Grove of Academe" from the title sequence, H. D. invokes her past retreat into a timeless realm by writing an appreciation of St. John Perse. She clearly admires his classical art: "this retreat from the world,/ that yet holds the world, past, present,/ in the mind's closed recess" (*HD* 27). But at this stage of her life, she can no longer find this pause an ultimate refuge:

> you showed me how I could cling
> to a Greek rock and how I could slide away,
> but did you show me how I could come back
> to ordinary time-sequence?
>
> (*HD* 44)

Many aspects of these poems show H. D.'s acceptance of her life, of history, of her responsibility to work for change. The details from present day events, her body consciousness, her rejection of the rosary of sesame in favor of "The days' trial,/ reality"—all confirm our sense that her project now is "to recover identity" and to use that recovery for the benefit of civilization. The child, *Esperance*, is her image for the work of artistic creation which may consume the artist but which "lives in the hope of something that will be." It is "the past made perfect." She in no way denigrates the lived life of history. Hermione, who stands for both H. D.'s earlier persona and her child Perdita, perhaps, "lived her life and lives in history" (*HD* 112). Now H. D. approaches what Julia Kristeva describes as the third stage of feminism in Europe: "*insertion* into history and the radical *refusal* of the subjective limitations imposed by this history's time" (195).

At the beginning of this essay, I said that the structural properties of H. D.'s temporal development might operate as a paradigm for the change some women have experienced in their relation to history during the modern period. Like many creative women, H. D. began with a sense of being an outsider to history. Time was the antagonist, history the signature of an oppressive patriarchy. As she developed, her vision of the temporal took on first, in the palimpsestic phase, a more androgynous aspect. In the end, it seems, time appears genderless and thus corresponds to the visionary project Julia Kristeva applauds finally in "Women's Time."

At the end of "Women's Time" Kristeva advocates what she calls the "demassification of the problematic of *difference*." By this she means "showing what is irreducible and even deadly in the social contract" (209), but in the interest of seeing where difference is not irreducible, where the evolution of civilization may require a sense of continuity as well as divergence in the experience of the two sexes. Kristeva advocates "this in such a way that the habitual and increasingly explicit attempt to fabricate a scapegoat victim as foundress of a society or a counter-society may be replaced by the analysis of the potentialities of *victim/executioner* which characterize each identity, each subject, each sex" (210).

In spite of her commitment at one level to detailing the battle formations in the war between the sexes, H. D. was ever ready to see the male as a friend and ally as well as an enemy. In fact, much of H. D.'s struggle with the meaning of time demonstrates her continuity with the male Modernists rather than her complete divergence from their practice.

We can see this continuity, for instance, in the appeal of the mythic for both H. D. and her male counterparts. Thomas Mann, in *Freud and the Future*, points to a higher truth embodied in the actual, a truth which marks individual lives with the imprint of historical parallels, making them both a formula and a repetition. Pound, Eliot, and Yeats each found a mythic expression of the temporal potent to reveal the larger contours of historical progression and connect them to vital moments in the past. Like H. D.'s Holy Ghost in "The Walls Do Not Fall" of *Trilogy*, the myth or dream they all delineate is meant to be

> ... open to everyone;
> it acts as go-between, interpreter,
>
> it explains symbols of the past
> in to-day's imagery,
>
> it merges the distant future
> with most distant antiquity. (*CP* 526)

We can certainly say that the angle of H. D.'s encounter with these matters was in part determined by the times in which she lived. We can also say that her relationship to "Father time" was daughterly instead of merely filial. It was rebellious but not dismissive. In her quest for the wisdom belonging to male "gods"—Amen, Zeus, Christ, Freud—she sought to appreciate as well as appropriate the positive attributes of their legacy. "Take me home, Father," the speaker says to Amen, in *Trilogy* (*CP* 527). Formalhaut's temple, to which Helen returns in Egypt, is "not far/ from Theseus, your god-father,/ not far from Amen, your father" but Helen's vision, like H. D.'s is "dedicated to Isis,/ or if you will, Thetis" (*HE* 212), to the potency of the female enlightened spirit.

H. D., like Emily Dickinson, ultimately dedicated her life to love and art, repeating in her own words the earlier poet's formulae: "my business is circumference" and "my business is to love." However, H. D.'s quest found its recompense in her reclamation of an identity committed to meaningful and public work, an identity-model spuriously offered to women in the nineteenth century but only perhaps genuinely possible in our own time. We can see this claim being asserted in the birth of the child as she pictures it in "Winter Love": a male child with a female inheritance, the child of art whose project is the rectification of imbalance, mutual destructiveness and male teleology.

Like Julia Kristeva in "Women's Time," H. D. saw herself as a visionary. But her "spiritual realism"—as she called it— united history with metaphysics at the end of her life. In her desire to help others, in her reconciliation with time, in her unashamed linkage between biography and myth, in her dedramatization of gender conflict, H. D. moved beyond her early and middle phases. As feminists of a different generation, we may or may not wish to claim her resolutions as our own. Nevertheless, her work like Julia Kristeva's offers useful imaginings to a world in many ways bereft. *Esperance* is H. D.'s gift to a barren time.

NOTES

1. The past ten years has seen an explosion of criticism of H. D.'s work. In this brief citation I will mention only a few important works: Susan Sanford Friedman's *Psyche Reborn: The Emergence of H. D.* (Bloomington: Indiana UP, 1981); Rachel Blau DuPlessis's *Writing Beyond the Ending* (Bloomington: Indiana UP, 1985); and *H. D.: The Career of that Struggle* (Bloomington: Indiana UP, 1986); Alicia Ostriker, *Writing Like a Woman* (Ann Arbor: Michigan UP, 1983); and the centennial H. D. issue of *Contemporary Literature* edited by Friedman and DuPlessis, Vol. 27, Winter 1986.

2. *HERmione* (New York: New Directions, 1981), p. 76.

3. Barbara Guest, *Herself Defined: The Poet H. D. and her World* (Garden City, N. Y.: Doubleday, 1984), p. 246.

4. *The Letters of Emily Dickinson,* ed. Thomas H. Johnson and Theodora Ward, 3 vols. (Cambridge: Harvard UP, 1958), p. 473. Similar reflections appear in letter #246 to Edward S. Dwight in which Dickinson is bemoaning the death of Dwight's wife: "I cared for Her—so long—she spoiled me for a ruder love—and other women—seem to be bristling—and very loud," p. 389.

5. *Hermetic Definition* (New York: New Direction, 1972), p. 19; all subsequent references to this volume will be given in the text as *HD* with page reference following.

6. *The Kristeva Reader*, ed. Toril Moi (New York: Columbia UP, 1986), p. 191; further references will be given in the text.

7. *Collected Poems 1912-1944*, ed. Louis L. Martz (New York: New Directions, 1983), p. 30; hereafter references will be given in the text as *CP*, page reference following.

8. *The Gift* (New York: New Direction, 1982), p. 10; references hereafter appear in the text as *G*, page reference following.

9. *Tribute to Freud* (Boston: Godine, 1974), p. 13.

10. *Helen in Egypt* (New York: New Direction, 1961), p. 271; hereafter references will appear in the text as *HE*, page following.

11. Frank Kermode, *The Sense of an Ending* (New York: Oxford UP, 1967), p. 72.

12. Albert Gelpi, "Hilda in Egypt," *Southern Review*, Vol. 18, New Series (April 1982), pp. 245-47 passim.

LINEAGE

Margaret Walker

My grandmothers were strong.
They followed plows and bent to toil.
They moved through fields sowing seed.
They touched earth and grain grew.
They were full of sturdiness and singing.
My grandmothers were strong.

My grandmothers are full of memories
Smelling of soap and onions and wet clay
With veins rolling roughly over quick hands
They have many clean words to say.
My grandmothers were strong.
Why am I not as they?

From *For My People*, originally published by Yale University Press, 1942.
Reprinted by permission of the author.

6

Memory and Myth: Woman's Time Reconceived

Patricia Jagentowicz Mills

Memory is the mediation between the psychological and political spheres of life, and critical remembrance is the impetus for woman's liberation. That is, woman's consciousness-raising, a process of re-forming female identity and social life, is motivated in its critique of woman's domination by traces of memory. As we reclaim our lives by re-creating a shared understanding of the world, we reclaim the memory of pain and possibility embedded in myths that reach beyond the given socio-historic world. Here we find that understanding is not merely a function of the historical development of reason from *mythos* to *logos*. Rather, woman's memory is embedded in myths which remain alive and elucidate aspects of civilization that would otherwise remain unexplained; these myths give us access to experience outside the purview of phallogocentric, instrumental rationality. Memory, therefore, serves as something more than the attempt to recall a lapsed utopian moment, the attempt to recall a golden matriarchal age of amazonian women, for memory is a temporal continuity which is a function of reason and imagination: it is woman's past as recaptured in the present. Thus, myths are not naive or unreflective stories—they are tales known to us only insofar as we re-member and re-make them within the project of consciousness-raising to become the matrix of our liberation.

Our appropriation of myths as a self-conscious project is especially important for the problems of self-knowledge and self-identity. Myths are what we create and re-create in order to understand what we are and how we are in the world. The dominant myths of our culture articulate the relation between civilization and sexuality, between rationality and bodily desire, between the reality principle and the pleasure principle. But these myths have become reified universals; they are the patriarchal tales of Oedipus, Odysseus, and Prometheus, in which man is shown to march through time in a journey of self-discovery while woman is forced to remain outside of historical time, confined to time out of mind. Woman is never seen to achieve an independent ego, an "I," and her desire remains subject to, and defined by, male desire. What patriarchal myths reveal are relations between man and woman in which woman is defined in terms of male sexuality, male desire—defined *for* man, not for herself. They are stories of woman's domination and self-alienation. What is required from a feminist perspective is an immanent critique of the dominant patriarchal myths which weaves and re-weaves tales of the creation of the female self through a critical appropriation of female mythic figures.

The project of reclaiming myths from a feminist perspective has already begun. Much of this scholarship focuses on the homosexual nature of female desire. While this is important work, I believe that it is also necessary to understand the power and deformation of female heterosexual desire in our recovery of female eros as the ground of self-identity and sisterhood.[1] I offer a critique of the tales of Oedipus and Odysseus, those mythic journeys to selfhood that color our understanding of self-identity, and color it male. Within this critique I focus on several female figures, including Antigone and Medea, as representing a way to understand female identity formation within patriarchy while pointing beyond woman's domination.

The answer to the riddle of the Sphinx which Oedipus offers is an answer of patrilineal descent: a son grows to become a man and takes the place of the father. Thus, male self-creation is the central problem of the myth in which Oedipus eliminates both his father, Laius (whom Oedipus kills), and his mother, Jocasta (who commits suicide when she realizes that she has engaged in an incestuous alliance). In addition, the Sphinx, who may be seen to represent matriarchal forms, is defeated by Oedipus and kills herself as a result of the encounter with him. Thus, while fathers are perpetuated in their sons, mothers are merely the vessels of reproduction that self-destruct when their sons grow to manhood.

Seen in this light, the Oedipus myth is a myth of male development within patriarchy and a denial of woman. For this reason the myth cannot explain female development as a process of self-creation but presents it as one of self-destruction. It is no wonder that Freud had such trouble trying to make this myth "fit" female identity formation—there is nothing in the myth to offer any help. If the Oedipus complex is the foundation of psychoanalysis, as Freud and many others believe, then it must be concluded that the foundation is essentially flawed: it *may* explain male development but it cannot explain female development as creation.

For an understanding of female identity formation it becomes important to move behind Freud's account of the Oedipal myth to reclaim the myth of Antigone, the myth of the forgotten daughter of Oedipus.[2] In the nineteenth century the ideal relationship between man and woman was thought to be the brother-sister relationship, a relationship of equality. Nineteenth century man searched for his psychic/spiritual twin or "soulmate," and the sister came to represent the perfected Other as self. Thus, the myth of Antigone held sway over the nineteenth century psyche in a way that the myth of Oedipus does today. When Oedipus replaced Antigone as the dominant cultural myth the importance of a male-female relationship of equality for the development of identity was denied. Psychic life was now understood in terms of the relations of inequality. George Steiner, in his book *Antigones*, recounts the consequences of the paradigm shift inaugurated by Freud: "Between the 1790s and the start of the twentieth century, the radical lines of kinship run horizontally, as between brothers and sisters. In the Freudian construct they run vertically, as between children and parents. The Oedipus complex is one of inescapable verticality. The shift is momentous."[3]

In the *Antigone* by Sophocles, the central conflict occurs between Antigone and Creon (her uncle and king) but the central relationship is that between Antigone and Polyneices, her brother: Antigone's enduring sense of duty to her dead brother grounds the tragedy. Sophocles shows that the brother-sister relationship, as a uterine or matrilineal relationship, exerts the primary claim on Antigone. She declares: "If I had suffered him who was born of my mother to lie in death an unburied corpse, in that case I would have suffered. ... Not for my children, if I had been a mother, nor for my husband, if his dead body were rotting before me, would I have chosen to suffer like this in violent defiance of the citizens."[4]

The reason the brother exerts the strongest claim on Antigone is because he offers her the only possible relationship of equality with a man in the given society. With a father, a husband, or a son, a women is in a position of actual or potential domination by virtue of patriarchal law and custom—she is not an equal Other. After a long and loving servitude to her father, the blind Oedipus, Antigone is refused her one request which is to be able to look upon his grave after his death. She is never his equal and he refuses her claim upon him once he is beyond needing her. Although less obvious than the father's authority over the daughter and the husband's authority over the wife, the son's domination of the mother is reflected in both cultural and religious texts: for example, Penelope must endure the vigilance of her son Telemachus during Odysseus' absence just as later the Virgin Mary will bow before her son, Jesus. A son, when grown to manhood in patriarchal society, rules the mother. Because the father-daughter, husband-wife, and son-mother relationships are relations of male domination, a woman necessarily has ambivalent feelings about them. She finds her one glimpse of a truly equal relation with a male in the relation with her brother. If a brother mistreats or exploits his sister she has the option of drawing away from him. With a father, a husband, or a son, such a retreat or abandonment is much more difficult: in these relationships there are legal and social obstacles as well as the moral and religious ones attached to the brother-sister relation. Given that it is easier to dissolve the bond with a brother, a woman's love for him is less threatening to her freedom and her sense of identity.[5]

Antigone must reconcile her obligation to the family, the obligation to bury her brother, with the demands of the political sphere represented by Creon. Her tragedy is that no matter which course of action she chooses she cannot be saved. If she defies the law of the Greek *polis* and buries Polyneices, she will die; if she fails in her sororal duty, she will suffer divine retribution and loss of honor. She defies Creon and in so doing brings the claims of the brother-sister relationship into the public world in opposition to the political authority which rests on patriarchal domination.

Thus, Antigone enters the *polis* on behalf of a familial relationship of equality between man and woman and this act of entering the political arena allows her to transcend the traditional limits of womanhood which would confine her to the sphere of the family. By openly insisting on the rights of the brother-sister relationship within the *polis* Antigone begins to recreate herself. In this way she represents the history of woman's revolt against the public world of patriarchal privilege. She is the precursor of the women who, in the recent past, proclaimed the personal as political; she represents female self-creation through the assertion of female identity within the public world. Like the myth of Oedipus, this is a myth of tragedy and ends with Antigone's suicide. But even this act can be seen as an act of defiance gainst male domination. By choosing to kill herself, Antigone does not allow Creon to have the ultimate power over her fate: she takes her own life to refute the power of the patriarchy over her.

Antigone defies convention by moving out of the family to act in the public world and in so doing has the potential to create a new identity for herself. But she dies from the effort. She cannot live out the contradictions of her life. Man is able to endure the duality of life, the duality of public and private, *polis* and family, through his relation to woman who maintains and sustains him. Woman's relation to man, however, does not offer her a way to make this duality tolerable. Once Antigone moves out of the family, there is no relationship to man capable of sustaining her. Thus, the *Antigone* gives an account of a failed attempt at female self-creation within patriarchy.

There is, however, within this mythic tale a relationship that is often overlooked but is extremely important: the relationship of Antigone to her sister, Ismene. When Antigone asks Ismene if she will help bury their brother, Ismene refuses out of fear. She cries out:

> Think how much more terrible than these
> Our own death would be if we should go against Creon
> And do what he has forbidden! We are only women,
> We cannot fight with men, Antigone!
> The law is strong, we must give in to the law
> In this thing, and in worse.[6]

Later, Ismene, motivated by feelings of sisterhood, overcomes her fear of patriarchal power and attempts to share the responsibility for burying Polyneices. Antigone protests that they both need not die for something she alone has done, to which Ismene replies: "What do I care for life when you are dead?"[7] Although fear of the patriarchy causes Ismene to waver, her final decision to do what is required is rooted in the familial devotion between sisters, not the brother-sister relationship. But Antigone rejects Ismene's show of solidarity. One could interpret this rejection as a response to Ismene's initial cowardice when confronting male political power. However, I believe that Antigone's rejection of Ismene is best understood in light of the fact that patriarchal society attempts to set women against each other so that we learn to see ourselves primarily in relation to men. Even if the brother-sister relationship can be said to be one of male-female equality, the sister-sister relationship must be seen as central to any attempt at female self-creation. Through her rejection of Ismene, Antigone reveals the patriarchal world as one in which women are said to achieve an identity only in relation to men and not through their relations with women. In refusing Ismene's gesture of sisterhood Antigone finds herself abandoned and alone in the patriarchal world with no alternative but suicide. Without the solidarity of sisterhood female rebellion leads to self-destruction rather than self-creation.

From a feminist perspective, there is another mythic parallel that is as compelling as that between Oedipus and Antigone: it is the one between Odysseus and Medea. The mythic journey of Odysseus found in Homer's *Odyssey* has been reclaimed in the twentieth century as a myth of the development of male consciousness. In the *Dialectic of Enlightenment*, Horkheimer and Adorno analyze Odysseus as the paradigmatic figure of the atomic or possessive individual forced into exile to find himself. Odysseus leaves Ithaca and battles nature to achieve a self but, in the process, he denies his own needs, his own place within nature, for the sake of self-preservation. He makes a journey through alienation to a return in which women serve merely as instruments for his development. However, in Odysseus's relations to the Sirens, Circe, and Penelope, we find a narrative of woman as mother, lover, and wife within patriarchy.[8] Most importantly, when we examine the myth of Medea as the counterpart of Odysseus we find a comprehensive account of the profound fear of woman's desire that lies behind the process of male identity formation.

In the myth of Odysseus the voice of the Sirens may be seen to represent the male's perception of woman as the first Other. Thus, the Sirens represent for the male the all-powerful mother figure. The desire to yield to the Sirens represents his desire to yield to the pleasure principle, to give up responsibility for the self—a desire that signals death to the male ego, as symbolized by the close association of womb and tomb. We do not know what happens to the Sirens once Odysseus manages to resist their power and sails past them. But we may surmise that, like the Sphinx in the Oedipal myth, once defeated, once heard without inducing surrender, they self-destruct. If we see the Sirens' song as the call of the all-engulfing mother—the first (M)Other— then we may interpret the self-destruction here as another account of the way in which woman as mother is sacrificed to the development of the male ego. Just as the maternal figures of Jocasta and the Sphinx self-destruct following their encounters with Oedipus, the Sirens are defeated by the developing male ego represented by Odysseus. From woman's perspective this encounter signals the loss of female power embodied in the mother.

The death of matriarchal power is clearly illustrated by Odysseus' trip to Hades, where he views the mother figures that have become completely impotent. From a psychoanalytic point of view the visit to Hades may be seen as Odysseus' descent to the realm of the unconscious, where a final death blow is dealt to the mother's power to allow a rebirth of the male. That is, Odysseus descends to the land of the unconscious, the land of the pleasure principle, the land of the mother, and emerges from this land reborn beyond her power.

Odysseus' interlude with Circe the enchantress is an account of the male's perception and fear of woman as an active, sexual being. Circe tempts Odysseus' men into giving themselves up to sexual pleasure and then turns them into pigs—creatures whose association with the sense of smell evokes an association with debased forms of sexuality. But these creatures retain their consciousness of once having been men. Thus, to succumb to Circe is seen by the male as a reversion to the animal in which one remembers once having been an autonomous individual, an ego, an "I." But a careful analysis of Circe's transformation of men into pigs shows it to be a simple reduplication of the transformation inflicted on woman in patriarchal society: just as woman is reduced to mere animal nature, to an animal defined by sex and forced to "smell out" sex for her survival, as prostitute or wife, so Circe reduces the male to mere animal nature, yet leaves him conscious of his humanity.[9]

Taking the initiative in her encounter with Odysseus, Circe invites him to her bed. She represents for man, woman, not as mother, as womb, but woman as sex, the lover with the *vagina dentata*, the bitch/witch who lures men into her trap and through the power of her sexuality destroys them. Odysseus has been given an antidote by Hermes (the god of commerce and the market) that nullifies Circe's power. Through this act of male solidarity Odysseus becomes immune to Circe's magic, the magic of female sexuality. But Circe's sexuality is felt to be so powerful that it creates a form of male castration anxiety which remains alive even after Odysseus has successfully resisted it. Thus, Odysseus confronts Circe with sword in hand, making her swear that if he has sex with her she will not take away his courage or his manhood. This oath sets up the double standard: male promiscuity is to be protected while female promiscuity is to be prohibited. Though married to Penelope, Odysseus indulges in sex with Circe but denies both women their sexual freedom.

The relation between Circe and Odysseus portends the "civilized" marriage contract of bourgeois society which transforms love between woman and man into a contractual relation of exchange. Circe gets Odysseus into bed with her but it is a loveless encounter in which neither Odysseus nor Circe experiences the pleasure of full sexual surrender. The renunciation by Circe of her power over Odysseus, the power of female sexuality, entails a form of frigidity: confronted with the male's threat of physical violence coupled with the threat of his withdrawal from the union, woman gives herself to man physically but withholds herself emotionally.

In the Circe episode, the defeat of female desire is achieved through trickery and the threat of violence. This recalls the fact that the right to ask a man into bed has been taken from all women and given back only to those who sell pleasure for a living: it recalls the mutilating chastity that man requires of woman. In the patriarchal world, any woman who "seduces" a man is seen as a whore, a hooker, a prostitute; and the seduction succeeds only at a great price—woman's submission to male domination.

What Odysseus wants to ensure with Circe's oath is that he will not be mutilated for *his* acts of promiscuity. In sex outside social laws, in illicit sex with women, the male fears a reversion to the animal, a symbolic mutilation and death of the self. What woman risks in illicit sex in patriarchal society is actual death. We see this clearly in the account of Odysseus' return home when he orders his son, Telemachus, to kill all the women servants who have engaged in sex with Penelope's suitors. Odysseus instructs Telemachus to kill the women by running them through with a sword. But Telemachus invents an atrocious death for them.[10] Before hanging the women to death, he forces them to clean up the blood and remove the bodies of their lovers, the suitors slaughtered by himself and Odysseus. Thus, the women are made to do a cruel and brutal form of "housework" or "domestic labor" before they are herded together to face death for the little bit of pleasure they have had in Odysseus' absence.

While Odysseus forges an identity through his encounters with the Sirens and with Circe, his long-suffering wife, Penelope, waits at home for him. Penelope represents woman as alienated nature whose subjected sexuality is defined in terms of private property. As such she is the archetypical bourgeois wife. The bourgeois world links sex and property so that no woman can afford a spontaneous reaction to any man: she must always size a man up as a potential husband before reacting. Given that a woman's life rests in the hands of the man she marries, she cannot afford to choose carelessly nor can she afford any mistakes after marriage. Thus, woman is not an equal Other as lover but must strive for equality in a relation of exchange in which she exchanges the rights to her body for economic security.

The marriage between Penelope and Odysseus is said to be a unity that promises permanence in life and solidarity in the face of death: it promises a mythic "haven in a heartless world." However, Odysseus conceals his identity from Penelope when he returns from his journey because her fidelity to him is to be tested. He reveals himself to his son and father and son conspire to keep Odysseus' identity secret. Thus, the male bond is simply reasserted while the male-female bond is put on trial. Odysseus has rights over Penelope because she is his property, and these rights must be safe-guarded at all times. Penelope responds to Odysseus' test with a test of her own. She says: "If this is Odysseus we too shall surely recognize each other ... for there are tokens between us which only we two know and no one else has heard of."[11] She then proceeds to describe their marriage bed as if it can be moved. This enrages Odysseus because he himself has made the bed immovable by carving it from an olive tree which remained rooted in the ground and building the bedroom around it. This incident reveals that bourgeois marriage is no mythic union of two into one. Rather, it is a mediated relation in which the marriage bed, as the symbol of the bond between sex and property, stands between man and women to keep them apart.

Penelope lives without sexual pleasure for nineteen years and knows that she cannot act on any desire she might feel for any one of the suitors without risking death. While Odysseus spends a year in an adulterous liaison with Circe, Penelope's chastity is strictly enforced. The exchange relation, in which Penelope must remain faithful to Odysseus, is an unequal one in which female desire is sacrificed on the altar of marriage. After Odysseus is convinced of Penelope's loyalty and fidelity, he finally embraces her as his own. But within this embrace the echo of the death cries of the women servants killed by Telemachus rings in her ears. The death of these women, women who have died for their pleasure, comes as no surprise to Penelope; she has made her bargain with the patriarchal world and knows its rules and its limits. Although Penelope betrays no woman, she has no particular allegiance to womankind, no sense of female solidarity. Her fate, like the fate of every bourgeois wife loyal to her husband, is one of alienation, sexual repression, and isolation, a fate for which she sheds incessant tears.

In this myth, home figures as a source of identity for man, but it is a place that he must leave; for woman home signifies the denial of the self, yet it is a place she cannot leave. Whereas Ithaca marks a point of departure and arrival in the mythic development of Odysseus' self-consciousness, it represents a fixed landscape of work and domination for Penelope. During Odysseus' absence Penelope has been surrounded by male suitors vying to replace Odysseus as lord and master. Since Penelope is unable to confront male power directly, she does it indirectly, by telling the suitors that she cannot choose a new husband until she has finished the burial shroud for her father-in-law, Laertes. Then she proceeds to weave the shroud all day and unweave it at night. Through this subversion she keeps the suitors at bay. In addition to her loneliness and toil, Penelope suffers from eventlessness, the trauma of woman trapped at home doing the same thing day after day.[12] While Odysseus journeys toward the unknown in search of a self, Penelope's future is known: it is the "given" of family life as predictable and routine. The weaving and unweaving of the shroud in this tale represents the rhythm and tedium of woman's domesticated life.

Man encounters the pain of exile, of alienation, but woman endures the pain of place, of coerced immobility. If the journey gains meaning for Odysseus from the return, it is because Penelope remains home to recognize him on his return. Penelope makes no journey—she is allowed no journey—and her self-consciousness is not nurtured or sustained by Odysseus. In the *Odyssey*, man's mobility requires woman's immobility. This myth of male identity formation requires woman's confinement to the family, the private realm, and does not allow for the development of a female self through and with an Other.[13] If Penelope were to journey with a crew of women to find herself, if she were to move out of the private realm into the public, Odysseus' journey would have neither source nor goal, neither origin nor telos. The quest for male identity, the journey through alienation to a return, requires that woman not experience the journey.

Greek mythology, however, does portray two women who leave their "proper" place, and both suffer for it. Antigone, as we have seen, leaves home insofar as she enters the public realm on behalf of the private; there is no relationship to a male to sustain her and she dies for her audacity. But a more provocative example of the woman who defies the patriarchal world order emerges in the myth of Medea.

Medea is the female equivalent of Odysseus in that she is the female exile, but she can never return home and no man waits there for her. Medea is not Greek; she is a foreigner from Colchis, whose exile issues from her passionate, all-consuming love of Jason. She betrays her father to help Jason obtain the golden fleece, and her brother is killed as he pursues the couple in their flight from her homeland. Euripides has Medea claim responsibility for the fratricide, which presages the infanticide she later commits. In other versions of the myth she is only Jason's accomplice in the murder. Nonetheless, Medea's love for Jason clearly transcends her love for, and loyalty to, her family of origin. And Medea accepts the fate of eternal exile as the condition of this love. Thus, she represents the fate of woman in patriarchal society who, in the name of love, must leave her parents' home to become a stranger in her husband's house.

Medea follows Jason to Corinth and has two sons by him. But once she has become a mother, accepting motherhood as a consequence of her great love, Jason betrays her by marrying Glauce, the daughter of the king of Corinth. This king fears Medea's powerful magic and, with Jason's consent, condemns Medea to a second exile. She is now to be exiled with the responsibility for two helpless children. Medea foresees only slavery for herself and her sons. She refuses this fate and takes her revenge. After the king of Athens agrees to accept her into his city she kills Glauce and her own children.

In her plight Medea appeals to the women of Corinth. She knows and delineates the situation of domination that the women share. Not only are women forced into marriage, a marriage for which they must have a dowry, but once married they are condemned to the life of the family while the husbands move freely in the public world. Medea's appeal for understanding from the women, however, entails no plea for female solidarity in action. Medea sees herself as one who is alone. The fact that she is not Greek is central to this mythic drama. True, she appeals to the Greek women by making common cause with them in their domination, but she sees the fate of Greek women only to refuse it: she will not be condemned to home and hearth. She says: "Let no one think me a weak one, feeble-spirited,/ A stay-at-home, but rather just the opposite,/ One who can hurt my enemies and help my friends;/ For the lives of such persons are most remembered."[14] Medea articulates the separation of public and private spheres and her dissatisfaction with it. She finds no solace in motherhood or family life in a patriarchal world. She prefers the individual battle for recognition in the public world to the solitary pain of the private realm.

Woman's desire and passion were tamed in the Greek world to allow for male promiscuity. In their subjugated forms, contained and confined within marriage, they no longer threatened the male. But Medea represents the sexually assertive woman who seeks her own pleasure. Jason accuses her with these words: "For the sake of pleasure in the bed you killed (the children)/ No Greek woman would have done this."[15] When Euripides tells Medea's story he places the infanticide at the center of the drama. Medea is depicted as a wild woman, "mad" with revenge, a woman willing and able to kill her family when roused to anger. She represents for man the violence of female passion that has not been "civilized," female passion prior to male domination. In a patriarchal world that subjugates woman's desire and denies her a sense of identity, a sense of self, woman's rebellion takes on terrifying overtones for the male.

Although Medea acts on her desire for the Other, she does not kill her children for the sake of *sexual* satisfaction. What is central to the myth, from woman's perspective, is man's betrayal of woman in *love*. Jason's betrayal creates a violent separation that destroys the unity of the marriage. Medea responds by destroying the children who objectify this unity. Out of the pain of betrayal Medea searches for a way to inflict pain on the one who has betrayed her. When Jason says that he cannot believe that she was motivated by pain to kill their sons, she asks: "Is love so small a pain, do you think, for woman?"[16] Medea kills the children to create the same violent rupture between Jason and his children that he created between him and her. Rather than kill him or internalize her "madness" in a self-destructive manner, she externalizes her pain and seeks to recreate within Jason the pain she experiences.

Medea represents monogamous married love, the union of two into one. But this does not mean that she accepts female chastity prior to marriage. Rather, she stands for the free rein of male and female desire prior to marriage and for monogamous marriage. Jason, on the other hand, stands for female chastity before and after marriage and for male promiscuity. Here we see a fundamental conflict between male and female perspectives on desire and marriage. And we find a challenge to the idea that *woman's* desire is promiscuous: in this myth it is man who is fickle and inconstant.

Medea loves Jason and sacrifices everything for him; her love is without bounds. Jason's love is a calculated gesture to ensure the success of his quest for the golden fleece. This gesture is abandoned when he has the opportunity to realize his ambition to move up in the world by marrying into the royal family of Corinth. Because Medea has chosen Jason for her lover and not waited to be chosen first, betrayal is her fate. Since Jason's betrayal of Medea all women fear to choose first, and all male claims of fidelity and love are suspect.

In summary, it is important to reassert that when we reclaim the mythic tales of female figures we do so in order to recreate ourselves with new vision. We re-memorize the distant past in order to ground our present attempts to achieve a liberated future. In these tales we find woman overpowered in her relation to man as mother, lover, sister, wife and daughter. But, most significantly, inscribed in these accounts of domination is the affirmation of the touchstones of the women's liberation movement concerning the relation between the personal and the political and the potential of female solidarity.

Unlike Penelope, Antigone and Medea leave home. Antigone leaves home a virgin-sister in order to recreate herself in terms of her sublimated relationship to her brother while Medea leaves home in order to assert heterosexual desire. Where Penelope endures the alienation and isolation of the marriage based on exchange, Antigone and Medea challenge the division between the private realm of the family and the public world of patriarchal privilege which consigns woman to a domesticated routine. For both, the personal is political: their tragedies reveal the content of male domination. But their challenges fail to mediate the relation between public and private because they are solitary battles waged solely on behalf of their relations to men.

Medea, like Antigone, courts disaster because she has no allegiance to other women. Her exile is total: it is an alienation from home and from other women. In the *Antigone* the potential for female self-creation is defeated because of the failure to respond to the gesture of sisterhood. Antigone's final moment of defiance is self-destructive: she does not survive her battle for self-creation. In the tale of Medea there is a move beyond self-destruction but not beyond destruction *per se*. Medea survives only at the expense of her children, and, therefore, at great cost to herself. Where Antigone had the potential to respond to Ismene, Medea has no other woman in her life except the one who has been set in competition with her by Jason. Had Medea been able to see the Other woman as self, to make common cause with Glauce, Jason would have been rendered powerless. Medea might not have been able to reclaim the love relationship with Jason but she would have created the ground for a new form of female self-identity, one based on female solidarity.

These myths are cautionary tales which reveal the cost to women who choose to battle the patriarchal world alone. They are traces of memory which reveal that without female solidarity women are destroyed or become female copies of the male individual—atomic, aggressive, alienated from self and nature, and therefore, self-destructive. Thus, we must remember the Sphinx and the Sirens, the maternal figures rendered impotent through their contact with the developing male ego; we must remember Circe, the lover defeated by male violence and chicanery; we must remember Penelope, the wife trapped and traumatized within the family circle; we must remember Antigone as daughter and sister: bereft and denied her wish to mourn at her father's grave, finally destroyed by her devotion to her brother; and we must remember Medea burning with love and desire only to be betrayed and abandoned because she dared to choose first.

Embedded in these tales, however, is also the promise of liberation. They show that to move beyond destruction and defeat we must remember that the pre-condition for our liberation is the forging of bonds among women. Thus, there is a link between mythic memory and the memory of consciousness-raising as a process of re-creating the female self. By taking the bond of sisterhood beyond its natural setting in the family to make it a political bond we created a profound challenge to the division between the public and private worlds. At the same time, as we met in small consciousness-raising groups to reclaim our lives by recalling a shared past of domination, the re-creation of the self through and with other women created a challenge to the atomic, possessive individualism of patriarchal society. The displacement of consciousness-raising from the small group to more generalized social and cultural forms must not entail amnesia. We must not forget the powerful lesson of sisterhood. We must remember that we moved beyond the renowned but solitary figures of Antigone and Medea. We must remember the two women who embody the memory and hope of sisterhood—we must remember Ismene and Glauce.[17]

NOTES

1. See, for example, Susan Cavin, *Lesbian Origins* (San Francisco: ism press, 1985), and Luce Irigaray, "Language, Persephone and Sacrifice," in *Borderlines*, Winter 1985-86.

2. The relationship between Oedipus and Antigone is rooted in the incestuous house of Thebes, making Antigone Oedipus's sister as well as his daughter. Mary Renault believes Antigone resolves the dilemma of her relationship to Oedipus by remaining "daughter in her heart, keeping faith with her childhood." See Mary Renault, *The Bull from the Sea* (New York: Penguin, 1980), p. 63.

3. George Steiner, *Antigones* (New York: Oxford University Press, 1984), p. 18.

4. Sophocles, *Antigone*, lines 465-511 and lines 901-20. The emphasis on the uterine relationship in the Greek text is obscured in contemporary translations but revealed in the Oxford translation of lines 465-511. See Antigone in *The Tragedies of Sophocles: In English Prose*, the Oxford translation, new edition, revised according to the text of Dindorf (New York: Harper & Brothers, 1880), pp. 178-79. Many modern translations omit Antigone's speech in which she defends her decision to bury her brother yet says she would not make the same sacrifice for a husband or son (lines 901-20). It can be found in *Ten Greek Plays in Contemporary Translations*, trans. Shaemus O'Sheel and ed. L. R. Lind (Boston: Riverside Press, 1957).

5. Robert Seidenberg and Evangelos Papathomopoulos, "The Enigma of Antigone," *International Review of Psychoanalysis* Vol I (1974), pp. 197-205.

6. Sophocles, *Antigone, in Drama: An Introductory Anthology*, alternate edition, ed. Otto R. Reinert (Boston: Little, Brown & Company, 1964), p. 2. While the Oxford and Lind translations are important for revealing the uterine relationship and the speech comparing the brother to the son and the husband, I prefer the Reinert edition for general accuracy in translation.

7. Ibid., p. 14.

8. My account of this narrative is based on a feminist appropriation of Horkheimer and Adorno's reading. See Max Horkheimer and Theodor W. Adorno, *Dialectic of Enlightenment*, trans. John Cumming (New York: Herder and Herder, 1972), especially pp. 59-60 (Sirens); pp. 69-74 (Circe); pp. 73-75 (Penelope); and pp. 75-76 (mother-figures in Hades).

9. Ibid., pp. 70-71.

10. Ibid., p. 79. Horkheimer and Adorno see this episode as an account of generalized brutality rather than an account of an atrocity directed specifically against women.

11. Homer, *The Odyssey* (Harmondsworth: Penguin Books, 1961), p. 343.

12. Robert Seidenberg has coined the term "trauma of eventlessness" to describe the absence of significant stimuli that can overwhelm a woman. See Robert Seidenberg, "The Trauma of Eventlessness," in *Psychoanalysis and Women*, ed. Jean Baker Miller (Harmondsworth: Penguin Books, 1974), pp. 350-62.

13. Alkis Kontos, "Memories of Ithaca," in *Ethnicity in a Technological Age*, ed. Ian H. Angus (Edmonton: Canadian Institute of Ukrainian Studies, 1987). Kontos gives a moving analysis of Odysseus' journey as the journey of an exile; however, his reading ignores the plight of Penelope.

14. Euripides, *Medea*, in *Women in Drama*, ed. Harriet Kriegel (New York: Mentor Books, 1975), pp. 22-23.

15. Ibid., p. 36.

16. Ibid., p. 37. The power of this tragic tension is revealed in the painting of Medea by Delacroix.

17. This article is an extrapolation of my analysis of myth in *Woman, Nature, and Psyche* (New Haven: Yale University Press, 1987) and is reprinted here with permission of Yale University Press.

7

The Hard Work of Remembering: Two German Women Re-examine Nationalsocialism

Marie-Luise Gaettens

> She believed that you must work at your past
> as you work at your future ...
> Christa Wolf, *The Quest for Christa T.*

In the seventies, after a thirty-year lapse of silence, German women authors in great numbers began to re-examine the Nazi past. They did so through a great variety of media: film, novel, theatre, and oral histories. This development is connected to the change in the political climate in Germany in the sixties: the radical questioning of post-war German society and the emergence of a women's movement. Alexander and Margarete Mitscherlich had argued convincingly in their influential book *The Inability to Mourn*,[1] which had come out in the early sixties, that there was a deep correlation between the conservative political climate of post-war Germany and the fact that the vast majority of Germans were avoiding any confrontation with their past under Nationalsocialism. The Mitscherlichs insisted that only by working through the past individually and collectively could German society open up to genuine social change.[2] In her most recent book, Margarete Mitscherlich reiterates this argument concisely: "When denial, repression, and de-realization of the past take the place of working through it, the compulsion to repeat the past becomes inevitable, even if it can be covered up."[3]

On the part of women, the interest in the Nazi past was connected to a new political awareness of women's specific position in society. Their preoccupation with the past represented a collective attempt to develop a historical conscience of their own—to comprehend their patriarchal legacies. Particularly for women engaged in cultural production, the Nazi era had created a devastating rupture in their already marginalized cultural tradition. Sigrid Weigel summarizes this:

The task of reconstructing women's cultural history extends into the phase of recent German political history which shows a painfully clear break in tradition. National Socialism's obliteration of the women's movement, the workers' movement and the avantgarde had dire consequences for the literature by women. After 1945, only a few for the most part conservative or Christian women, maintained any continuity of literary production from the Weimar Republic, while the socialists, feminists and avantgarde literature were largely stifled and "forgotten." The younger, especially the politically aware women saw themselves without a heritage.[4]

While this analysis applies primarily to the Federal Republic, women authors of the German Democratic Republic also began to re-examine women's past and present position in society in their works of the seventies.[5] Weigel argues that in the absence of an independent women's movement, GDR women began to explore their lives primarily through the medium of literature.[6]

The work of memory is of particular importance for women as their historical experience is largely excluded from the dominant historical discourse.[7] Years of the privatization of women's lives have produced a situation in which women's history can be found primarily in the context of the autobiographical; and as "private" memory, it is left out of the "serious" writings of history. The authors of the essay "Popular Memory: Theory, Politics, Method" conclude: "It is not only unrecorded, but actually silenced. It is not offered the occasion to speak."[8] Women who "take the occasion to speak" thus work against a long tradition of privatization and silence. In making their historical experience public, they unearth a repressed aspect of history: women's lives in patriarchal society. Women are not "without" history; rather they have their own history with its specific relationship to the history of the dominant. Women's relation to dominant history is simultaneously one of exclusion and participation. This means that while they themselves are oppressed, they are also complicit.[9]

The word "women" has to be used with great caution, particularly with respect to Nationalsocialism. The condition of being both inside and outside the male order with respect to Nazi society applies to women who by their ethnic, religious and social background also belonged to the dominant group. Women who were persecuted for racial and/or political reasons had a very different position in Nazi society, and the word "complicity" with respect to them has a different meaning, if it has one at all.

I would like to focus on the works of two authors: Ruth Rehmann's *Der Mann auf der Kanzel (The Man in the Pulpit)*[10] and Christa Wolf's *Patterns of Childhood*.[11] In each, a woman has grown up under Nationalsocialism in a family which conformed to Nazi rule. Both authors belong to the generation (Rehmann was born in 1922, Wolf in 1929) that was perhaps the most profoundly shaped by Nationalsocialism, its schools, youth groups and general political climate. While this generation is not responsible for the crimes of the Nazi government, it seems especially important for them to come to terms with the Nazi past in order to break out of the patterns of thinking formed during that time. It is precisely this recognition of how profoundly she has been shaped by Nationalsocialism that Wolf offers as her main motivation for writing *Patterns of Childhood*. Wolf asserts that the citizens of the GDR have also failed to confront their past.[12]

While Wolf retraces her own childhood under Nationalsocialism, Rehmann is primarily concerned with her father's political response to Nazi rule. Rehmann's father, a conservative, Protestant pastor, belonged to the group of German professionals who firmly closed their eyes to the murderous policy of the Nazis. Reconstructing her father's response to the Nazis requires that Rehmann overcome the separation of her two memory systems: her public, "political" memory, in which she is well aware of the oppressive nature of the Nazi rule, and her cherished "private" memory of her father, as an exemplary father and pastor. Rehmann's project can thus be characterized as the decompartmentalization of her memory. It is precisely this compartmentalization which has enabled Rehmann to avoid asking the most disturbing questions about her father's past—a past to which she as his child is intimately connected.

Like so many German families, the Rehmanns' memory crucially disfunctions when it comes to the Nazi past:

> The family's memory no longer works. The lines are interrupted: Nazi era, the war, the collapse of Germany. How does one pass on fathers who were neither Nazi criminals nor resistance fighters? How does one get them alive and as individuals through the barrage of stereotypes and judgements? How can one protect them from the distortions of images of horror and wishfulness? How can one explain the differences between the actual past and the recollected past without falling into the trap of making tearful excuses ... I-was-too-little, I-did-not-see-anything, I-was-not present.[13]

Throughout her project, Rehmann avoids the temptation to smooth over contradictions: while she shows the pastor as a lovable father, she also exposes his narrow-minded, conservative nationalism and his disregard for working-class people, for people of other religions, and for women. Neither does she claim distanced objectivity towards the character in her work. Instead, she draws the reader's attention to the fact that character and author are closely connected and that movable boundaries exist between them. She articulates this through shifting forms of address: the pastor is sometimes called Reinhold, sometimes the father or the pastor; the daughter is sometimes cast in the first person singular and sometimes addressed as the child. The figures of the past and of the present are thus clearly separated. The titles father and daughter, furthermore, emphasize the structural relationship between the two.

In Wolf's *Patterns of Childhood* past and present identities are also clearly differentiated. This method makes the constructedness of the characters transparent and rejects the notion of a unified subject transcending the disruptions of time. It articulates instead that time ruptures the subject. In both texts we witness a woman in the process of reconstructing the past: her search for sources, her conversations with other participants, her reflections on the past and present, and the process of her remembering. Memory does not exist as a given array of material at the disposal of the author but is presented as an ongoing, strenuous process, in which the remembered past is not identical with *the* past. Both authors are aware that the habit of remembering in anecdotes often functions as a way to avoid confronting the ambiguities and the disturbing aspects of the past. Wolf analyzes the ideological uses of these ready-made anecdotes, "miniatures" as she calls them:

> These miniatures are for memory what the calcified cavities are for people with tuberculosis, what prejudices are for morals: patches of once active life now shut off. At one time one was afraid to touch them, afraid of burning one's fingers on them; now they are cool and smooth, some of them artistically polished, some especially valuable bits have cost years of work, for one must forget a great deal and re-think and re-interpret a great deal before one can see oneself in the best light everywhere and at all times. That is what we need them for, the miniatures.[14]

We resort to these miniatures when the process of memory seems too painful. They reduce the past to consumable bits and thus provide false peace with a past that is all too distressing and that demands self-questioning. Rehmann and Wolf demonstrate that the process of deciphering the past always requires the active engagement of the historical subject—a position they assume for themselves as women, despite patriarchal denial. Both encounter patriarchy on two levels in their projects: in the past, where patriarchy is a crucial component of fascism, and in their present or as they necessarily confront the patriarchal structures of history-telling.

In the reconstruction of her father's past the daughter confronts a powerful, perhaps the most powerful, figure of patriarchy. In patriarchal society, the father is the representative, and ultimately the embodiment, of the political, social, and cultural order. All of which are founded upon the exclusion of the daughter. Lynda Booth analyzes the structural inequality between father and daughter in patriarchal society:

> In the four-cornered nuclear enclosure which is the source of Western ideologies about the family, the father weighs most and the daughter least. To consider the daughter-father relationship means crossing the greatest amount of ideational space and juxtaposing the two figures most asymmetrically proportioned in terms of gender, age, authority, and cultural privilege. All these asymmetries are ones which are controlled by the idiom of presence, which defines the father, and absence, which identifies the daughter.[15]

In engaging in a critical evaluation of her father's relation to the dominant order, the daughter trespasses upon an area she has no right to enter. She is an impostor and fundamentally lacks the authority for her project. It is thus not surprising that becoming her father's author arouses powerful fears in the daughter. At the beginning of the book Rehmann enters her old hometown from the wrong side, the side on which little girls were not supposed to walk alone. As she begins her project, the daughter has a terrible nightmare:

> They were standing around my bed, looking down at me. I was lying naked and asleep, their small, clever heads and their furtive glances upon me. They thought that I was an imbecile, me and my senseless dream-muttering. Despite an inordinate effort, I was not able to order it and make it reasonable.[16]

The topography of the city evokes the topography of the female body, with its sexual parts that have to be hidden. Her female sexuality disqualifies the daughter from speaking, and her family, as a censoring presence, looks down on her. Her speech and her naked body are thus sources of embarrassment for the daughter. Her relationship with her father is of crucial importance in positioning the daughter in the cultural order. Rehmann, who was her father's favorite as a child, realizes as she reaches adolescence that something about her nevertheless displeases her father:

> But there is something about her growing up that annoys him; it is never mentioned, not even hinted at, referred to only through this cool ray of displeasure, which is always directed at the same hidden spot, which obviously cannot be loved, not even by God and which therefore should not be.[17]

It is significantly the absence of the father that leads to Rehmann's return to her hometown—a return that forces her to confront her father's past: "The discussion (whether they should visit the town or not) began at the height of the *Siebengebirge*. It was as usual a lengthy and controversial debate in this family without a father, without the word of power."[18] The word of the father is the word of power that regulates and rules. It prevents the family's discourse from straying into forbidden areas, and limits it to the areas of the private that block out unpleasant historical truths. The discourse of the patriarchal family depends on the division between the private and the public in order to keep the hegemony of the father intact. Thus it is no coincidence that it is the daughter who causes the breakdown of this neat separation. She does so reluctantly, however, for she has internalized the official version of the family's history. It is a former member of her father's congregation who forces Rehmann to examine her compartmentalized memory. Unasked, this parishioner proudly shares one of her fondest memories of the pastor with the daughter:

> She still has it clear before her eyes, as if it had happened only yesterday, the pastor, his Catholic colleague and the SA mayor next to each other on a stage, beautifully decorated with swastikas and flowers. The pastor movingly thanked God for the happy turn in German history—an image of unity between patriotic church and Christian state.[19]

The terrible pronouncement "unity between patriotic church and Christian state" and her father's participation in this act force Rehmann to re-examine her memory of her father—a memory that she has so neatly separated from its historical context. Rehmann begins to retrace her father's life in order to understand his acquiescence to the Nazi state. She examines her father's upbringing in a parsonage in Imperial Germany. In Rehmann's reconstruction of her grandfather's house, we see the rule of the quintessential *paterfamilias* who presides with benign authoritarianism over his large family. It is an image that evokes Martin Luther, reminding us of the centrality of the patriarchal family to Protestant dogma. Completely enwrapped in paternal care during his youth, Rehmann's father will forever remain a good son who unquestioningly defers to his fathers: his natural father, the Emperor William II, and God. Strict hierarchy structures all these relationships. Rehmann describes the pastor's communications with God in authoritarian, even militaristic terms; in the morning the pastor receives his daily orders from God and at night God surveys his day. The biological father receives his authority from his identification with the heavenly father. For both relationships the terminology is strikingly similar: to serve, to respect, to obey, to punish, to fear, to examine, to forgive.

The "father of the land" (*Landesvater*), the Emperor, rules over matters of the nation. Herbert Marcuse has pointed out that in Protestantism all figures of legitimate authority are based upon the model of the father. In turning all masters into fathers, their authority is not only strengthened but also made permanent.[20] This also means that the figure of authority can only be male and, in the pastor's case, must be Christian and a member of an elevated social class. Women, Jews, and working-class people do not qualify for positions of authority.

The pastor's conformism to Nazi rule is rooted in this conception of authority and his inability to question it. Thus he revealingly utters the following to a member of his congregation who has joined the oppositional church which is resisting the identification of the protestant church with the Nazi state: "What you do goes against the authorities. ... I cannot do that."[21]

Their fundamental lack of any authority dispossesses women, Jews, and the working-class of their right to their own voices. The pastor's notion of authority is thus complicit with the Nazis' increasing denial of rights to these groups. It also makes it impossible for the pastor to hear their voices in the face of Nazi oppression. One night in 1938, the pastor is visited by his Jewish friend Jacobi (their friendship is possible because Jacobi has converted to Christianity). Jacobi is thoroughly distressed and talks agitatedly with the pastor. Rehmann remembers hearing her father say to Jacobi that he should not believe these rumors. The pastor dismisses the deportation of Jews as a mere rumor because it has not been announced by the authorities. To the words of a parishioner who points to the existence of concentration camps he responds by calling such statements *Latrinenparolen* (toilet slogans). He undercuts criticism from the female vicar who challenges his nationalistic concept of religion by denying her the status of a woman; she is turned into a freak. A "real" woman would not have challenged his authority.

Rehmann convincingly depicts the formation of the pastor's nationalistic, patriarchal world-view, one that was profoundly shaped by the imperialist spirit of turn-of-the-century German *Kaiserreich* and that served as one of the bases for the emergence of the Nazi movement. Yet as a reader one also notes an overeagerness on Rehmann's part to be fair to her father. Particularly at the end of the book, daughterly guilt completely overcomes Rehmann. In the face of her father's death, she loses her perspective on Nazi rule during World War II. Her son's response to her project accurately points out the danger of such a subjective evaluation of history:

> There are so many stories of this kind, he said. They are told in a truthful manner by people (that) one respects. Each one of them tosses and turns a little piece of guilt for such a long time that it becomes completely humanly understandable, yes almost endearing. ... Yet it did not just happen out of the blue, it was produced, not by one or a few, but by many almost all. I ask myself, where did it go (the unspeakable guilt) in all your nice and sympathetic stories? Where does it hide, in a fold of the coat that you so carefully spread over it?[22]

Rehmann responds that this is the result of being a "biased witness," one who is never able to separate herself neatly from her character, but whose examination "cuts into her own flesh." This response exemplifies Rehmann's awareness of her own complicity, for the daughter also kept her eyes shut to the Nazi atrocities. She remembers being completely indifferent to the deportation of a Jewish classmate's father. By integrating into the text this argument with her son, she grants the reader a degree of critical distance from her account and draws his/her attention to the fact that the past is not re-constructed from a disinterested perspective. For Rehmann our own entanglement in history makes it impossible for us to produce an objective account; we must therefore constantly examine this entanglement, re-examine our memory and the motives that underlie its selectiveness.

Yet Rehmann's difficulty in studying her father also points to the general difficulties daughters experience in writing about their fathers. The profound cultural imbalance between father and daughter shapes these texts significantly. Weigel points to a fundamental contradiction inherent in daughters' writings about their fathers. On the one hand, writing about the father is an emancipatory act: the daughter claims for herself the right to speak and breaks the father's prerogative over the word. On the other hand, the daughter constructs herself as an author precisely through the paternal presence from which she claims she is freeing herself. Thus she ultimately claims authority for her authorship through her father.[23]

Furthermore, by writing women enter into the cultural order which is dominated by the word of the father. They are forced to follow the discursive practices established by the fathers. Weigel elaborates the contradictory position of the daughter:

> As a female author, a woman breaks into the paternal domain, which presupposes his recognition. If she challenges his exclusive power over the word, she rebels against her own subjugation while simultaneously following his rules, without being able to take up his position.[24]

This fundamental contradiction has to be faced by every woman author; it is simply more apparent in "fatherbooks."

In *The Man in the Pulpit*, paternal presence clearly dominates maternal presence. As the title makes clear, her intention is to come to terms with her father. Yet in doing this, the text inadvertently reproduces the condition in our culture in which the presence of the father depends upon the absence of the mother. Rehmann writes about the relationship between the father and mother: "He never notices the order she creates, that serves first of all his work, his peace, his well being."[25] Life in the parsonage disintegrates whenever the mother is sick and not able to provide the necessary framework for the family. It is only on these occasions that the family becomes aware of her work; yet whenever she returns to it, the family is relieved and able to forget her again: "The mother is back again and can be forgotten."[26] Despite Rehmann's insight into the constellation of the patriarchal family, she has nevertheless internalized this configuration. While she constructs the pastor's character as full of complexities and contradictions, the mother remains a one-dimensional figure. As opposed to the pastor, we know little about her past, her interests, her wishes. In Rehmann's text desire flows only in the direction of the father. Rigid and repressed, the mother upholds the order of the house with stern authority. Ceaselessly vigilant over her family, she seems determined to put an end to any form of pleasure: "Children are supposed to leave festivities when it is nicest; they should by no means be among the last guests, when festivities 'degenerate,' when barriers fall down, on the whole they are supposed 'to keep their distance' ..."[27]

Instead of mediating between paternal authority and the children, she relentlessly implements the word of the father, and constant, unfaltering self-control has made it difficult for her to forgive others: "She finds it more difficult to forgive sins than he does. Her conscience retains resentment for a long time; for as long as she is able to remember. Even though she wants to believe that God has forgiven, she cannot feel it."[28] She is able to express desire only in a sort of otherworldly longing. In the summer she longingly watches the swallows sail away in the air; when she is moved by music, her face takes on the expression of Iphigenia—a powerful cultural image which, particularly through Goethe, influenced women's definition of themselves in terms of self-sacrifice. Accordingly, Ulrike Prokop argues that most women of the mother's generation resolved the impossibility of self-definition in a patriarchal society by defining themselves solely in terms of sacrifice. This in turn made many middle-class women susceptible to Nazi ideology.[29]

In Rehmann's mother we encounter a zealous fulfillment of duty that turns into a kind of tyranny, combined with a deep sense of inadequacy. She thinks: "... in essential matters the father was always her superior."[30] Though no admirer of the Nazis, the mother shares the pastor's old-fashioned nationalistic views. Yet in her character we also see links with the Nazi concept of womanhood: she is industrious, self-sacrificing, authoritarian within the family, but defers in all public matters to her husband. The Nazis' propagation of strict gender roles in fact helped them overcome middle-class resistance.[31]

The pastor's notion of authority made it impossible for him to conceive of his own active participation in the process of history-making, an abstention from which the Nazis profited. In contrast to the pastor's authoritarian concept of history, Rehmann believes that history requires the active participation of all historical subjects. She engages in her memory work in order to understand her own formation by history, a prerequisite for breaking the hegemony of the past.

Christa Wolf also stresses the importance of attending to the past. The opening lines of *Patterns of Childhood* express precisely this: "What is past is not dead; it is not even past. We cut ourselves off from it; we pretend to be strangers."[32] The past is a continuous process and constantly reaches into the present. "Is not dead" reinforces the notion that the past is not a closed entity, but continues to live within us. Yet we try to separate ourselves from our past—an attitude that is particularly notorious with respect to fascism. Our pretense that we have nothing to do with our past creates in us estrangement which produces self-alienation. Only by working through our past, by remembering, do we bring movement into the petrified sedimentations that history has deposited in us and thereby open ourselves to change: "To confront one's past experience is necessary in order to remain productive."[33]

Yet history has caused a deep split in the subject, which expresses itself in the split between the second person singular and the third person singular. In *Patterns of Childhood* the figure of the past is clearly separated from the figure of the present. The figure of the past is called Nelly and she is addressed in the third person singular. Yet even the subject of the present cannot address herself as "I," but instead addresses herself as "you," which results in self-interrogation: "The person who has learned to see himself [sic] not as 'I' but as 'you.' A stylistic particularity such as this can't be arbitrary or accidental."[34]

While Rehmann structures her text around a male genealogy, Wolf creates a female genealogy in *Patterns of Childhood*. Wolf's work of memory centers on four generations of women: Nelly, the largely autobiographical figure of the past who grew up under Nationalsocialism, her mother Charlotte and her grandmothers; in the present, the narrator/author and her daughter Lenka. Lenka, a child of the GDR, serves as a contrast to Nelly and is the figure to whom the narrator wants to communicate her past experience. Through Lenka the dialogue with the past is extended into the future. Yet this dialogue does not work smoothly:

> Charlotte worries about her daughter's truth mania, while Nelly, perhaps not consciously, increases her efforts to guess Herr Warsinski's expectation of her. It turns out to be difficult to discuss the subject with Lenka. Herr attempts to understand this child are bound to fail. The idea that one might crave the favor of one's teacher is simply foreign to her, she considers it is the height of insanity.[35]

Despite the difficulties, the dialogue between the women of the past and present creates a strong female bond. The realities between mother and daughter represent the central relationship in the text. The narrator realizes how vitally she has been shaped by her mother: "Although the daughter refuses to admit that the compulsion to use her mother's gestures, looks, and words grows stronger as she grows older. She catches herself at imitations she would never have thought possible."[36] The significance of this relationship for the production of this text is most succinctly characterized by Virginia Woolf's phrase: "... a woman writing thinks back through her mothers."[37]

Yet, as with Rehmann, writing about the past stirs up powerful anxieties in Wolf. This is again revealed to the narrator in a dream. In Wolf's dream the mother is the central figure who could be hurt by her daughter's writing. In this dream the narrator's dead mother has returned, and the whole family, the dead as well as the living, has gathered around the table. The narrator separates herself from the family's unity by going into the kitchen to do the dishes. She closes the door because she wants no help: "Suddenly, a shock that penetrates even the roots of your hair: in the big room on the table lies the manuscript, with, on the first page only one word, 'Mother,' in large letters. She'll guess your purpose and feel hurt."[38]

For Wolf too, writing about the past and turning one's family into characters poses a constant danger of violation. For Wolf this potential violation can be avoided only if the scrutiny of others extends to oneself: "Because one acquires the right to material of this kind by personally involving oneself in the game and by keeping the stake sufficiently high."[39] The author herself has to be willing to undergo a process of change in the act of writing if she wants her readers to be affected. She rejects the notion of the distanced author who rules over her characters.[40] While writing about the past is possible only if she uses the third person for the figure from the past and thus distances herself from her ("to remain speechless, or else to live in the third person") this also turns the figure into an object, a product of an uneasy relationship to the past:

> You're not only separated from her by forty years; you are hampered by your unreliable memory. You abandoned the child, after all. After others abandoned it. All right, but she was also abandoned by the adult who slipped out of her, and who managed to do to her all the things adults usually do to children. The adult left the child behind, pushed her aside, forgot her, suppressed her, denied her, remade, falsified, spoiled, and neglected her, was ashamed and proud of her, loved her with the wrong kind of love, and hated her with the wrong kind of hate.[41]

Growing up under fascism has profoundly affected the relationship to the past—it is shaped by self-denial, hypocrisy and the authoritarian structures that underlie all relationships. Even though the child Nelly is introduced in the process of uttering the word "I" for the first time, for the narrator the ability to say "I" remains a utopian dream. The development of Nelly's ability to say "I," which is connected to the development of her ego is also the process through which she internalized the norms and values of the Nazi society in which she grew up.[42] In the process of learning a language identity is formed, and the child positioned within ideology.[43] Wolf draws our attention to the subject's formation within an ideological system. History is thus not only located outside of the subject, but vitally shapes the constitution of the subject. For Wolf only a subject aware of her own development is in possession of history.[44]

Wolf's focus on the different generations of women undercuts the patriarchal tradition of the father as the representative of the family and of continuity residing exclusively in male lineage. Such male genealogy culminated in the Nazis' notorious trees of Aryan descent. The memory of the father allows a critical evaluation of patriarchal history; it does not perforce unearth the repressed memory of the mother. Yet this memory crucially shapes a woman's relation to history. Virginia Woolf describes the "split" vision of women as they encounter history, which in the western cultural tradition is inextricably bound to nationhood: "Again if one is a woman one is often surprised by a sudden splitting off of consciousness, say in walking down Whitehall, when from being the natural inheritor of that civilization, she becomes on the contrary, outside of it, alien and critical.[45] In general, their governments arouse highly ambivalent feelings in women: they encounter not only their own representation but their own exclusion. Yet the split vision also points to women's identification with patriarchal governments and the specific nationalism with which they grew up. In Wolf's *Patterns of Childhood*, the memory of the mothers leads to an exploration of women's specific relation to history. While the female genealogy provides a subversive counter-structure to the Nazis' strict sense of patrilineage and points to a future utopian state of female bonding, the women of *Patterns of Childhood* are also integrated into Nazi society and complicit with it.

The memory of the mother leads to an even older memory—Cassandra, the embodiment of female resistance to war, the seer who forewarned her society of its impending destruction. Charlotte shares Cassandra's strangeness, which precludes her fully integrating into the existing order:

> Cassandra behind the counter in her store; Cassandra aligning loaves of bread; Cassandra weighing potatoes, looking up every once in a while, with an expression in her eyes which her husband prefers not to see. Everything we do is an accident. An accident this husband of hers. These two children about whom she has to worry so much. This house, and the poplar out in front of it, completely alien.[46]

As Cassandra foresaw the disaster of the Trojan War so Charlotte foresees World War II. In 1935, faced with her husband's great business venture—a second grocery store—she unexpectedly proclaims: "You work your fingers to the bone and run yourself ragged, and along comes another war and blows everything to smithereens."[47] Just as no one listened to Cassandra, so too no one listens to Charlotte; instead, her foreboding is dismissed as an unhealthy predisposition to gloom. But, unlike Cassandra, Charlotte pays no heed to her own warning, engaging in her husband's business venture, running his store with unfaltering energy while he serves in the army during the war.

For Wolf, Cassandra's treatment prefigures what will happen to women in the 3,000 years from pre-Christian to current times: they are silenced and objectified.[48] In Charlotte, Wolf points to a painful inarticulateness which makes it impossible for her to express her own needs and desires, or to explore her own position in society. During the course of Nelly's childhood, Charlotte punishes her family more and more frequently with long bouts of silence, her only way of expressing her discomfort with and resistance to the existing order.

Through her mother, Wolf remembers a silenced, non-synchronous tradition of women. In *Three Guineas* Virginia Woolf speaks of the memory of one's mother as a vital source of resistance to the patriarchal order.[49] It is precisely Wolf's focus on a female tradition that puts her out of step with the GDR's definition of history. Throughout the book the narrator argues with her brother Lutz about the significance of the past and about the present state of society. Lutz, who can best be characterized as the voice of sane, pragmatic, male socialism, warns against too much subjective involvement in the re-construction of the past. Satisfied with his insights into history, gained through the official historical writings of the GDR, he refuses to engage in the arduous search for memory which the narrator undertakes. What is ultimately at stake in these discussions, though never expressed, is the subversive poten-tial of memory. For as Lutz defines it history is that which has already been interpreted and serves to legitimize a specific social order and state.[50] Wolf's act of memory is thus also a subversive act against the present social order: the questions she asks about the past led her to question the present—the society which still does not allow women as subjects.

Wolf seeks to move beyond the facts of history to the intricate formations which history produces within the subject. Wolf retraces in Nelly a chain of associations revealing the deep ramifications of patriarchal sexual repression and fascist racism, history engraved in the historical subject. The realization of this is so painful that it can only be stated in parentheses:

> (It's a touchy matter to this day to inquire into the connection—it must have established itself at that time—between the nameless Jew boy, whom Nelly has come to know through Leo Siegman, and the white snake. What does the pale, pimply boy have to do with toads, spiders, and lizards? What do they have in turn to do with the ardent, fanatic voice calling out from the flaming woodpile on that summer solstice night: 'We pledge to stay pure and to consecrate ourselves to Flag, Führer, and Fatherland' ...)[51]

The encounter with an exhibitionist, with slimy, crawling animals which Nelly associates with the male sexual organ, the story Nelly heard about a Jewish boy whom his fellow student felt "the natural inclination" to hit, and the powerful appeal by the Nazi youth movement to remain pure, form the network of Nelly's sexual identity. In her work on memory, Wolf resembles an archeologist who excavates the different layers that history has deposited in the subject.

The words "pure" and "normal" in particular mark the intersection of female sexual repression and racism under Nationalsocialism. While the Aryan German girl learns in the League of German Girls to remain pure (a purity essential to her standing in the social order), Jews and other ethnic groups are designated impure by their very nature. Thus Jewish people are called vermin by the Nazis—a term which serves to legitimize their murder, since vermin are usually killed. Sexual repression is required of girls like Nelly if they are to be considered normal: "It came to Nelly in a flash that her mother must be right. Not to be normal is the worst thing by far..."[52] Charlotte presents to Nelly, as a negative example, a girl whom she considers oversexed. For Charlotte female sexuality is something negative and dirty which needs to be firmly controlled and is best not talked about: "Nelly will control herself. That's what every human being has to learn. ..."[53] Women are in greater danger than men of forfeiting their humanity through sexual transgression; thus self-control has to be even more firmly implanted in them. The subject constitutes herself through control and thus integrates the repressive social order into her most intimate self. Adolescent sexual curiosity thus becomes laced with deep feelings of guilt: "Guilt and concealment were forever tangled in Nelly's mind and furrowed a deep rut studded with glitter-words."[54] "Glitterwords" because the eyes of the adults begin to glitter whenever one of these words is uttered. A look at these words reveals that sexual and racist terms are completely entangled: infertile, carnal, not normal, alien to the species, predisposition, a slave to ...

Such "harmless" words as "normal" assume under Nationalsocialism an explosive, racist meaning. Gisela Bock argues that the Nazis' sexual policy was a powerful control mechanism over all women. Bock demonstrates that compulsory sterilization, the heartpiece of Nazi eugenics policy, was implemented against groups regarded as racially unfit, the mentally and physically disabled and women who did not conform to the Nazis' sexual norms. Bock elaborates: "Among women only the good housewife and industrious mother could be sure to evade sterilization. Unwed and poor mothers with too many children, women on welfare, and prostitutes could not be sure."[55] In the course of Nazi rule unfit to procreate became unfit to live: the eugenics policy was the important first step to mass murder.

Girls like Nelly, however, are offered a compelling compensation for their sexual repression: the opportunity to exercise power. Few other forms of government have ever offered young people such a degree of power as the Nazis did, out of their accurate perception that it would bind them to the system. The intelligent, well-adjusted and ambitious Nelly thus becomes a leader in the League of German Girls. In this capacity she belongs to the elite and is able to direct and punish others. Nelly, who is thirteen or fourteen years old and herself rather slovenly, inspects her fellow playmates' closets very much like a miniature army general, punishing them publicly if they do not meet her standards. Nelly's eager support for the Nazi youth organization has been efficiently erased from the narrator's memory:

> Where Nelly's participation was deepest, where she showed devotion, where she gave herself, all relevant details have been obliterated. Gradually one might assume. And it isn't difficult to guess the reason: the forgetting must have gratified a deeply insecure awareness which, as we all know, can instruct our memory behind our backs, such as stop thinking about it.[56]

Wolf unearths a deep connection between sexuality and power in Nelly's development. Her work of memory aims to reach those aspects of history which are the most repressed and require the subject's deepest self-probing. The confrontation with the past thus erupts into grief for unrealized possibilities.

Examining history, women encounter the violence that structures so much of the European past. In the essays about her work *Cassandra*, Wolf describes the pain of the historical encounter:

> An act of violence inflicted on a woman founds, in Greek myth, the history of Europe. My pain for this continent is in part a phantom pain: not only the pain for a lost limb, but for limbs that have not yet been formed, not developed, for unlived feelings, unfulfilled longing.[57]

An identity so deeply rooted in sexual repression, power, and control leaves Nelly with an enormously diminished emotional capacity which can never be fully regained in later life. It is for this reason that the ability to say "I" must remain a utopian wish.

Within the context of Nelly's social and sexual formation, we encounter Charlotte as a powerful figure who forces Nelly into the patriarchal order. Here female genealogy does not function as a counterstructure to the male order but rather as a powerful vehicle for installing the female within this order. Women have internalized the word of the father and hand it on to their daughters. Charlotte, though not a Nazi, facilitates Nelly's entry into the Nazi system: "Charlotte Jordan thinks one shouldn't feel above doing what everybody else does. Nobody has ever died of it yet."[58] As a legacy from her own childhood, she passes on to Nelly such norms as sexual and emotional repression, such values as cleanliness, industriousness, and obedience—all of which help Nelly to excel in the Nazis' educational institutions. Charlotte, like Rehmann's father, exemplifies the overlap of basic patriarchal values and many fundamental Nazi values. The conservative sexual politics of the Nazis indeed gained them the support of large numbers of middle-class women who felt threatened by the new ideas about women and the family developed during the Weimar Republic.[59]

Charlotte's education decrees normalcy. One of Nelly's aunts, Aunt Dottie, does not fulfill the requirement, since she is mentally retarded. She thus becomes the victim of the Nazis' euthanasia program and is murdered. Dottie's sister becomes sick with grief but the family remains completely silent about the death: "More suspicious than anything, however, was the fact that Charlotte—who was fond of saying about herself that she would always call a spade a spade—that Charlotte clammed up completely."[60] The narrator reflects on this self-imposed silence, a fearful silence no doubt, but one that made the family ultimately complicit in Dottie's murder: "It's hard to determine which has to come first: the readiness of people to have their hearts prepared to sanction murder or the coffins that are being wheeled past them."[61] In her self-imposed silence Charlotte, instead of being identified with Cassandra, can only be identified with those Trojans who allowed no word against the war.

The memory of the mother reveals the contradictory relation of women like Charlotte to the dominant order. Through her identification with Cassandra Charlotte is within a tradition of female resistance to the male order, but she is also an example of how muted this tradition has become. She represents female self-censorship of perception and speech. In their flight at the end of the war, Charlotte hands a bowl of soup to a concentration camp survivor. She asks him why he was incarcerated, to which the man replies that he is a Communist. Full of surprise, Charlotte insists that nobody was put in a concentration camp simply for being a Communist:

> Nelly was surprised to see that the man's face was able to change expression. Although he was no longer able to show anger, or perplexity, or mere astonishment. Deeper shadings of fatigue were all that remained accessible to him. He said as though to himself, without reproach, without special emphasis: Where on earth have you been living? Of course Nelly didn't forget his sentence, but only later, years later, did it become some kind of motto for her.[62]

It is a motto which carries the message *not* to become like the mother—to unlearn many of the things which Charlotte's influence taught. Although otherwise curious, Nelly early learns to remain silent, not to ask questions about certain matters such as politics and sexuality. The eight-year-old already knows to remain silent about the maid Elvira's confession that she is a Communist, though Nelly does not know what that means. She knows not to tell about her encounter with an exhibitionist, not to ask about Dottie's death, not to ask about the Jews she has seen carrying their sacred objects out of their burning synagogue, not to ask about the diapers that are secretly given to a woman in the foreign laborers' barrack. Wolf shows very convincingly how the silence of millions is crucial to a system like the Nazis'—a self-imposed silence which is passed on to the children. As a consequence of such an upbringing the subject develops an elaborate system of self-censorship that damages perception and makes experience retreat into the far reaches of the mind, where it is safely stored away in "encapsulated vaults," severed not only from the world but from the individual's conscience as well:

> But twenty-nine years later you have to ask yourself how many encapsulated vaults a memory can accommodate before it must cease to function. How much energy and what kind of energy is it continually expending in order to seal and reseal the capsules whose walls may in time rot and crumble. You'll have to ask what would become of all of us if we allowed the locked spaces in our memories to open and spill the contents before us.[63]

The breakdown of these memory barriers does not happen automatically; it requires active agency. What can be remembered automatically are the "miniatures with captions" which safely pass self-censorship because they pose no danger to our sense of identity, having been neatly separated from their unsafe context. Wolf aims to get beyond this kind of memory, which she calls "this system of treachery:"

> The news blackout hasn't been lifted. Whatever passes censorship consists of preparations, encapsulations, fossils with a terrifying lack of individuality. Ready-made parts whose manufacturing process—in which you took part, you won't deny it—must be brought in the open.[64]

This fundamentally conformist memory reinforces our accommodation to the existing order and through it the subject participates in the social production of memory as a legitimizing ideology for a social order based on forgetting —particularly the lives of women. Through the self-censorship entailed in ego-development, women internalize this system of amnesia upheld by the society in which they grew up. Memory that reaches beyond "this system of treachery" requires a movement which goes against the grain. This movement, slow and arduous, breaks down the "encapsulated vaults:"

> Suddenly you know that everyone knew. Suddenly a wall to one of the well-sealed vaults of memory breaks down. Snatches of words, murmured sentences, a look—all kept from recreating an incident which one would have had to have understood. Dying like flies.[65]

This kind of memory produces unwanted insights, precisely because it dissolves the protective barriers erected to keep our identity safely within the bounds of the social order. The profound resistance to memory thus stems from the threat it poses to this "comfortable" identity. Yet, as Margarete Mitscherlich argues, the painful process of remembering has to be undertaken in order to dismantle the hegemony of the past.[66] For Wolf this serious preoccupation with the past is necessary if one is ever to change. Memory instigates moral consciousness.[67]

It is crucial for women to attend to memory; through it they encounter the repressed aspect of history—the patriarchal gender sytem with its inherent oppression of women. Through their memories, women gain the critical perspective necessary to break out of their conformity to patriarchy. Their memory also points them to the silenced stories of women's lives—a necessary source for a non-patriarchal future.

NOTES

1. Alexander and Margarete Mitscherlich, *The Inability to Mourn: Principles of Collective Behavior*, trans. Beverly R. Placzek (New York: Grove Press, 1975).

2. Ibid., pp. 13-14.

3. Margarete Mitscherlich, *Erinnerungsarbeit Zur Psychoanalyse der Unfahigkeit zu trauern*. (Frankfurt/M.: Fischer Verlag, 1987), p. 14. My translation.

4. Sigrid Weigel, "Woman Begins Relating to Herself: Contemporary Women's Literature," *New German Critique*, Vol. 31 (1984), pp. 53-94.

5. Sara Lennox, "Nun ja. Das nachste Leben geht aber heute an Prosa von Frauen und der Frauenbewegung in der DDR," *Literatur der DDR in den siebziger Jahren*, ed. P. U. Hohendahl and P. Herminghouse (Frankfurt/M.: Suhrkamp Verlag, 1986).

6. Sigrid Weigel, "Overcoming Absence: Contemporary German Women's Literature," *New German Critique* Vol. 32 (1984), pp. 3-22.

7. Marielouise Janssen-Jurreit and Ute Fervert have examined standard German history books and found that women are almost completely absent in them. Marielouise Janssen-Jurreit, *Sexismus*, 3rd ed. (Frankfurt/M.: Fischer Verlag, 1986); Ute Fervert, *Fraun-Geschichte Zwischen Burgerlicher Verbesserung und Neuer Weiblichkeit* (Frankfurt/M.: Suhrkamp Verlag, 1986).

8. Popular Memory Group: "popular memory: theory, politics, method." *Making Histories*, ed. Richard Johnson, et al. (Minneapolis: University of Minnesota Press, 1982), p. 207.

9. Sigrid Weigel, "Double Focus," *Feminist Aesthetics*, ed. Gisela Ecker, trans. Harriet Anderson (Boston: Beacon Press, 1986), p. 61.

10. Ruth Rehmann, *Der Mann auf der Kanzel Fragen an einen Vater* (The Man in the Pulpit: Questions to a Father), 3rd. ed. (Munchen: Deutscher Taschenbuch Verlag, 1986). All quotes from Ruth Rehmann's book are my translation.

11. Christa Wolf, *Patterns of Childhood*, trans. Ursule Molinaro and Hedwig Rappolt, 2nd ed. (New York: Farrar Straus and Giroux, 1984).

12. "Diskussion mit Christa Wolf," *Sinn und Form*, Vol. 28 (1976), p. 860. My translation.

13. Ruth Rehmann, op. cit., p. 15.

14. Christa Wolf, "The Reader and the Writer," *The Reader and the Writer Essay Sketches Memories*, trans. Joan Becker (New York: International Publishers, 1977), pp. 190-191.

15. Lynda Booth, "The Father's House and the Daughter in it," *The Structures of Father Daughter Relationships*, unpublished manuscript, p. 2.

16. Ruth Rehmann, op. cit., p. 12.

17. Ibid., p. 135.

18. Ibid., p. 9.

19. Ibid., p. 13.

20. Herbert Marcuse, "Studie uber Autoritat und Familie," (1936), *Ideen zu einer Kritischen Theorie der Gessellschaft* (Frankfurt/M.: Suhrkamp Verlag, 1969).

21. Ruth Rehmann, op. cit., p. 127.

22. Ibid., p. 181.

23. Sigrid Weigel, *Die Stimme der Medusa Schreibweisen in der Gegenwartsliteratur von Frauen* (Dielmen-Hiddingsel: tende), 1987, pp. 160-161. My translation.

24. Ibid., p. 165. My translation.

25. Ruth Rehmann, op. cit., pp. 92-93.

26. Ibid., p. 94.

27. Ibid., p. 96.

28. Ibid., p. 95.

29. Ulrike Prokop, "Die Sehnsucht nach der Volkseinheit," *Die Uberwindung der Sprachlosigkeit Texte aus der neuen Frauenbewegung*, ed. Gabriele Dietze, 2nd ed. (Darmstadt: Luchterhand, 1981), p. 119.

30. Ruth Rehmann, op. cit., p. 95.

31. Renate Bridenthal, Atina Grossmann and Marion Kaplan, *When Biology Became Destiny Women in Weimar and Nazi Germany*, ed. Bridenthal, Grossman, and Marion Kaplan. Introduction (New York: Monthly Review Press, 1984), p. 22.

32. *Patterns of Childhood*, p. 3.

33. "Diskussion mit Christa Wolf," p. 878.

34. *Patterns of Childhood*, p. 118.

35. Ibid., pp. 100-101.

36. Ibid., p. 90.

37. Virginia Woolf, *A Room of One's Own* (San Diego, New York, London: Harcourt Brace Jovanovich, 1957), p. 101.

38. *Patterns of Childhood*, p. 10.

39. Ibid., p. 158.

40. Christa Wolf, "Die Dimension des Autors. Gesprach mit Hans Kaufmann," *Lesen und Schreiben Neue Sammlung*, 4th ed. (Dortmund: Luchterhand, 1983), pp. 73-74.

41. *Patterns of Childhood*, p. 7.

42. Bernhard Greiner, "Die Schwierigkeit 'ich' zu sagen: Christa Wolf's psychologische Orientierung des Erzahlens," *Deutsche Vierteljahresschrift fur Literaturwissenschaft und Geistesgeschichte*, Vol. 55/2 (1881), p. 331.

43. Kaja Silverman, *The Subject of Semiotics* (Oxford: Oxford University Press, 1983), pp. 30-31.

44. Ortrud Gutjahr, "Erinnerte Zukunft Gedachtniskonstruktion und Subjektkonstitution im Werk Christa Wolfs," *Erinnerte Zukunft: 11 Studien zum Werk Christa Wolfs*, ed. Wolfram Mauser (Wurzburg: Konigshausen und Neumann, 1985), p. 75.

45. Virginia Woolf, *A Room of One's Own*, p. 97.

46. *Patterns of Childhood*, p. 165.

47. Ibid., p. 111.
48. Christa Wolf, *Cassandra and Conditions of a Narrative: Cassandra*, trans. Jan van Heurck (New York: Farrar Straus Giroux, 1984), p. 227.
49. Virginia Woolf, *Three Guineas* (New York, London: Harcourt Brace Jovanovich, 1969), pp. 78-79.
50. Weber, in Wolfram Mauser, ed., *Erinnerte Zukunft: 11 Studien zum Werk Christa Wolfs* (Wurzburg: Konigshausen und Neumann, 1985), p. 86.
51. *Patterns of Childhood*, p. 135.
52. Ibid., p. 57.
53. Ibid., p. 58.
54. Ibid., p. 57.
55. Gisela Bock, "Racism and Sexism in Nazi Germany: Motherhood, Compulsory Sterilization, and the State," in Bridenthal, op. cit., p. 287.
56. *Patterns of Childhood*, p. 229.
57. Christa Wolf, *Cassandra*, p. 233.
58. *Patterns of Childhood*, p. 254.
59. Bridenthal, op. cit., p. 13.
60. *Patterns of Childhood*, p. 198.
61. Ibid., p. 198.
62. Ibid., p. 332.
63. Ibid., p. 69.
64. Ibid., pp. 152-53.
65. Ibid., p. 69.
66. Margarete Mitscherlich, op. cit., p. 13.
67. Ortrud Gutjahr, op. cit., p. 75.

Lunge*   *Erin Moure*

All of a sudden you find out there isn't enough time.
You find out there was never enough time.
You find out you shouldn't have washed the dishes.

Over & over, so many dishes, the wet cloth, the spill
across the counter, window, bird out there
or not, the clean house, begin

& you find out you shouldn't have bought the clocks.
You shouldn't have bothered buying clocks.
You never had what they had to measure.

You leap up & throw them face-down into the trash.

There is not enough time to cry about this.
The pain in your back is very deep
and pointless.
You find out that all this time they said
you were part of the working class
there was no time.
The real working class in this country was always unemployed,
& you always had a job, the same one.

You find out there is no such thing as enough time
& still you don't have any of it.
You shouldn't have craved the arms of women.
You shouldn't have slept with men.
You shouldn't have dreamed *Philosophy*, or
the heart monitor screen in your apartment bedroom,
just like in emergency.
It's all shit. Merde. This, & hey, & you others.

Time for the medicine. You fast cure. You fuck-up mad dog. You You.
You lunge over the table. In mid-lunge. Going for the adrenalin again,
going for keeps, prose, boots, the sandwich you couldn't eat, you bit &
spit out, you thought it would make you sick again. Lunge for the dog's
stale portion of sleep, your legs straight off the chair, your hair stuck out,
the clatter of the chair falling backward, zone five, zone six, the sound
of

Your arms make

Amicus, object,   referrent

Points   of or-   der

* From *Domestic Fuel* (Toronto: House of Anansi Press, 1985).
Reprinted by permission.

8

Hélène Parmelin and the Question of Time[1]

Maïr Verthuy

A necessary introduction

Hélène Parmelin (a pseudonym) is a contemporary French novelist. She was born in Nancy to Russian parents who, after having been imprisoned by the Czar for revolutionary activities, managed to escape to the West. Raised in Paris, she spent a few years before World War II in what was then called Indo-China with her first husband; during the war, in France, she was involved in the Resistance; for some thirty years after that, she remained a vociferously critical member of the French Communist party and was then, as she is now, active on all political and human rights issues. She started writing while in Indo-China, and also had a long career as a journalist, but her first novel was published in 1950. Since then she has published seventeen more, as well as a variety of short plays, and books on art and politics. She lives in Paris.

My choice of Hélène Parmelin requires perhaps some explanation. On the one hand, in spite of her tremendous output—and although I consider her to be among the greatest twentieth century French writers—she is not as well known as one would expect; on the other, she is not really, in any sense which I might today give the word, a feminist. Those facts may well be the two sides of a single coin.

She is not particularly well known, I think, for one very basic reason: she has always stood outside, even against, literary or political fashions. That does not mean that she eschews political stands or that she avoids the literary questioning characteristic of her century; she merely does both in her own way. To take but one example of the latter: when she first started publishing, the non-Communist world in France was just discovering the laconic style of Hemingway and the American thriller (hence Albert Camus), whereas the Communist world was plunged deep into Zhdanov-type socialist realism (hence André Stil); Parmelin, on the other hand, while politically a member of the Communist party, had just discovered Dos Passos and was very much influenced by his fresco-style writing. Inevitably, she was rejected by both sides. Her situation has been complicated by the traditional rifts in French

94

society, journalism, criticism. Because she was a member of the Communist party, neither the Socialist nor the right-wing press was interested in what she wrote; because she did not write according to the norms of socialist realism, the Party considered her writing to be revisionist. It's called falling between two stools. One may wonder why, when she finally left the Party, she did not receive from society's mainstream, as others have done, the welcome due a "prodigal" daughter. The answer is that she refused to beat her breast and act like a prodigal, merely stating that she had joined the Party in order to defend human rights and had left it for the same reason.

One may add to that, I think, the fact that she does not write in a traditionally "feminine" manner, although I will argue later on that she writes very much out of her woman's experience. She has always written about the whole world: about politics, wars, soldiers, uprisings, police brutality, newspapers, love, miners, unions, journalists, painting, madness, broadcasting, obsessions, writers and writing, accidents, births, deaths, the public and the private world, all of it. Most of her main characters are men. One could say then that she writes like a man. I don't think that's true except insofar as she assumes she has the right, which she exercises, to write about anything she pleases, just like a man. Not many women have achieved that. The critics must have found that difficult to deal with, particularly if you consider that she also in effect confused the issue by writing at the same time about babies and cleaning and recipes, as if they too had as much right to exist as all the "male" concerns she addresses.

As a feminist, I must admit having my own difficulties with her writing. It naturally disturbs me that almost all her main characters are men; that thinking like a man seems important to her; that the female characters appear to have fewer sympathetic traits than the males. I can explain the latter away by pointing out that she is describing people as they are and not as they could be and that, in a sexist world, for obvious reasons, women may be, or may be perceived to be, the more scatterbrained, the less adventurous, the less *significant* sex. I can explain the former by saying that since most of her protagonists are intended both to be neutral observers and to travel a great deal, it would not have been realistic until recently to use a female in such a role.[2] It seems to me, nevertheless, that both these explanations, while perfectly true, skirt the main issue.

I once gave a paper on Simone de Beauvoir entitled: "If Only a Woman Were More Like a Man!"[3] That wish seems to me to characterize de Beauvoir's approach to the woman question. While I don't believe that Parmelin's attitude could be described in quite the same way, it seems fairly clear that both women have been influenced by a political philosophy and a culture that present the Caucasian male as the norm. All colonial powers, and France was nothing if not a colonial power, believed they had no better model to offer the conquered and colonized than the conqueror himself. "La différence" is a very recent concept. Traditional Marxism (Existentialism, etc.)

was no better. It offers a model of progress based on the bourgeois values of the nineteenth century and founded its idea of equality for the sexes (or the "races") on the opportunity offered women (Blacks, Jews, etc.) to raise themselves to the heights attained by their male (Caucasian) counterparts.[4] The rhetoric portrayed an ideal human being (the Caucasian male) transcending sex (or ethnic origin). To pursue that ideal was to be a feminist (antiracist, etc.) because it purported to refute age-old ideas concerning biological inferiority. That, I believe, is largely Parmelin's model. It's a generational question. It works better in her writings than it does in Marxist organization because she has not in fact applied it completely (and because she is a great writer). Unlike de Beauvoir, she does not despise maternity, for instance, perhaps because she is a mother. She does, in other words, deal with the specificity of women's condition, although it is not clear that she identifies with that rather than with the vague human ideal discussed above.

A question of time

> The world unfolded by every narrative work is always a temporal world. Or, ... time becomes human time to the extent that it is organized after the manner of a narrative; narrative, in turn, is meaningful to the extent that it portrays the features of temporal experience.[5]

The temporal "experience," as Ricœur so aptly calls it, has undergone profound changes in the twentieth century. Einstein's theories on relativity and the new *quantum* theories they generated, have completely overturned our ideas about fixed time and space. We now know, for example, even while we continue to think in traditional patterns, that, far from constituting two distinct, linear and three-dimensional phenomena which can be measured objectively according to certain fixed laws, time and space form a single four-dimensional continuum with a number of specific and hitherto unsuspected characteristics, not the least of which is that time is perceived differently according to the speed at which the actual observer is moving. There have also been new discoveries about the nature of matter itself. The atom is no longer believed to be the smallest possible building block, for instance. In other words, we have long since left a mechanical, linear, fixed world in which one could study objective phenomena, to enter an ever-expanding, profoundly unitary world (or universe, or galaxy, galaxies even), which is in some sense holistic, where the observer can no longer be separated from that which is observed.

These changes, of which we are all to some extent aware, even when we know little or nothing of the laws of physics, are not without consequences for fiction. While a goodly number of authors continue to write according to a traditional (and reassuring) model, others, more in tune with their times, are trying to capture this newer reality in their writing, or, to use Ricœur's words, to capture this new *experience* of reality, since the observer has now become part of the equation.

The phenomenon is not new, of course, or recent. In our own *fin de siècle*, it is approaching its one-hundredth birthday. Ever since H. G. Wells and *The Time Machine*, first published in 1895, science fiction, a genre which more and more women writers have come to dominate, has been preoccupied by the possible characteristics of time, and some of the speculations which may at first have seemed far-fetched are now, in many cases, either banal realities or close to realization. Science fiction is not even the only literary genre to be concerned with time. As far back as the 1920s, in the writings of James Joyce, T. S. Eliot, Virginia Woolf, Ivy Compton-Burnett, to name but a few English-speaking authors, we can see how theme and structure have been influenced by a new sensitivity to ideas about the fluidity of time and space. Even so, we had to wait until the sixties and seventies for the "new physics" to permeate almost all major Western writing and for a number of important writers, many of them women, to make it the subject of their writing.

Hélène Parmelin belongs to this latter category, as the question of time, tied in naturally with that of space, is fundamental to her writing. From the anguished waiting for the French deportees returning from Nazi camps that plays so large a part in her first published novel, *La Montée au mur* (Remembering Our Martyred Dead, 1950), to the "Headmovie" of her latest novel, *La Tortue surpeuplée* (The Overcrowded Tortoise, 1987), we can follow the progression of her efforts to render the lived experience of time, the modern temporal experience. With a single exception—*Le Monde indigo* (The Indigo World, 1977), in which the action lasts about a year—the objective duration of events is very brief, despite the often considerable length of her novels. The shortest period, the time it takes to drive from Paris to Brussels, is that of *La Gadgeture* (Gadgetworld, 1967), which is one of her longest texts. In most of the others, the action lasts but a few days, although, in two or three of her books, the action can last up to three months.[6] Time expands and contracts at the author's desire.

But the challenge of rendering subjective time, which she is certainly not the first to take up, is also not the only challenge she accepts. We see her preoccupation with the relationship between exterior and interior time, between the present and the future, between the time it takes to think, the time it takes to write, the time it takes to read, and with the question of simultaneity. She attempts, as she proceeds with the exploration of her writing, almost to deny time while transcribing it, and to freeze it without stopping it. To get a good sense of the way time is dealt with in Parmelin's work, it might help to think of a diptych, with one panel representing time as it is lived by her characters and the other representing time as experienced in the writing process. Such divisions are not always easy to maintain, but they make it easier to approach the question.

Time as lived by the characters

One aspect that Parmelin explores is time's elasticity. In *Léonard dans l'autre monde* (Léonard in Another World), for instance, published in 1957, she is already creating the different densities of time her characters experience, sometimes hanging heavy, sometimes disappearing in a flash. "Time slid by without moving a step," she says, more than half way through the novel, and readers must indeed react sympathetically to the statement on the same page: "Léonard would have been extremely surprised to be reminded that less than twenty-four hours had elapsed since his arrival." But when Léonard, an intellectual and bookseller, leaves his working class in-laws and their family crisis to return to his own milieu in Paris, where he engages in his normal activities—the bookstore, writing, political involvement—then, in his familiar routine, time flies. Its passage is no longer marked by hours and minutes but in other ways; by seasons: "Léonard did not return to St-Honoré for the Christmas holiday" (p. 308); by his achievements: "in early December, in his apartment in rue de Tournon, Léonard finished his important study of the Commune" (p. 301); by interruptions: "Three weeks after the first letter, Léonard received ..." (p. 303).

Time measured by the clock or the calendar seems to have meaning only in certain circumstances. Actual time is rarely mentioned in the novel, and even then almost always in approximate terms, except when the author wishes to stress its unpleasant aspect, as, for instance, when Léonard is learning about the miners' lives:

> Outside, though it was still dark, the mining-town was stirring. The sound of heavy, measured footsteps could be heard. A retreating army marched noisily through the streets.
> What's that?, said Léonard.
> The miners are going down. It's four o'clock.
> But it's Sunday!
> Some of them have to go and work anyway. (p. 113)

Right through her fiction, the concept of time expanding and contracting according to the emotions or preoccupations of her characters reappears. In a fairly recent novel—and the only one of which it can be said that the central character is a woman, although women are present at the center of most of her novels—*Le Monde indigo*, the action of the whole book lasts, as has already been said, something less than one year, and yet approximately half the novel, some 330 pages, is devoted to the account of *one* day in the life of Cramponne, who cleans for a living. Cramponne has temporarily abandoned her studies in order both to read freely and to see more of the world around her; she is good at the job and enjoys it; cleaning, as the author points out, is something women want to get rid of because it's unpaid labor undertaken on top of their other duties. So Cramponne cleans for money.

Part of the description is taken up with the details of her work: "She's reached the silver, that she's cleaning with paste. And a dollop on the rag. Rub rub rinse. And a dollop on the rag. A nice shine. It's going well. Rub rub

rub" (p. 287). "The loo is the only thing I wear gloves for, said Cramponne mildly. Let me explain. First you remove all the water from the bowl with a sponge. When it's empty, you clean it with your favourite scouring powder. If there are still some deposits, I've a good tip for you. I use an emery-board, you know, for filing your nails, and when I rub that on the reddish stain, it disappears. And when it's all clean, I flush until there's no foam left" (p. 283). Although these actions fill the bulk of her day, and Parmelin reproduces very carefully both the substance and the rhythm of such activities, they do not loom large in Cramponne's perception of her world. Much more space is given over to her thoughts or, as we shall see, to the thoughts and activities of those around her, which range over not only large physical areas but also over long—and short—periods of time. The time spent cleaning the silver or the refrigerator may well have some objective existence—Cramponne is paid by the hour—but her experience of that time is as limitless as the thoughts she sends winging around the world.

Parmelin has other ways of expressing the non-linear quality of time. The first is to make it indivisible, so that past, present and future coexist. Thus History is absent from her universe and is replaced by the past, a past that lives primarily in the thoughts or words of the characters, thereby becoming part of the present, possibly even the crux of the action. It is through their "today" that we learn of their yesterdays.

In *Léonard*, for instance, in what appears to be a traditional author's device, Léonard discovers what happened before his departure from Paris through letters written by a brother-in-law, Ambroise. But, in reality, Léonard is remembering the letters while on a train. It is therefore his memories and not the letters themselves that bring to life earlier events; a kind of interior monologue. Further on in the novel, the events described in the letters and others following from them are retold by some of the other characters, and so the past becomes absolutely protean as it is transmitted from one person to the next, endlessly transforming the tableau that is presented to Léonard.

We are then, she says, for all intents and purposes, our memory, our past, which is inseparable from us in each today and tomorrow that we live and is intensely personal. Thus Franek, married to Léonard's sister-in-law, Zélie, wishes to transform her, to deny or wipe out any possibility that she might have had an affair with another miner. He does everything in his power to extract Zélie's memory from her like some aching tooth, to replace it by his own, to restore her to some lost virginity. But Zélie knows, without being told, that if she submits she risks her death as a person, that relinquishing this part of herself to another endangers her life. And so she remains silent about certain things. It is her only act of resistance.

The present contains the past, but it also contains the future, as Cramponne notices when she watches the May Day parade in Paris: "The future world is present in the bellies of the pregnant women, those that are round, pointed, sticking out, balloons either ballooning long skirts or hoisting the minis up in front. They are the foremost point of the family outings, parents arm-in-arm, everyone calling the children to heel, grandpa and grandma pulling or pushing the strollers" (p. 20). This is also evident from the numerous references in various novels to the children who will be born after various amorous encounters, whether the protagonists are aware of the consequences of their actions or not. Frequently, demonstrating how the future is created in a thousand different ways, she even describes the connections that will be formed at a much later period between two characters who have not yet met in her fictional universe. On a more sombre note, *La Femme-crocodile* (The Crocodile-Woman) describes two Spaniards, a brother and a sister, of whom the author writes: "Tomorrow morning, a bricklayer from Marseille who is now watching a game on television, will overtake on a bend in the road, hitting a chicken truck head-on. The brother will be killed instantly. The sister will be disfigured" (p. 84). That is another of the tricks used by Parmelin to emphasize the indivisibility of time.

Another aspect of her writing which is incompatible with the idea of linearity is her use of circular time. Even in her early novels, where the stories seem to have a traditional ending, we learn that appearances are deceptive and that the endings are merely optical illusions. In *Léonard dans l'autre monde*, all such pretence of organization disappears. The events follow each other but lead to no conclusion, no transformations, no "happily ever after." Léonard takes a train north; after three days he returns to Paris where he takes up his usual routine. Zélie, her unidentified nervous breakdown ended or suppressed, picks up her life again, with the same worries, the same friends, the same dissatisfactions as before. Miners die, others take their place. The novel starts, the novel stops. This way of writing does not negate the importance of the death of a miner or of a woman's distress, nor does it seek to inculcate a philosophy of despair in the face of destiny or the absurd. It serves other purposes.

The first of these is to demystify the very idea of a plot. Nathalie Sarraute, reluctant spokeswoman of the Nouveau Roman of the fifties and sixties says that the reader: "distrusts ... a plot which, wrapping itself around the character like a bandage, under the appearance of cohesion and life, gives it the rigidity of a mummy."[8] Indeed, except in the detective novel and other para-literary genres, the modern view rejects these neatly presented packages, reassuringly written according to a pre-established formula. Stories, as Jean-Paul Sartre notes,[9] are reworked and narrated after the event; superfluous details are eliminated in order to give a semblance of significance to a series of disparate events; they do not correspond to the actual experience. Hélène Parmelin gives us life: chaotic, contradictory, knowing no beginning and no end, life as it is lived.

It must be emphasized that this circularity is far from being pessimistic; on the contrary, it demonstrates the fundamental optimism of the author. Her position is that life goes on, and the fact that it stops for one person should not blind us to that reality. This is quite different from such novels as the very moving *Weekend à Zuydcoote* by Robert Merle, in which the whole universe stops with the death of the narrator (how could it be otherwise in this first person narration?). Where Merle rages against death itself, Parmelin, with pain, accepts and integrates it into existence, as a vital process that assures the continuity of the world.[10] The death of one worker does not stop the work nor the death of one woman the pregnancy of others. On the contrary. In the end, as we see in *Léonard*, everything goes on: work: "Franek's work is very difficult right now" (p. 302); the struggle for better working conditions: "Nestor sent off a short letter describing the burial. He added the speech he had given which denounced the silicosis-producing coal dust and which had been published in *The Tribune*" (p. 304); births: "Later he received the announcement of the birth of a son to Narcisse and Maria" (p. 308); in fact, life: "In Paris, Léonard lived his small portion of the life of his times, between peace and war" (p. 308).

Circular time also permits other aspects to come into play. Like Léonard, many of her other characters undertake journeys. Cramponne returns to Toulon to visit her grandmother. In *Le Perroquet manchot* (The One-Armed Parrot) and *La Tortue surpeuplée*, to name but two more works, the protagonists undertake a journey the end of which brings them back to their starting point. In general, all these travellers return after a renewal that allows the person who has undergone a painful or difficult experience to pick life up where it was left off. They are changed because they have lived or learned something, yet unchanged because they are true to themselves. The character is frequently confronted by death, be it that of a friend, of a passing acquaintance, or of a complete stranger. The death is a shock or a tragedy, but, when the journey is over, life goes on as before, nothing has really changed. In this context, it is essential to emphasize the stress the author places on the idea that death from natural causes is part of life itself. People die, they are mourned, life continues. This is true for the characters already mentioned, as it is for many of the mothers and wives she describes, for a variety of her characters.

In one sense, these deaths, present within a continuity, resemble Wittgenstein's rope. The rope is made up of many threads, but none of them run from beginning to end. Each is attached to another, and the whole is made up of all the threads of differing lengths, connected to each other. If the rope is Life, each thread is one of its constituent lives. This impression is reinforced by the author's deliberate repetitions. She reintroduces characters, themes, quotations and events from one novel to another. In both *Le Taureau-matador* (The Bull-Matador) and *Aujourd'hui* (Today), characters peer through holes they've made in the wall; Aunt Marie-Egalité in *Le Taureau-matador* and Joseph in *Aujourd'hui* both repeat constantly: "And to think that (somewhere) at this very moment (someone) ...;" Sébastien in *La Manière noire* (Sombre Thrills) and the father in *Le Soldat connu* stuff themselves with garlic; in *Aujourd'hui* and *La Manière noire*, the same woman appears pushing a baby carriage. A complete list of such common threads would be superfluous.

One can undoubtedly explain the simultaneism[11] that characterizes Parmelin's work by the desire to describe the complexity of the links that exist between humans and which are reminiscent of Geoffrey Chew's theories on the nature of the universe.[12] We are not only the sum of our own actions but also the sum of other people's. Somewhere, something ties us all together. Although one could illustrate this from almost any of her novels chosen at random, and although *Le Guerrier fourbu* might be considered in some ways the best example,[13] *Le Monde indigo*, with its cleaning heroine, seems particularly appropriate here.

This book is constructed like a series of intersecting or partly overlapping circles, the element common to them all being Cramponne, who is its central character and motor. Eight basic worlds are presented to the reader: that of the author, who, in a series of what she calls "interchapters," explains to the reader in exactly what circumstances she is writing the novel; that of Cramponne's "grandmère Arsène," who raised her and who lives outside Toulon; that of a writer friend, Malingaud; of her lover, Lagrénée; of three of the families who employ her, the Bertholet, the Duponchois and the Taladore; of Gildas, another friend, this time an actor. We are invited into each and all of these worlds, either as we accompany Cramponne, physically—in the sense that she is actually described as being with them—or mentally, when she thinks about them. The characters also have independent lives involving a great many people, which the author narrates, so that a number of events are unfolding before the reader simultaneously. The circles are not, of course, hermetically sealed. Cramponne's stories about her employers or her friends and family circle freely among the other groups and some may end up in one of Malingaud's novels; Lagrénée's daughter, Aglaé, visits Cramponne to reproach her for entering into a liaison with her father; some things filter through at quite a different level: "Boris, who is listening to this, taps his forehead, *toc toc*, just like Vincent Malingaud. And indicates that enough is enough. How strange that his gesture, *toc toc*, should have spread from Jules Malingaud to his son, from him to Broque and Barilero, on to Cramponne and Lagrénée. And from there to his wife, Julie, and Aglaé and thence to the maid, Gloria. Who uses it non-stop" (Vol. 1, p. 273).

As well as these intersecting circles, Parmelin uses juxtaposition. For instance, when describing the May-Day parade, which Cramponne is watching, she naturally enumerates all the groups involved but she also enters into detail about the lives of some of those either taking part or watching, other than the characters we have already met. In some cases, there is no apparent connection with Cramponne or any of her friends and employers, except their common presence at the parade; in others, links appear as time goes on. We learn, for example, that one of the masked soldiers demonstrating in favour of a soldiers' union, Paul Lorrain, who has already appeared in *Le Soldat connu*, is in fact a friend of Lagrénée's son and corresponds with Stanislas when he goes to Iran. Readers understand from Parmelin's writing that, in reality, apparently parallel lives require time rather than infinity in order to converge.

On the writing side

Since writing, and *a fortiori* reading, can only exist in time, this second half of the diptych constitutes a major challenge, since Parmelin wants to transcribe in her texts (and thus in time) all the thoughts and images that come to mind in less than the blink of an eye. We traditionally think of our thoughts as "flowing," rather like "pancake batter," as the author says in *La Gadgeture* (p. 11); what could be further from the linearity that image evokes—batter sliding slowing to its destination—than the bombardment of thoughts and images we all constantly experience?

This is how she describes it in *La Femme-crocodile* (The Crocodile-Woman):

> As for the crocodile man ... during that very moment, those very seconds, those brief yet immense rifts in thought—because what is most difficult to grasp in the thought process is not the space it covers but the rapidity with which it moves— the image of Pope John XXIII flashed through his mind, and that's how he ended up in the Vatican. (p. 157)

This is followed by nineteen pages of description of various aspects of a visit to the Pope made by the female narrator—maybe—after which she continues: "And if the story of this visit seems to have taken a long time, well, it didn't happen like that in the mind of the man sitting in the café .... The whole thing was contained in the word 'Pope'" (p. 176).

She emphasizes this theme in her most recent book, *La Tortue surpeuplée*, in which a male character who has disappeared into a parallel life with a young woman called Zaza tries several times to explain what happens at such moments:

> How can I explain in a few words the magic power of the mind that creates in one's head at supersonic speed an accumulation of memory, of the present, of ideas. Without condensing them, without omitting anything. Without adding anything either; just all simultaneous. A humanly embodied computer that's superior to all the electronic brains. That combines circumstances, places, the essence of sentences, feelings, total images ... All it took was one word, Caroline, and a passing thought for the way she always said: "Give me until ..." and, in the space of one step in the hallway, something ... created a whole world in me, and then disappeared, mission accomplished. (p. 202)

He looks for a word, tries a few, then comes up with: "Headmovie" (p. 204). Afterwards, from time to time, he uses it, and a whole world is conjured up for the reading audience, with no need for additional detail: "Here I am, Headmovie-ing right into Jonathan's innocent pranks," (p. 217); "I reacted against the word 'arse' for a split second in Headmovie conceptual mode" (p. 260). The less the author says, of course, the shorter the span of time that elapses between the act of reading and the time required for the images evoked by the text to take shape in the reader's mind. As soon as Parmelin develops the content of her Headmovie, however, then the problem resurfaces. In other words, while this term, rather better than any other, helps us to understand the immediacy of what happens, using it does not eliminate the time required for the narration itself. To that extent, the results of her efforts are ambiguous, but is not the author herself—after all, she created the word Headmovie—fully aware that only the visual can ever hope, however vainly, to escape temporal restrictions? The very existence of such ambiguity, however, reveals at least a partial victory; first, because she raises the issue of the spread between the problem of quantitative writing and qualitatively lived experience, and second, because through her spiralling strategy (for instance, she abandons the Pope only to pick him up seventeen pages later), she creates for the reader the illusion of perfect correspondence between the act of reading and the experience described.

"I'm going to write a novel while living it," says Faubourg in *La Manière noire*; this is the other major challenge taken up by Parmelin: the attempt to make the writing and the living of the writer coincide. It is the time aspect of that challenge with which we are concerned here.

From her very early novels on, she plays with the idea of negating any separation between the two, writer and written, without reaching a solution, but it was not until *La Manière noire* that this theme was developed more fully. At the heart of the novel, there is Faubourg, a writer, who bears a strange resemblance to Parmelin, in the masculine mode, of course. He lives his life intensely; the action of the book lasts only a few hours, yet we live or re-live the events of May '68, the FLN[14] reception in October of that same year, taxi-rides, late-night meetings, unhappy love-affairs, betrayals, inflatable dolls, and so on and so forth. Faubourg wants *simultaneously* to see, to record and to write everything. Rationally, readers are aware of the impossibility of such an endeavour; Parmelin herself says: "When you want to know how you fall asleep, either you fall asleep and don't find out, or you keep watch and stay awake all night" (p. 45). Clearly Faubourg will not start to write his book until Parmelin finishes hers, since the events she describes are those that he and his friends are living and that he wants to recount.

Yet somehow the book creates the impression that everything is happening at the same instant, that we are reading as the author and her character write. Faubourg, who could be speaking for Parmelin, says to Galuchat:

> You know I always write about the present. Today. My time and my characters' time are the same. They go through what I go through. They are involved in the same situations. They are multiple, and I try to describe the simultaneous truth of the world. (p. 387)

In one sense, his statement is justified. Like so many women and men in Parmelin's novels, Faubourg is a writer. Before sitting down to his desk, he thinks about what he will write, and, even if he gives the appearance of wanting to include *everything*, he still must, of necessity, make some selection in the formless mass of events and persons that present themselves to him. At some point:

> Suddenly, everything around him falls into place in response to his all-consuming thought process, as if from then on everything he sees and hears bends itself to his will, taking on the shape he needs to include it in La Manière noire. (p. 129)

In these circumstances, one might say that life and writing coincide even before the sitting down to write, rather as a pregnant women is a mother even before giving birth. It is Faubourg's consciousness that is important; as long as he's aware, in all senses of the word, the novel is in the process of being written:

> That's life. The main thing is to start La Maniére noire and to get on with it. ... The main thing is to have begun it, to be already inside it. To live it and to write it at the same time, in any case, he said hypocritically, that's the thing. Everything I write at the very moment becomes something that, after all, I live. (p. 544)

Since consciousness is now, as we saw earlier, part of the equation, how can we deny the reality that Faubourg affirms?

The presence of the word "hypocritically" warns us, however, that what he says is not entirely true, or, at least, if it's the truth, it's not the whole truth. Parmelin here dissociates herself from her character or superimposes her consciousness on his. Unlike him, she is omniscient, she can reveal information he has no access to. She ponders on the Soviet astronaut who is circling the earth, reminds us that Patrick and Hermetz are engaged in erotic games without Faubourg's knowledge. To write as she does, Faubourg cannot be satisfied merely to transcribe his actions; the role of creativity, of art, must not be forgotten. Quentin explains that very clearly in *Le Diable et les jouets* (The Devil and the Toys):

> Literature is not merely written, it is lived as such, consciously or otherwise. *Living is not enough, however, as it is the act of writing that gives life an opportunity to become literature.* (p. 254)[15]

In other words, one needs TIME. Parmelin gets into, to use an expression she uses to describe Faubourg, writing games, games that are absolutely serious, and through which she explores a number of her concerns. Does she, in fact, wish to warn us that these are indeed games? To live and to write are certainly in some measure synonymous for her; her work, which rejects any pretence of objectivity, proves it. But writing, she also tells us, needs time, reflection, shaping. Or perhaps, ever the conjurer, and with a conjurer's rapidity, she is trying to convince us she has succeeded where her character has, at least in part, failed!

A non-vicious circle

Although this paper has been mainly concerned with the aesthetic aspects of Parmelin's treatment of time, the question of the author's sex seems to me to be very much part of the equation. In the introduction, I made it clear that her world view can only with difficulty be called feminist and offered some explanation for what appears to me to be her stance. That does not mean, however, that she is not writing out of a woman's experience. On the contrary, whatever she may believe about the androgyny of writers or the nature of the ideal human being, unlike Simone de Beauvoir who seems to have little acquaintance with the experiences of most women, Parmelin lets her woman consciousness and experience inform both the content[16] and the form of her writings.

In the temporal context, that attitude is extremely important, since the correspondence between the language of New Physics and the lives of most women seems nigh on perfect. Women who have always been interrupted, even while working, by the constant demands of their entourage; who have always taken responsibility for maintaining family connections (oh, the Christmas or Hanukkah cards, the annual letters, the birthday or anniversary gifts!); who have never genuinely succeeded in separating the sexual act from what precedes or follows; who have borne the children that maintain the human race: women have perhaps never lived linear time as men have, never believed the world could be reduced to the individual, to the atomic, or that our actions have no repercussions, never been able to consider life as mere "matter," never known the universe other than through living continuity.

If then, for Parmelin, time is both real and a game, if objective reality is replaced by subjective interaction, if the present contains both past and future, as a woman may contain both her mother and her child, if time is circular and continuous and the world a mass of inseparable simultaneity, surely then we may conclude that to write as a woman is today to encompass time as we now understand it.

NOTES

1. This article is a modified version of a chapter in the book I am currently writing about Hélène Parmelin's fiction. The original was written in French and, as I am absolutely incapable of translating my own work, I wish here to express my gratitude to Lucille Nelson (a graduate of the French Department's translation programme and a member of the Simone de Beauvoir Institute, Concordia University, Montreal) who produced the excellent translation which is the basis for this text. I am also grateful to the students from my seminar on time and space in the works of Duras and Parmelin whose insights were crucial to my understanding of this question.

2. Cf. Maïr Verthuy, "Y a-t-il une spécificité de l'écriture au féminin?," *Canadian Women's Studies/Les Cahiers de la femme*, Vol. 1, no. 1, Fall 1978.

3. Sydney, Australia, June 1984.

4. One need only think here of Jean-Paul Sartre's book: *La Question juive*. This is still read by many people as "progressive," although what the author prescribes is total assimilation! Jews are acceptable on condition that they are no longer Jews.

5. Paul Ricœur, *Time and Narrative*, Vol. 1, p. 3, translated by Kathleen McLaughlin and David Pellauer. University of Chicago Press, 1984, 288pp.

6. This concentration of time is reminiscent of the French classical theatre which did not allow any plot to extend beyond 24 hours. I believe, however, that there is a crucial difference. Whereas Parmelin is attempting to render subjective time, the intention in the

sixteenth and seventeenth centuries was to maintain as exact a correlation as possible between the (real) time of the spectators and the (fictional) time of the play, in order to translate the concept of time as fixed, as identical for everybody, because, or so I hypothesize, they were unable or unwilling to accept the simultaneous existence of two different time-sets.

7.   All translations from Hélène Parmelin are either Lucille Nelson's or mine.

8.   Nathalie Sarraute, *L'Ere du soupçon*. Paris, éd. Gallimard, 1956.

9.   Jean-Paul Sartre, *Situations I*(Paris).

10. I am currently working on a paper that is based on the hypothesis that, whereas men and boys seem to see themselves automatically at the center or hub of the universe, women seem largely incapable of the same feat. I am interested in the consequences of that attitude for literature and feminist theory. It would help to explain why men apparently have a more apocalyptic approach to death than women.

11. Simultaneism: a technique which juxtaposes in time events or happenings from people's lives which have no apparent connection but which may converge or influence each other without those involved necessarily being aware of it. Dos Passos, the well-known progressive American writer, was one of the first to develop this technique; Parmelin was very much influenced by his writings.

12. G. F. Chew, "Bootstrap: A Scientific Idea," *Science*, Vol. 161, 23 May 1968, p. 93.

13. The worn-out warrior of the title is Guillaume Lacharrée, a war correspondent, now a patient in a clinic in France, because, with an unusually acute sense of reality, he can no longer separate war zones from peace zones or pretend that the whole world is not in some way involved in conflict:

   The horror of it, Doctor, is that I feel the war in myself, and to such an extent that it's as if I were there. In any case, I don't see the difference. The proof is that even as I speak I am so conscious of being on the Pei-Me plateau with you that there's no difference between being there and not being there. ... For the others, the war comes and goes. When it's finished in France, it goes to India or Africa. For them, it's over. But for me, they all come here. All those wars. Whether I'm really in them or not, what difference does it make? ... It's the same things happening. Hey, I can prove it. Listen to the planes overhead ... (p. 276).

14. Le Front de libération national, the representatives of the Vietnamese resistance to the US forces and their puppet government. In 1968, their delegates in Paris were officially recognized for the first time.

15. Emphasis added.

16. One need only think of Cramponne cleaning the loo to be convinced.

9

Urania—Time and Space of the Stars The Matriarchal Cosmos through the Lens of Modern Physics*

Heide Göttner-Abendroth
translated by *Lise Weil*

THE CONCEPT OF TIME IN MATRIARCHAL SOCIETIES

Urania is the muse of astronomy. She is also a woman, a goddess. Is this only a coincidence, or mere masculine projection? My research into matriarchal societies indicates otherwise.[1] The account I present here of Urania the muse has a firm basis in fact.

The moon goddess stood in the center of the ancient goddess cults of the Eastern Mediterranean. She was a triad, the first trinity.[2] In the social structure and in the rituals of the highly developed matriarchal societies of that region (ancient Egypt, Crete, prehellenic Greece), her figure was reproduced as the triple star of the queens, whose highest mission was the cult, or in the tripling of the trinity to a nine-headed staff of priestesses, who directed the fate of these first city-states. In the matriarchal theacracies the cult positions were the most influential, and there was no division of religion, art, science and politics as there is today. The first priestess of the moon cult was not only the tribal queen or the representative of the city-state, she was also the best dancer of the nine. For the high points of the cult as of social life were the great celebrations in honor of the moon goddess during the season cycles, and at these celebrations, in connection with all other forms of art (music, song, rhapsodic speech, architecture, ceremonial costume and rich food), there was dancing—long, lusty, and to the point of exhaustion.[3] The nine wild muses of Parnassus—before the patriarchal God Apollo tamed them

* This article first appeared in *Feministische Studien* Nov. 1982 (Beltz Verlag, Weinheim und Basel). It was published in translation in *Trivia: A Journal of Ideas* No. 10, Spring 1987.

and usurped their arts—were really only a staff of priestesses who identified with the tripled trinity of the moon goddess of Mount Parnassus. There were similar staffs of priestesses on Mount Helikon and on Mount Olympus, representing the local moon goddess—until she too was conquered by a patriarchal god, Zeus, who crushed every resistance with his "lightning bolts" and rose to become the highest father of the gods.

Everything that we designate as "art and science" today was present in the ecstatic dances of the moon priestesses, the muses. As mothers of the cult and of their mountain people, as the freest goddesses of creativity and of the entire region, they danced unendingly and thus resembled the wild orgiastic Maenads. Most remarkable were their ceremonies of "danced time," which imitated upon the ground the movements of the stars. Urania, queen of the nine, was in charge of these ceremonies.

These dances were now lawless and they did not take place just anywhere in the open country. There were designated dance sites, and these sites were the earliest astronomical observatories. The simplest form was a circle of stones—nine, eighteen or twenty-seven, depending on the size of the circle. In the middle of this circle there usually stood a stone obelisk, a pointed menhir, which had many meanings: altar of the goddess, stone Herm as symbol of the hero—the masculine partner in the dances of the nine-fold goddess, giant index finger for the moonlight or sunlight falling into the circle. For these circles were not just observatories, but also stone moon calendars and sundials. Through the fixed position of the outer stones and the shadows of the inner stone, moon- and sunrises and moon- and sunsets were observed. These calendars served to divide the months by the moon and the years by the sun. For example, a special pair of stones always marked the most important sunrise at the winter solstice, the rebirth of the light: the sun rose towards the solstice over the horizon exactly through the narrow crack between the stones. For the moon ceremonies with their meaningful dances did not take place randomly, but at certain set moments in the complicated interplay of moon and sun in the sky which influenced the growing seasons on earth. Even in the simple matriarchies, it was the phases of the moon observed by the naked eye which determined the dances. In the highly developed matriarchies of the Near East and the Mediterranean up until the end of the Bronze Age, time was divided by the harmony of the three central heavenly bodies: mother earth—the ancient cthonic goddess, her daughter the moon—the younger astral goddess, and her son, the sunstar, who, being a man and a hero, was not considered divine. The time phases of the ceremonial ritual dances were, first, the equal days and nights of spring till the next full moon (Ostara), the time when vegetation returned—the ceremony of the hero's initiation into his dignity through the goddess. After that came the phase of the summer solstice till the next full moon (Litha), when vegetation reached its peak—the ceremony of the holy wedding of the goddess and her hero as fertility partners (hieros gamos). Following this was harvest time, the equal days and nights of fall till the next full moon (Mabon)—the sacrificial ceremony for the crops and the hero-king. The mythic year of nine months ended with the winter solstice up until the next full moon (Yule), when vegetation rests beneath the earth and waits for its return—the ceremony of the rebirth of the light and of the hero-king, whom the Triple Goddess now holds on her lap as a small child. The remaining three months were considered a time of silent preparation for the coming mythic year, which begins again with the equal days and nights of spring.

This time has so much to do with women that it was itself considered to be female: Urania, or heavenly time. For the bodily processes in woman concerned with fertility—for which she was highly revered in matriarchies as the giver of life—run synchronously with the clocks of the heavenly bodies. The menstruation cycle runs synchronously with the phases of the moon, and the pregnancy cycle of nine months is embedded in the mythical year from Easter till Yule (vernal equinox till winter solstice). Presumably, the erotic acts of these peoples in the community, at least on the sacral level, were adjusted to these cycles, and everything obeyed this synchronous "inner clock" of women.

Recognition of such an "inner clock" was, however, possible only by way of comparison with the outer clock, the stone observatories, which determined the place and time of the dances and gradually over millenia turned the dance site into a giant calendar. Such dance-site calendars can still be seen today in partly or completely preserved stone circles in Ireland, Scotland, and England.[4] The most splendid example of a moon and sun calendar is Stonehenge in the south of England. Many of them existed in France and Germany too. In Germany they were called "Trudenrings" (rings of the Trudes or Druids) or later "Witchrings." In France examples can still be found in Brittany, though there they are connected with other complicated forms of menhirs (e.g., rows, parallel lines, and waves). The stone circle is only the simplest form, and the calendar-builders did not stay with it. They also built multiple concentric circles from which rows of stones went out like snakes, then formed concentric circles again. Such a giant installation, surrounded by earth walls like an amphitheater, is the 6,000-year-old Avebury Ring in the south of England. Stonehenge, 4,000 years old, is relatively young by comparison.

Another form for the dance sites was the labyrinth, which imitated the movements of the dancers. The basic model here is the spiral: around to the left from the outside into the center of the circle, then around to the right, dancing out from the middle. This double-spiral path was an image for the moon-goddess, who seems to travel in a spiral leftwards around the earth until she stands full and round in the zenith in the middle of the sky, and then seems to spiral to the right until she disappears near the sun as the new moon. Thus, the mystical spiral was the image of the goddess herself with her double power: to go from darkness to light or from death to life and conversely, from light to darkness, from life to death. Death as a definite end did not exist; it was only transformation into new life, an intermediate stage before rebirth. Thousands of such spiral symbols adorn the stones of the megalithic graves, as well as cult objects like vases, pitchers, belts, bangles and headdresses. They decorate sacred rooms in palaces, as well as insignia and runic writing in the oldest archeological documents all over Europe and the Near East. And the earliest forms of the labyrinths—which were nothing other than cultic dance sites—were simple spirals.

Such labyrinths or dance sites were spread all over the Eastern Mediterranean. Today some can still be found intact as stone or grass labyrinths in what were then remote zones of France, England, Germany, Scandinavia, and Russia. Mostly they are called "Troy castles," and even in patriarchal times it has been known that women danced or rode in them. The majority of these labyrinths were either destroyed by the devotees of patriarchal religion or buried when their temples and churches for the new gods were built on top of them. Only a few labyrinth patterns have been imitated in the great cathedrals of France as ground decorations, for example, in Chartres, Bayeux, Arras, Amiens, Saint-Quentin, Reims, and Sens—all on the original site and in the original size.

The calendars were the sacred objects *par excellence* for matriarchal peoples: time made manifest. Only through them could the dances which took place fulfill their magical purpose: namely, to favorably influence the phases of the moon, the cycle of the sun and vegetation on earth. This was the sole purpose of the four great ritual celebrations, for the agrarian matriarchal societies depended directly on the flourishing of vegetation. Agricultural magic was not understood as a replacement for observation and calculation—in fact, these peoples conducted natural and astronomical studies in great detail, and were the first to do so in human history. Rather, it was a way to enter into communication with nature. For this one had to be guided by her readiness, her constellations, and here observation and calculation were essential. But these peoples saw nature and the cosmos not as an experimental subject, but as a living being, one whose will could always change in the end. Thus it was necessary to communicate with her through symbols in order to make oneself understood, to express one's wishes, to make clear to nature that she should keep to her once calm intention: that is, to let spring, summer, fall and winter come. This purpose was fulfilled by the magic celebrations which were preceded each time by precise calculations, as can be seen in the astronomical time of these peoples, now turned to stone.

The calendar-temples in their spiral form were at the same time a representation of the cosmic space in which all visible heavenly bodies move about the earth in an apparent spiral. *And time is nothing other than the movement of planets and stars in space. For this reason, the representation of time was also that of spiraling movement.* This means more than the simple juxtaposition of "cyclical" versus "linear" time, where "cyclical" time connotes dull, futureless circles in place, while "linear" time is supposed to correspond to progressing and progressive historical consciousness. Both concepts of time are ideological constructs. In contrast, the concept of spiraling time seems more realistic, for it rests on concrete observation of the movement of stars in space. Moreover, it is more complex, since it connects the circling motion with the progressing movement of always further-reaching spirals. This concept of time slid seamlessly into these peoples' concept of history; historical time was for them also a cycle, which, through gradual evolution, took on the form of a spiral. Scientific and historic time were in this sense undivided.

The smallest historical unit of time was the cycle of moon phases (months), a larger one was the cycle of the sun year, after that came the Great Year of a hundred moon months (Great mythical Year), and the largest historical unit was the world age (eon). According to them the world ages, whose echo we still hear in the myth of the "golden," "silver," and "iron"ages, also developed in spiral fashion one from another. Thus, the conception of history as nonlinear, noncyclical dynamic process is the earliest form of dialectic. Demonstrably, the first philosophical debates on dialectics in antiquity arose from reflections on the philosophy of nature, and these originated in the spiraling conception of time—which we might well call a "dialectical" conception of time—of the matriarchal ages.

THE PATRIARCHALIZATION OF TIME

With the dismantling of matriarchal mythology and, along with it, of the matriarchal world view in antiquity, the complex, spiraling concept of time of the matriarchal peoples was also destroyed. For this concept was determined not only by the stars, but also by woman: she was the divine rebirther, who with every birth symbolically began the cycle of the seasons on a new level. She was the eternal creator of life, who with every birth again challenged death as definitive end. Out of her monthly cycles, yearly cycles, life cycles, human history emerged into the world ages.

The radical destruction of her role in the early patriarchal warrior societies dissolved this structure. Man stood on his own two feet and insisted on his own strength; every dependency on woman, especially that of having been physically and mystically reborn from her, was denied. With this, the spiral conception of time went under, to be replaced by one that was aggressively linear, that knew only a straightforward succession of advancing deeds. After the first European patriarchies were established, the dimension of time was split and became doubly ideological. The time of the ignorant "barbarians," whose strange customs were jeered, was now called "cyclical" and assigned the negative value of dull, backwards, ahistorical. The time of the new patriarchal peoples by contrast was rational-linear, adorned with all the positive values of the new spirit. Indeed, the historical consciousness of early patriarchy outdid itself in the enumeration of genealogies of ruling houses, all pure father-son genealogies, and in similar lists of the succession of dynasties and kingdoms.

Strict linear time also had its perils, for within it the idea of rebirth, which characterizes all matriarchal religions, dropped away, leaving the idea of death as a definitive, horrible end. From now on, the shadows of Hades, the terrors of Orkus, whence there is no return, haunted the people of antiquity. There was no hope of rebirth—since this would be a relapse into "cyclical" time.

This process of splitting off and devaluing, which represses whatever doesn't fit the new world picture, forcing it into the past, into the lower stratum, into the unconscious, is later to repeat itself with great frequency—no longer with spiraling time, but with the ideological ambivalences which remained even in "linear" time. The first ambivalence has already been mentioned: the new glorified linear-historical consciousness of the patriarchal dynasties, which strictly absolved man of all connection to natural and female cycles, but also entailed the irrevocable end of the individual. The latter paved the way for acceptance of the syncretic salvation religions of Hellenism with their outlook on rebirth, among them early Christianity, which led ultimately to the victory of Christianity in the late Roman Empire. Life is now extended beyond death by way of a single resurrection in the hereafter, rather than repeated births in the here and now, and, in parallel fashion, historical time receives its extension in eschatology. But this patriarchal reconstruction of religion now occurs on the ground of linear time: life, death, and individual resurrection, like the piecing together of history as salvation history, strictly follows the scheme of the unique straightaway. Conscious opposition to nature, which is subordinated to the concept of "the supernatural," exists alongside conscious opposition to woman as a creature chained to the "natural" and "cyclical." These ideas sustain the Middle Ages. However, through the combining of history with salvation history, linear time, at the beginning of modernity, encounters another split—this one between historical time and scientific time, whereby the latter disposes of all religious remnants in the concept of time.

With the rapid growth of the mathematical sciences there sets in a rigid metricization of linear time. Previously, time had remained primarily inside mythic and religious contexts; despite a number of calendar reforms directed at the old "heathen" division of the year, the "churchyear" with its ceremonies by and large repeated the matriarchal season cycle. With the introduction of metrical time, a sharp boundary is drawn against this religiously padded historical time, setting off negatively valued historical time as less rational, just like the supposedly "cyclical" time of prepatriarchal societies. Splitting off and devaluing persist still today in the codex of sciences where the non-metricizable, historical sciences are judged against the hard sciences as second-rank, imprecise, narrative, and basically only half-scientific.

Exact, metricized scientific time is the ideal left over from this double split in the dimension of time, although in traditional philosophy a theoretical dialectic which saw time as spiraling process rebelled against it. The metricization of time preceded a revolution in astronomy: the discoveries of Copernicus and Kepler, known as "the Copernican revolution," showing that the heavenly bodies do not circle around the earth, that the earth turns around the sun and rotates on its own axis. This was the modern explanation of day and night and the seasons, and it served to devalue all previous conceptions of time as dull ignorance, stemming from mythical and religious prejudices. The heliocentric world view which dethroned the earth and made the sun the focal point, at the same time elevating man (sic) to the measure of all things, gained victorious acceptance. With the Copernican revolution a completely new concept of day came into being, one which no longer has anything to do with the visible day as the phase of light which becomes longer or shorter. Day is now defined as a rotation of the earth and, as such, becomes the basis of the new time measurement. This astronomical day is called a "sidereal day" and marks the span of time which passes before a distant fixed star sighted in the sky surfaces at the same exact spot. This definition is independent of the length of light or darkness; it now becomes the constant abstract unity on the ground of which the first mathematical timekeeper, the clock, is introduced.

The exclusive focus of the following centuries was the progressive perfecting of this mathematical timekeeping clock. Astronomy consists solely in meeting the technical requirements of its science: to develop increasingly far-sighted telescopes and increasingly precise clocks. However, typically enough, the development of precise clocks was advanced not only by the pure science of astronomy but by a much mightier force in the patriarchal state structure: the admiralty. Seafarers instantly recognized the enormous importance of an exact chronometer for navigation. Government promotions and the awarding of high prizes were begun, at the admirals' instigation, and finally led to Englishman John Harrison's glorious deed: the invention of a clock capable of synchronizing the European and American continents to within a minute. In 1761, a schooner sailed with this clock from London to Jamaica and back, and on its return it was established that Harrison's clock deviated from London time by only 56 seconds.

We can understand the full extent of the admiralty's ambitions only once we recall that the centuries after the Renaissance were characterized by the discovery and conquest of all the continents on the globe by European seafarers, and the erection of great, world-wide colonial empires—especially England. In light of the early signs of imperialistic advances on the part of the modern European nations, the exact measurement of time was no pure science and no mere technical game, but, in the hands of the admiralty, a strategic instrument, an indirect weapon of war. Not only were historic and scientific time split here, but even more concretely, quantitative and qualitative time. The former, as demythologized time, fell into the hands of scientists, technicians and admirals as described above; the latter stayed with the people in the vague concepts of "morning," "afternoon," "evening," "midnight," and so on.

This changed with the industrial revolution. As all labor processes became increasingly rationalized and technologized, quantitative time established itself on a broader basis. Everyone had to have a watch so that he could orient himself by travel schedules, work schedules, by time-clock and assembly-line time, by hourly wages and piece rates, down to the minute. For quali-tative time there remained only the devalued niches in industrial society; it ranked outside the paid wage scale as "free time," which explains the enjoy-ment of a "day off," and the vacation joys of "summer," "winter," or "Easter." It is worth noting about this last division of the time dimension that it is above all women at home, the remaining peasant classes, or the picturesque peoples of the tourist zones in poorer countries who are responsible for this holiday recreation within the framework of qualitative time. For these people "still have time."

In spite of all this, quantitative industrial time lags way behind the time measurement capabilities of modern physics (nuclear physics, geophysics, astrophysics), which marches ahead in the straight perspective of linear time and the ideal precision of the unambiguous mathematical scale—until it runs into unforeseen problems.

THE CONCEPT OF TIME IN MODERN PHYSICS

As the astronomers got their clocks to run more and more accurately, they made a rare discovery. From old charts which reached back to the year 1700, they determined that the moon, up until 1750, had simply traveled too quickly around the earth—that is, its orbiting time ran over the calculated average. After 1750, however, its orbiting time slowed down and in 1800 reached a low after which it gradually increased again. In 1880, it was again at the calculated speed, but did not maintain it; interrupted by a few swaying motions, it gathered increasing speed, traveling once again too quickly around the earth, as it continues to do today. This strange acceleration of the moon, like its equally strange deceleration of over a hundred years, confused astronomers, until they began to investigate the movements of the other planets during this same time. It turned out that in terms of their speed of movement, they had behaved just as strangely as the moon, and this solved the riddle. It was the earth's rotation which was subject to these swaying motions and so produced an apparent acceleration or braking effect in the planets and stars. The earth's rotation and its movement around the sun mani-fested irregularities as its ideal elliptical path through the various constellations with their neighboring planets was disturbed by their forces of attraction. This was a fatal realization for the specialists in mathematical time, for the "sidereal day," which had been defined as the constant fundamental unit of metrical time, now proved to be inconstant. The earth's rotation became inadequate as a unit of time measurement and they had to start looking for a new and truly consistent measure. The search for even more precise, more abstract time led at last to the invention of the atomic clock. Now the absolutely regular vibration of the Caesium atom became the tiny basic unit, permitting such unimaginable precision that even a millionth part of a second can be broken down into exactly equal parts.

These clocks too were produced not for the sake of pure science, but for technological-military use, astronautics. Thus, it is first and foremost the Luftwaffe generals who demand increasing funds for the perfecting of time measurement. Here the goal is weatherproof and disturbance-free homing systems for planes and rockets, for U-boats and space probes—none of which, as we know, have a neutral, value-free civil function.

In addition to bringing strategic-military "progress," always the top priority in patriarchies, this most abstract time brought astonishing things to light, and, quite suddenly, these led back to the concrete. The accuracy of the atomic clock made visible phenomena which recall the matriarchal myths. The determination to measure the irregularities in the earth's rotation precisely, down to tiny fractions of seconds, led to the discovery that the earth turned a bit faster in winter and slower in summer, and that the change in its rotation thus synchronized with the seasons of the northern hemisphere. The measurements of the atomic clock brought an even further irregularity to light: namely, a steady, very slight slowing down in the earth's rotation, caused by the braking effect of the tides, which, through the attraction of the moon, surge steadily against the continents of the rotating earth. This braking effect is miniscule, to be sure, but, measured over long periods of time, it is noticeable. Thus the geophysicists discovered that two hundred million years ago, when dinosaurs ruled the earth, the day had only 23 hours and there were 385 days in the year. Four hundred million years ago, as the first plants put down roots along the coasts, the year had 405 days, each of them lasting only 21.5 hours. In the (certainly unforeseeable) future, the days will become longer and longer.

Biologists now assume that a day of 30 or 36 present hours would bring our entire biological environment and ourselves fatally out of balance, for it would expose a connection which is presently invisible, although it affects and directs all our bodily and spiritual functions. Only in the last three decades has modern metrical science discovered this connection—or rather, rediscovered it, now in mathematical instead of mythical language: it is called "the biological clock."

What this means is that the alternation of sleep and waking, of activity and rest, does not *follow from* the alternation of night and day. Over time, plants, animals and humans in laboratories and artificially isolated rooms exhibit the same alternation in the same 24-hour rhythms as the creatures outside. The self-sufficiency and independence of this 24-hour period led biologists to suspect that it was "inborn," embedded in our cells, consisting of very definite elementary chemical processes which run down with great regularity and represent a standard of time, a "biological clock." This clock is so precise that all beings are capable of "measuring" the length of daylight through the changing seasons to within a few minutes. Instinctively or unconsciously, human beings have adapted to these periodic changes in our environment. This becomes acutely noticeable in, for instance, long-distance flights against the movement of light on the earth; sleeplessness, nervousness and uneasiness linger for days after a flight from west to east, which goes against the "biological clock." On the other hand, to orient oneself by this clock, to live *with* the rhythmical exchange of day and night, not against it in artificial light, etc., is balancing and calming and accounts for the relaxing effect of vacations.

This shows that the speed of the earth's rotation is not a matter of indifference to present forms of life, since they are all adapted to a 24-hour day and not to a longer one. When the day had 21 hours, the earth was filled with other life forms than today, for other climactic conditions and another light-time prevailed. An earth with a 30-hour day would have altered the light, time, and climate conditions so strongly that an entirely other form of life would be living on it—certainly not anything like today's. For this reason, biologists assume that humans can never inhabit other planets, since if nothing else the different time relationships would make survival impossible for us. The "biological clock" ties us to earthly time relationships in exactly those phases determined by the earth's rotation speed; this is all the more true of the "inner clock" of women, whose complex biological processes, in conjunction with our ability to give birth, indicate even greater adaptation to the monthly ordering of time. This sets a limit to all abstract time and to all abstract utopias.

In the wake of Einstein's relativity theory, many absurd things were both developed in theory and observed in practice. After Einstein, time becomes the fourth dimension of space (spacetime) and independent of speed. Here time is no absolute constant—time as such does not exist, only various times relative to a certain context. Thus "simultaneity" exists not in itself, but only relative to a context.

The relativity of time led astrophysicists to search for an absolute time unit which would be good for all zones in the cosmos under all movement conditions. How else could they describe all trajectories of time in the cosmos? This absolute time unit is absolute speed itself, the speed of light. The speed of light is a universal constant and thus alone suited to describe dimensions and trajectories in the cosmos—in light years. Here the relativity of time and space is taken fully into account: space is measured in time and time in speed. Just as the invention of the atomic clock indirectly eliminated traditional metrical time, which became inhuman machine time, and led to the reinvention of the "biological clock," so the relativization of time turns the classic-patriarchal linear conception of time upside down.

The speed of light as a theoretical constant also failed to salvage the linear conception of time, for it is only a vehicle by which to synchronize in theory the times of all the worlds in space. In actuality, the astronomer who gazes deeply into space is really seeing step by step into the past, into other times. This became clearer as the giant telescopes became more capable. After the discovery of all the nightly constellations, loosely directed by suns, as well as the starcover of the "Milky Way" directly around us, on whose edge our solar system races along, attention was directed to "extragalactic" objects, that is, to heavenly bodies outside our own spiral nebula, the Milky Way. If the light of the stars within our galaxy travels thousands of years before it reaches us—so that Nova explosions which occurred in the Stone Age on earth are just now becoming visible in the sky—the distances of extragalactic objects are virtually fantastic. Our "neighbor galaxy," the spiral nebula Andromeda, is about two million light years away. Between it and our Milky Way there is nothing in space, for suns do not exist in space, they are all found in star clusters, in galaxies, which are masses of spheres, masses of ellipses, or rotating spiral nebulae. We see Andromeda as it was two million light years ago, a glimpse into the ancient past. How it looks today is unknown, nor is it known if it still exists and has not in the meantime exploded. The "average" distances of galaxies is 60-80 lightyears, while galaxies of a thousand million lightyears are considered "remote," though they can still be photographed through the telescope. At the boundary of two thousand million lightyears, strange objects appear which seem to defy all known laws of nature. They radiate tremendous energy for their enormous distance from us, much too much for a normal galaxy and for the circumference which they presumably have. They are called "quasars" and, at two to 13 thousand million lightyears, many more have been discovered. In this realm, "normal" galaxies no longer exist—and this suggests the following solution to the puzzle. What is being observed here is the earliest past of the cosmos itself, as its shapes are still forming, as giant masses of material not yet galaxies are in the midst of an implosion, a gravitational collapse, which will lead to the first rotation and the birth of a galaxy. Here we are seeing not only to the edge of the cosmos, but also simultaneously way back, to its origins. The radio waves and light signals that reach us from the quasars are so old that they were sent out when our Milky Way was itself perhaps a quasar. In the meantime, the quasars have themselves turned into totally normal galaxies.

So, what the astrophysicists glimpse *simultaneously* through their telescopes are not various celestial objects, but various stages of time in space. They are literally seeing step by step into the past of the universe, and can see its formational stages. Time becomes here what it is after Einstein: spacetime, the fourth dimension of space. It surrounds us in the center with visible rings—and this is certainly no longer a linear conception. Here its relativity emerges: for the present is with us, on our globe, in our solar system, while the "younger" past is to be found in the stars of the other galaxies. The even more distant ones, which we see around us, existed an unimaginably long time ago. But, if the observer stood upon one of these distant objects, she would be in *her* present, and would see our system in its past stages: the earth still glowing or not yet completely in existence—or the Milky Way in the state of a quasar. So every world in space has its own time.

The galactic world picture of modern physics dissolved the linear conception of time for yet another reason: after Einstein, the cosmos is unbounded, but not endless. It has the form of a bent hollow sphere, which is finite, but in which one can move without bounds. In other words, from a three-dimensional point of view it is finite, but if one includes the fourth dimension, that of spacetime, it is unbounded—just exactly as unbounded as travel on the surface of a sphere. And just as one can never travel perfectly straight on the surface of a sphere, because of the curving of the sphere, so one cannot travel straight as an arrow in space, but must always follow the curved arc of the hollow sphere. Space is crooked, Einstein said, and nothing in it travels straight ahead—not even light. The distant light "ray" which finally reaches us is thus not linear, but bent. And what is time? It is, as absolute time, the speed of light, the speed of a light particle travelling a crooked path. Now, under these circumstances, can *it* be perfectly linear, straight as an arrow?

Galactic time surrounds us in rings and reaches us on a crooked path. Would it be too bold to call it spiral time? Spiral like all movements in the cosmos: that of the galaxies or of our solar system, which travels in a spiral in its galaxy, or of every planet in this solar system including the earth, which travels at once in a circle around the sun and a quasi-line in the galaxy. If the mythic-matriarchal world view derived its divine time-spiral from the apparent movement of sun, moon, and planets, so the galactic cosmos can now derive its scientific time-spiral from the real movements of bodies in space and the shape of the cosmos. (To the extent that anything described by the mathematical language of modern physics is "real"!) There ought to be physicists who acknowledge that, in the process of researching the greatest, unimaginably complex relationships in the cosmos, and the smallest, unimaginably complex relationships in the atom, the mathematical imagination, and the power of abstraction, gradually fails. This could mean the end of the career of mathematics.

Would that be a misfortune for Urania?

NOTES

1. See Heide Göttner-Abendroth, *Die Göttin und ihr Heros. Die matriarchalen Religionen in Mythen, Märchen, Dichtung* (Munich, 1980), and *Die tanzende Göttin. Prinzipien einer matriarchalen Ästhetik* (Munich, 1982), both published by Frauenoffensive.
2. See Robert Graves, *The White Goddess* (New York: A. A. Knopf, 1948), and *The Greek Myths I & II* (Harmondsworth: Penguin, 1955).
3. For material on the moon dances of the matriarchal peoples see Robert Briffault, *The Mothers* (London—New York, 1969, reprint).
4. Observation and explorations in Brittany, the south of England (esp. Cornwall and Wales), Ireland, and Scotland, where most of the remaining stone formations from the so-called "megalith culture" are to be found.

10

Copenhagen*

Margaret Davis

In the late 1920s my mother was living in Copenhagen as a typist. When the Fifth Solvay Congress was held, she found extra work typing up the notes of scientists who had gathered to discuss the importance of the new quantum theory. Because she was accurate and caught on to the terminology quickly, she was soon in demand.

Eventually she was hired by a German physicist of whom she knew nothing. Albert Einstein was then in the midst of the now famous debate with Niels Bohr on the nature of quantum mechanics. My mother's job was to type up his handwritten arguments, as well as to take down for transcription, those of Bohr. In this way she was exposed to the first consistent formulation of quantum theory which, under Einstein's influence, she initially discounted.

For one thing, she soon saw that, carried far enough, quantum theory would lead to the conclusion that all possible outcomes to a problem are equally real and coexistent. That is, that there are endless branches of reality in the realm of possibility.

Later, when her own studies of time and synchronicity had gained prominence, my mother explained it to interviewers this way: "Say a television represents the universe. The channels are worlds, or possibilities, which coexist, each unaware of the others. You select a channel. What you see before you represents reality. At the same time, all the other channels seem not to exist, but yet, they are there, they have not simply disappeared."

It was an episode in her own life that proved to her what Bohr's theory could not.

In the spring of 1928 my mother, after a series of personal tragedies (including the deaths of several close relatives), fell into a depression from which she found it almost impossible to lift herself. She worked only enough to sustain herself at the most minimal level. Restless, beset by insomnia, she took long walks, played endless games of solitaire, killing time. Then, inexplicably, she found herself drawn to works on philosophy, physics, and evolution: she began spending hours at the Library of Natural Sciences.

* "Copenhagen" was inspired by Mary Daly's book, *Gyn-Ecology*, in particular her passages on patriarchal notions of time: "Women are constantly tempted to measure reality in terms of the measurements of Father Time, which are linear, clocked. This is a trap .... Otherworld journeyers are time/space travelers, seeing through the senseless circles."

One day she approached the reference librarian for a rare volume on the biological implications of time. The librarian looked at her sharply. "I just pulled that book down for you yesterday. Didn't you say you wouldn't be needing it?"

At my mother's puzzled expression, the librarian looked at her more closely, then apologized. Apparently he had mistaken her for someone else.

Certainly it was not an episode worth noting, except that thereafter my mother began to be aware of something peculiar. Almost invariably the books she sought on the shelves were checked out. Or, if she needed a volume from the closed stacks, the librarian seemed always to mention having just retrieved that same title for her only a day before. And, in every book she opened, she found the same small handwriting throughout, a handwriting eerily similar to her own. By now she was reading advanced books in the subject, each one leading her to a more difficult, more exciting reference. It seemed improbably that these obscure works would be much in demand—as improbable as the idea that someone else had her precise interests and was keeping just one book ahead of her always.

An uneasy idea began to form in her mind.

She started going to the library at odd hours and on different days, but it made no difference. No matter what book she sought, she sensed that what she'd come to call her Other had been there first. Every book she found showed signs of having been put out for her, whether purposely or not she could not say. They lay out of order at the end of a row; or face up across their neighbors; or simply open, at her usual table, turned to the very page she needed. At times, when she sat down, she fancied she felt the heat of the Other's body in her chair.

Was she making too much of a number of coincidences? Or was she perhaps creating the coincidences herself? Perhaps she was setting the scene unconsciously, laying out a book, for example, then forgetting she had done so. But to what purpose? It seemed too elaborate a prank to play on oneself, and certainly there are easier ways to go mad.

One afternoon as she stood at the counter, a librarian said, "Oh, there you are at last. I thought you'd be back, that's why I kept it for you," and held out a wallet.

Instantly my mother knew that it belonged to the Other; she took it automatically. When she got outside her heart was pounding. She opened the wallet. The name on the inside was exactly hers, though certainly a case could be made for further coincidence, since it was not an uncommon name after all. Still, it was as unnerving as it was totally to be expected.

The address was that of a street with which she was not familiar. She found it after asking directions several times. The house sat between a bakery and musical instruments shop. There was a café across the street. My mother sat there for almost an hour, holding the wallet tightly in her lap. She noticed that no one paid her any special attention, though once a passing woman smiled at her.

My mother wanted to cry, "Who do you think I am?" but if she was indeed the double of this Other, not only in face but in name as well, an answer would have been of little use. The question, she realized, was not who, but what.

Finally she roused all her nerve and approached the house. She stood for a long time on the topmost step. Within, someone played the piano (my mother preferred the violin), the danse Zukav which she recognized. There was laughter from upstairs. At last, with shaking fingers, she pushed the doorbell. The piano stopped. Footsteps approached the door from inside. My mother held out the wallet and as she did so, heard a gasp behind her. At that moment, as the door began to come open, she turned her head knowing that on the sidewalk stood someone whose Other she was and who had followed her this far. She turned sharply. A young woman was running in a vaguely familar way across the street. The door opened. My mother dropped the wallet and ran across the street, as her Other had done.

Zen mystics say we never step twice into the same river.

After that she could not remember the name of the street to find it again, but it didn't matter. Copenhagen would change, she would change, the channels would turn, and everything would be different, as the restless manifestations of time invariably are.

11

Unreliable Allies: Subjective and Objective Time in Childbirth

Meg Fox

> Obstetricians in the past century taught that the safest treatment of uterine inertia was "tincture of time." Their view was naturally colored by the disastrous effects of instrumental and operative interference in those days. In modern obstetrics that concept retains only a modicum of truth, for the passage of time, if not well utilized, produces an ever-increasing fetal loss, or as Jeffcoate writes, 'Nature and time are unreliable allies.'
>
> (*Williams' Obstetrics*, p. 843)

From the masculine point of view of obstetrical caregivers,[1] those elements of childbirth which are most troublesome, and which they strive to overcome, are its unpredictability, its hiddenness, its irrationality, and its sexuality. (The reader will note that these are aspects of the "feminine" most troubling to the "masculine.") Thus the mechanism of defense against these fearful elements is to overcome expectancy: the modern obstetrician does not stand by the woman, waiting for the birth to resolve itself, but hastens to intervene. Not only is labor accelerated, or indeed induced, and the birth of the baby speeded by forceps, vacuum extraction, or Cesarean section ("from his mother's womb untimely ripp'd?"), but indeed the whole of the pregnancy (and now with new technologies of fertility, the whole of conception too) is subject to scrutiny and intervention, with the consequence that instead of beginning with the oneness of mother and child, and culminating in the separation of birth, the mother and child have come to be perceived as separate from the beginning, from the moment of conception, and are only united after the birth is completed, when in the luxury of the "bonding period," the baby is given to her mother to be held. The trend of modern obstetrics, in other words, has been to recapitulate in the mother the father's experience of conception, pregnancy, and birth. The fear of separation is overcome by exaggerating and universalizing it.

The history of modern obstetrics (which is also the history of male intervention in and control over the process of birth) is one of the substitution of the male model of productivity for the archetype of the creative and transformative mother. The process of birth, in this context, becomes a trial, a challenge, which the male hero must meet and subdue. So entirely have we focused on the fearsome aspects of birth, that our image of giving birth no longer retains any elements of the heroic struggle which redeems the mother goddess of other cultures.

It is important to acknowledge that birth is almost always painful and sometimes dangerous, facts which women in pre-technological societies at least could not ignore. Equally, it is important to struggle against the confinement of women to the narrow and devalued role of mother. Yet we must guard against adopting an androcentric attitude which views childbearing as unworthy of those who are fit for higher things. In the constitution of masculine heroics, pain and risk are defining elements. They form the oppositional framework within which the individual discovers and tests his strengths, and in being overcome, are proof of his strength, courage, ability. It is possible for birth to be such an experience of positive challenge, for a woman to discover under such conditions hitherto unsuspected reserves of bravery and fortitude. But when the challenge of birth is to be met, not by the woman herself on her own behalf, but by her hospital staff, it is they and not she who find in birth an opportunity for daring. As a process in which the mother can do little to help herself, birth becomes pure (and needless) suffering: the pains and risk are no longer *her* oppositional framework. The active, and heroic, participant in birth is now the obstetrician, who will rescue the mother from the experience of labor.

Pain becomes a central issue, for it alone is objective and real, more, it is the only feeling left of labor when all the sensations of power and heroism have been discredited. So the quest for effective maternal anesthesia has been an intimate part of the history of modern obstetrics. These medications are chosen because they "take away the pain," the sensations, the in-the-body experience, of labor. Instead of experiencing and remembering herself in vigorous activity, the mother now finds a blank space like that of sleep or unconsciousness, culminating not in the birth of the baby, but in awakening, like Sleeping Beauty, to find the baby all bundled up in a cot beside her bed. Like the inquisitive child fobbed off with stories of the stork or the cabbage patch, she is ignorant of how the baby got there. What does it mean to be without the memory of such a central and transformative event as giving birth?

Memory is the sign of the continuity of the self, the palpable connection between what we were and what we are. Without memory, identity is threatened: to live only in the present is to have only an animal existence, and to lose our former (and our future) selves. To remember is to regain, in one's consciousness, past, lost, time. But without the conscious experience, there can be no conscious memory of labor. Yet while the woman is unconscious, may there not be embedded in her unconscious a memory of birth, an unseen genie which she cannot consciously recall but which may yet grip her? The unwarranted side effects of all these drugs include disorientation, restlessness, hallucination, and loss of control, so that the women under their influence must be kept in bed, sometimes under physical restraint. So intoxicated, the experience of labor is of nightmare, and hellish time which does not pass.

If the psychotropic drugs cause a distortion or even a loss of the conscious memories of childbirth, local anesthesia causes a loss of the experience of labor itself. The experience which is substituted is a complex one. From the waist down, she is paralyzed; her body is a dead weight. Such drug-induced separation of consciousness from bodily awareness itself pushes the woman in labor into a void, where normal feelings and sensations are lost. She is not restored to normal consciousness, but to yet another alternative to ordinary reality. The depersonalized reality of a birth which is not felt, a baby pulled from a sensationless body, is ultimately a meaningless reality. For how can we grasp a reality which we have not encountered? In her complete passivity, the woman in labor now finds herself with nothing to do but pass the time until the baby is delivered. She is enmeshed in linear time, moving from moment to moment, accompanied by the ticking of the clock (and the pulsing of the electronic fetal heart monitor) from the onset of labor to the moment of birth. By means of her drug-induced lack of sensation, her experience of the labor is exactly that of her attendants: it is an objective and verifiable phenomenon, a chain of events which can be set in its proper place in time, a minor and finite disturbance of her normal life.

No one could be more acutely aware of the passage of time than obstetric hospital staff. Most of the measurements which are made of labor are time-bound, as are most of the judgements and courses of action dictated by the results of these measurements. First of all the timing of the labor itself must be taken. The woman is asked to recall the date of the beginning of her last menstrual period, and her estimated date of confinement (280 days later) is calculated. If she is more than fourteen days from that date, she is either in pre or postmature labor. Attempts will be made to halt premature labor, as they will be made to induce labor in a woman who has exceeded her term. The length of the labor itself is then calculated. The woman is encouraged to name a specific time when labor began (although this is often experienced as a gradual and subtle change from the normal cramps of late pregnancy), and her progress in cervical dilation is charted against the length of time she has been in labor, and compared with the average progression of dilation in time. Too slow a labor will be accelerated with drugs, which in themselves often produce contractions of such intensity that a women will require anesthesia. Attempts are sometimes made to slow a too-rapid labor (especially when expert help is delayed), both posturally and by the administration of drugs (both demerol and epidural anesthesia slow dilation). If the amniotic sac is ruptured (either spontaneously, or, in the hope of speeding delivery, artificially), the length of time elapsing before the birth becomes of special concern.

The frequency and duration of the contractions are also measured, and the woman (and increasingly, her partner) encouraged to keep a record of the contractions experienced before she has come into the hospital. Timing the contractions has indeed become one of the two chief occupations of the man who chooses to attend the birth of his child (the other is "coaching" his partner in the correct performance of her breathing and relaxation). The contractions too are compared to a standard, by which the woman herself as well as her caregivers set their behavior: she is to come into the hospital when they are five minutes apart and more than thirty seconds long. The baby's heartrate is charted against time, and increasingly, read out on a continuous fetal heart rate monitor, a device which further immobilizes the woman in labor, and leaves her, often enough, staring hypnotized at the flickering numbers on the display screen. She is constantly reminded of the passage of time: her caregivers take the count and try to estimate how much longer she will be. Though she is left alone for much of her labor (she is not perceived as needing any help once her anesthesia has taken effect, and if she has not yet had anesthesia, it is prescribed as the remedy when she can no longer cope on her own), her attendants appear at regular intervals, and regularly reassess her progress in labor.

Taking such a view of birth, the obstetrical caregiver reduces it from an archetypal and eternally recurring act to a mechanical and time-bound process. This serves to strip it and the woman in labor of much of their threatening power, and indeed to shift the locus of understanding and control from the mother to her "deliverer." It forces on the woman a model of self-control, which she must achieve either by correct application of the techniques of prepared childbirth, or by accepting medication. By insisting on the minute chronology of the labor and "delivery," the medical caregiver reconstitutes birth as a rationally apprehensible sequence of causally related events. Birth is fixed in an inflexible sequential framework, thus locating the laboring woman, and with her, her attendants, in time. While this has the effect of marginalizing and even subverting her experience of childbirth, the purpose which underlies such practices is actually to make her caregivers comfortable and reassured.

Whatever the emotions of the caregiver, whatever chaos of inner reaction to the character of the patient or her condition or the attendant's own fears and doubts, pleasures and pains, refuge from disorder is always to be found in the orderliness of the medical world.[2] In this context, time is reduced from a subjective experience to a rational, intelligible, measurable means of orientation, an essential part of the mechanism for coping with the inner turmoil of the caregiver (who after all is dealing with issues of life and death, miraculous healing power and dreadful helplessness). This painful state is literally covered over by the ceaseless demands and absorbing routines of medical practice. There is not time to linger over what's past: onward to new problems, new patients, new treatments. The present is thus materialized, filled with concrete evidence of one's productivity. But in dissociating the present so definitively from the past, the threatening aspect of the past, its deathly finality, is stressed. Then the breathless hurry of the present is only a reminder of its relentless rush into the past.[3]

In order to minimize this threat to the value and continuity of the present, a line of inheritance and respectful preservation is established. This historical sense conquers the transience of time, keeps knowledge of the losses it brings at arm's length. Yet the history of medicine is imbued with the progressivist attitude: discoveries are continual and the future is full of promise. Ever-new and ever-better technologies are replacing the treatments of the past. Such optimism for the future implies a glad willingness to bury the past, at once guilt-provoking and threatening (the future will bury you). The inevitable result of this state of affairs is that the medical practitioner is struggling simultaneously to remain in touch with an historical continuity and to overcome the finality of time, his own slipping into the past. He cannot let time slip away. So in the end, no medical caregiver has any free time, any time to spare for sitting with the laboring woman, sharing her experience. The obstetrician, with his thirty or forty deliveries per month, fills up his time with business, and with new beginnings: there is no time to savor the finality of birth, the end of his relationship to the pregnant woman; he is off to the next, and the next. In some measure this is true of everyone, no matter how low on the medical hierarchy: a breathless business and bustle pervades the hospital atmosphere.

The woman in labor leaves behind that quantifiable time which rushes past her attendants. The relentless rhythm of her contractions takes over the function of time-keeping, submerges objective, clock time in the eternity of bodily time, the endless succession of the heartbeat. (After all, we do not hear the silence after our heart has ceased beating.) And the woman in labor, forced by the intensity of the contractions to turn all her attention to them, loses her ordinary, intimate contact with clock time. This endless rhythm, like the succession of waves at the shore, the murmur of our breathing, the drumbeat of the heart, is a living symbol of a timeless, endless world. To allow oneself to be absorbed by this rhythm is to pass through that gateway, to allow oneself to be worked on by the experience, and to emerge from it a changed being, as the mystic emerges into a *vita nuova*.

This timeless state is also deathlike, as trances are sometimes said to be deathlike. The laboring woman, absorbed in her body's demand, is beyond the claims of ordinary reality. This, I believe, explains the anxiety-ridden, incessant demands placed upon the woman in labor that she re-enter the mundane world, come back from whatever realm she has entered. It is almost a parody of the bereaved lover's cry over the body of his beloved: "Speak to me!" At the same time that every attempt is made to encourage the woman in labor to become the passive recipient of medical care, a certain intense responsive activity is demanded of her. She must not slip away into her trancelike state: she must answer questions, report her sensations and condition, follow instruction. The woman in labor is not allowed to concentrate. It is clear that her entry into a timeless state is threatening to her attendants. It both disturbs their sense of the reliable, tangible character of time, and contrasts most uncomfortably with their acute awareness of time, evoking the conflict between the changeless and the threateningly changeable. Her state is a direct confrontation of the impossibility of controlling time by merely measuring and recording it. The medical practitioner feels obliged by anxiety to count out the time of labor but then cannot bear the anxiety this provokes, the graphic illustration it provides of the escape of all those grains of sand. The woman in labor must be made to reify and to share the medical time-bound perception of labor, or else she will devalue it, or worse, throw it to the winds.

In so far as it succeeds in this task, medicalized childbirth has no knowledge of the passion or ecstasy of birth, of its freedom and creativity. We would empty the actual act of meaning, and yet continue to use the words which describe it as metaphors for acts of the intellect and imagination. But we are not wrong to speak of artistic creation and the birth of a work. There is more labor in the intellectual process and more mind in the bodily than we are encouraged to perceive, and an underlying similarity in the state of mind required for both kinds of creativity.

Emerging from the birth experience, one feels changed, as the artist in the achievement of her creation remakes the person she had been. If we recognize the doubly creative aspect of birth—the bringing forth of new life and the transformation of the mother—we can only wish to enhance its transformative character, to respect the inner, psychic experience of birth, and to protect the mother's concentration and absorption. It is all too easy in our culture to reduce birth to a mere physical function, and to discount the importance or relevance of the psychic experience of the mother (and, as Leboyer has pointed out, of the child). As a culture, we may accept that some few women seem to find in childbirth an experience of mystical dimensions, though it makes us as uncomfortable as all other mystical and religious experiences. Further, the idea that birth may be experienced as creative seems romantic, and worse, retrograde. We are reminded of the sentimentalization which assigned to women a biological destiny. Yet it does not make sense to refuse a larger meaning to an event which changes not only a woman's body but her way of life and her self-definition. For then she is truly at the mercy of her bodily functions, threatened by the unwarranted side-effects of a physiological process which disturbs her normal functioning. The changes in her feelings and self-understanding which an experience as powerful as childbirth brings may, I suggest, be embraced as opportunities for personal growth, for new understanding. But if we deny or fear this aspect, if we desire to see birth as merely another aspect of business as usual, then we change the very meaning of birth itself. It becomes mere production. The analogy is no longer with artistic creation, but with assembly-line manufacture.

Then we regard labor with the eyes of the scientific management consultant, making a time-emotion study. Surely it is possible to complete this task more efficiently? We are answered with "the active management of labor," a concept developed in an extremely large and busy maternity unit (the National Maternity Hospital in Dublin), whose premise is that "the stress and morbidity of labor are related to duration"[4] and which ensure "efficient uterine activity by early artificial rupture of the membranes with oxytocin augmentation, if required."[5] With this new emphasis on efficiency and on rationalization, the obstetrician now becomes the "management," the baby the product, and the mother the means of production, the definitive labor force. In true capitalist style, the workers do not own the means of production, nor are they consulted by management in the goal-setting and decision-making process. The expectation is that the wages (in this case the best possible baby) are all that the labor force has any right to expect. The suspicion is that left to themselves, laborers will prove inefficient, or worse. The process is not expected to be creative, it is supposed to be effective, productive, time-saving. Decisions about the process are for the "speed boss" alone. Thus the acceleration of labor is intimately connected with the alienation of labor. Like the subjects of the Gilbreths, those pioneers in motion study, the laboring woman is supposed to strictly divide productive from pleasureable activities, to offset the dreariness of working passively in harness with a judicious period of what the Gilbreths called "Happiness Minutes." Once the new mother has met her quota, she is allowed a "bonding period" of about one hour in which to become close to her baby. Labor which is begun and carried out in alienation has no intrinsic satisfactions. There is no reason to experience it, for it has become useless suffering. In this context, the baby is a good to be consumed, and the less involvement the prospective consumer has with the drudgery of production, the more privileged she is.[6]

Fixing on a particular length of labor, like fixing on a particular date of confinement, as optimal, encourages the anxiety of both doctor and patient, exaggerates the stress of waiting, and the fear of birth itself. For now there is a newly emphasized aspect in which birth can go wrong: its timing. And this fear that birth will be ill-timed extends to contain all the other fears of what could go wrong.

I have tried to suggest that these fears have two aspects: the rational consideration of risks (for child and mother do not always come through the process safely), and the reactivation of our deepest inner fears, of separation and of death. The attempt to locate birth at a particular point in time, to "know" when the baby should be born, is an attempt to allay this anxiety by remaking what is uncertain and unknowable into something that follows established, unchanging rules. Not knowing what to expect, or when to expect it, seems to make the unknown more threatening, and to emphasize our own powerlessness. If we can resist this sensation by declaring that in fact we do know, and take charge over time by reducing it to a measuring device, then we expect to feel reassured. But in fact a curious thing happens: we do not resolve this conflict, we only reframe it. Instead of directly confronting our fears of death and separation we only have new fears to confront, new elements which slip away from our grasp. The struggle for control intensifies, and even minor deviations take on a newly threatening aspect: any little thing that escapes control seems to open the door for a total loss of control, for death itself.

Like the sorcerer's apprentice, the obstetrician attempts to make birth work for him, only to find his old difficulties dividing and multiplying into a thousand new ones. There is only one right time to be born, yet his ability to influence timing is limited. The pace becomes ever more frantic. The number of prenatal examinations multiplies as the due date approaches: from once a month, to once every two weeks to once a week, to twice a week (or more) if the date is past. With each re-evaluation of the pregnancy comes an all-too-brief period of decisiveness and finality: doubt has been relieved, a decision made, all is fixed and stable. But as term approaches, this fixity is ever more rapidly overturned. The sense of moving in the right direction, of reassurance, is broken by the passage of a few days. Everything is open to question again, and new means of stabilization and reassurance must be established. Time must be captured and submitted to the dictates of formulation. But it will not stay fixed. Time is always running away: there is not enough time.

The busy obstetrician exaggerates the scarcity of time by crowding his personal time with activities. The sheer number of his patients, the rapidity with which he must examine and dismiss them, the constant interruptions to this frenetic process by deliveries and emergency calls, all serve to make him unendingly conscious of the passage of time, the impossibility of finishing his tasks. By leaving himself no time, he makes himself extraordinarily conscious of time: he is tyrannized by time through his very efforts to manage it. Resisting finality by setting himself unending tasks, he yet grasps after finality by a process of continually making judgements. And these very judgements, with their ring of finality and decisiveness, echo the finality of death, are freighted with the fear of separation.

What I am arguing is this, that in a culture which can neither allow a healthy union between mother and child, nor support a gentle and self-affirming weaning from that early dependence, we cannot witness birth, the paradigmatic separation, with equanimity. We attempt to delay the finality of birth by inverting its meaning. If we can separate the mother and child when they are still locked in physical symbiosis, then the moment of birth, when the baby is given to the mother, becomes not the primal separation, but their first true union. The truly obsessional time-keeping of obstetrical care becomes a symptom of this need to keep the separation of birth at bay. Time is overvalued. It must not be wasted. Constant activity is required in order to overcome the fear provoked by the sense that time is running out. The anxiety of waiting is overcome by devaluing the mother and investing the obstetrician with magical powers.

In industrialized society, the woman herself is drawn into this recasting of rôles. Encouraged to see herself as privileged because she has new options opened to her, to see herself as empowered by new, more precise, and scientific understanding of the process of pregnancy and birth, she is in fact placed in a newly passive position. When pregnancy and birth belong to the mother, then pregnancy itself is an activity, the nurturing of the unborn child, the preparation on the part of the mother for her activity in giving birth and in mothering. Birth is a creative act. But when pregnancy becomes a delicate condition, it is reduced to a time of passive waiting for the child to be given to the mother, during which all activity and judgement properly issue from the obstetrician.

Waiting for the baby becomes waiting for a discrete, temporally precise, event. By knowing when her need for the baby will be met, she hopes to allay the anxiety of waiting: she can clearly anticipate the relief of her fears. From the perspective of the hospital staff, this relief is of primary importance. In this context the pregnant woman waits passively, patiently, for delivery. But her own inner experience of labor contradicts all the time-keeping of her attendants, makes the chronology of her labor meaningless to her. While the laboring woman's knowledge of time may be idiosyncratic, it may also be no less objectively real than the ticking of the chronometer, based as it is on a qualitatively different biological time from the biological time which the hospital staff is experiencing. The process of labor, after all, like all physiological events, has a rhythm of its own, based on internal stimuli, hormonal regulation, and indeed a whole host of mechanisms which are poorly understood. The harmonious interplay of these stimuli, in time, brings about birth. The timeliness of labor, its precision in unfolding, is therefore not less "real" and meaningful than the minute-by-minute passing of time which we can measure by the clock and by our heartbeat.

Labor is both something concrete and objective, a consensually validatable event, and something subjective, the inner, individual, psychic experience of the laboring woman. It happens within her body, it is an experience of her vital being, which includes and transcends the objective event which may be the object of ordinary sense-perceptions. As an experience, not a simple event, it will not be over and done with when the baby lies in her arms. It will become part of her self, and live on in her memory. The recollection of such crucial experiences is an essential activity of consciousness, of the making of individual identity. To repudiate this inner experience, and insist on the objectification of labor, is to encroach on the private and inner ground of female subjectivity, to violate the boundaries of the self, because it is finally an insistence on the unreality of our personal experience. To thus repudiate the subjective is to insist that the individual has meaning only in her usefulness for the state. It is to enlarge, to a horrifying degree, the cultural definition of women as objects for male use, to make of women's most intimate relationship to their bodies and their bodily capacities a matter of political expediency (Gena Corea's "mother-machine," Margaret Atwood's "handmaid").

Labor may be seen as a "time-event" (in Jaspers' words), like the hatching of an egg, the breaking of a chrysalis, which have their own time, which cannot be disturbed without disturbing the event itself. To observe labor as if it were the pursuit of a pre-set goal ("delivery"), which ought to adhere, in so far as it is normal, to a routine or protocol,[7] may only be to force a clash between two very different, and incommensurate, kinds of time. The observer of labor parallels his inner, beat-to-beat, experience of time in the recording of the forward motion of the clock. This is phallocentrically structured time, ejaculatory time, methodically proceeding towards a pre-determined goal, an experience of time in every way opposed to the recurrent waves, the waxing and waning, of gynocentric time. He is immersed in his ordinary life. Attending births is part of his daily work. But at the same time, the woman in labor experiences herself not as moving with time, but as moving in it. For her, time stands still, moments flow together, the past and the future do not lie still behind and before her. In place of sequence, and linear relation, there is an overwhelming richness of sensation, which pulls her attention from the outer world. She is immersed in the immediacy of her experience. Her body is no longer a neutral background for her consciousness.

In offering to restore the laboring woman to her ordinary self, they are offering to reshape the experience of labor from a "time-event" into "chronology," from an experience and expression of the woman's vital being into a series of objective, concrete events, which may have their proper place in series, but are nevertheless separate, distinct, and individual. Labor so understood becomes a succession of stages, a progression of centimeters of dilation. The result of this shift is paradoxical. Attempting to concretize labor, to make it follow a pre-set pattern, it is dominated by the past, by general clinical experience of labor. Neither the individual labor nor the involvement of the individual caregiver with this labor have the possibility of development, growth, self-realization. "What should be" is then not only impersonal, it is fixed, definite, decided, final. It is emptied of potentiality. In the attempt to alter the threatening, unquantifiable, open-ended quality of labor, to establish control through predictability, to make the time-experience of labor rational, they focus on the end of labor, its finite and measurable timing. This is an attempt to contain the experience of labor, and to bring its transformative and mutable nature into a proscribed form, to bring its time to an end. They want to break the cycle of contractions, to be able not only to get a woman into labor, but to get her out of it. But in the very act of so doing, instead of making time and change stand still, they exaggerate the inexorable separation, and then time is not held in check but is pressing in on us. This open-ended future which they attempt to grasp and mold into a timeless and changeless pattern then looms in grotesque finality over us.

So they have brought about a confrontation, in the very attempt to circumvent it, with the threatening aspect of time: time the devourer of all things. For if time passes relentlessly, as the ticking of the clock, the passage of the seasons, and the subtle changes of aging tell us, and we cannot inhabit an eternal present, if there has been a time before we existed, then we are confronted with death. This is Father Time, time with a scythe, who mows us down, and against whom nothing can really preserve us, take comfort as we might in the continuance of the race. Robbed of the individuality, and of the potentiality, of labor, neither the woman in labor nor her caregivers can experience birth, they can only know about it. They have lost the sense of their own constancy in time, and attempted to replace it with a concept of time, a correct knowledge of time. Birth is no longer an experience which they can live through, but only a strenuous schedule to which they must adhere.

But if a woman becomes an active participant in labor, embracing the experience as subjective and meaningful, then she has another source of time orientation available to her, body time, the rhythm of her vital functioning. She need not be pathologically disoriented in time. She may lose herself in labor without losing her identity, her sense of her basic continuity. And so intense is this experience of herself in her body, that it annihilates any desire for rational consciousness, for locating herself in the rationalized present in order to reassure herself that she is not slipping into the fading past or overwhelmed by the threatening future. Absorbed in the rhythm of labor, in the work of her own body she is in touch with a truly timeless present, a present free from the fearful distinctions, the relative time, of reason. In this way, the experience of birth is a passage, for its duration, into a realm beyond time, an experience of immortality. The laboring woman has lost touch with time as it passes and is totally absorbed by her bodily self. She is in the fullest possible possession of the universe of herself. As her body fills her consciousness, it pre-empts all other objects of perception, and in its fullness of life, death can have no share. Birth is not only release, it is recurrence and return.

NOTES

1. Diana Scully, Michelle Harrison, Suzanne Arms, Barbara Katz Rothman, and Ann Oakley, among many others, have levelled the criticism that the obstetric profession and the science of obstetrics are dominated by male practitioners, and that even as numbers of women are being incorporated into the profession, they are being co-opted by it, led to accept masculine attitudes and practices.

2. This orderliness is a reflection of the scientific emphasis on predictability and rational control. My criticism, of course, is that biological medicine has excluded from its field of legitimate inquiry both all subjects not susceptible to such predictability and control, and all methods not similarly constituted.

3. What I write of obstetrics is true of modern medical practice in all fields, and hence more likely a symptom of modern medicine than a problem in obstetrics per se.

4. M. E. D'Alton and D. K. Dudley, "The Active Management of Labor in the Primiparous Patient, in *Canadian Family Physician*, Vol. 32, (October 1986), p. 2129.

5. Ibid., p. 2129.

6. There is no more dramatic example of such separation, the mother as "maternal environment," the fetus as "product of conception," than in the case of a "surrogate mother" receiving in vitro fertilization from a donated ovum and donated sperm. But all women receiving modern obstetrical care are subject to a process of re-definition and objectification

of the pregnancy, a process which seems to offer control of the future, apparently sharing that control with the woman, while actually emphasizing her dependence. Her pregnancy is no longer her state, but an objective entity which will be treated by those whom technology has empowered.

7.   E. A Friedman in 1955 made a "Graphic Appraisal of Labor," charting mean duration which has become the standard of measurement for normality, and most active obstetric interventions are attempts to bring labor into conformity with this mean.

TIME

Rachel Vigier

It was for us
a cycle
until you marked a return—
notches on bone
later found and theorized upon
as marvels of primitive ingenuity
when it was us
you were feverishly measuring
calculating a life
carried by one of ours.
At first, we were surprised
by these crude measurements
and laughed as a group
at these plottings of our body.
It seemed not to matter.
You continued with this obsession
and we dismissed it.
When the moment comes
we will let you know
it seems we once said.
But you counted backwards
and now your measured fact
tells us what once
we knew beforehand.
The first mark of time
was against us
and you continue
to march your numbers
through our souls
where out of habit—
and weariness too—
we have made a place for you.

12

Teaching "Time": Women's Responses to Adult Development

Jerilyn Fisher

Life cycle theorists commonly chart adult development by studying different, successive periods which follow an age-related sequence of tasks and expectations. Most of these studies reflect male bias, basing their frameworks and conclusions on the milestones men cite in their descriptions of the developmental journey from one stage to the next. Feminist research and writing based on women's various experiences as they grow through time can promote necessary revisions of current life cycle theories. We need to continue our questioning of deeply-rooted patriarchal assumptions about timing and growth, assumptions that have been shaped and corroborated primarily by those observing men's life patterns.

This gender imbalance in writing and research about women's development looms large when one is charged, as I am, with the special challenge of teaching adult learners, the majority of whom are women. While one can generalize about returning students' enthusiastic and deeply anxious attitudes as they enroll, it is more difficult to encapsulate their wide demographic and personal diversity. Still, I can make certain general observations about the students I teach on a suburban New York City campus: a striking proportion of them are divorced, single parents, or remarried. Most are between the ages of twenty-five and seventy. More than eighty percent of these students receive tuition assistance. About sixty-five percent are White, thirty percent are Black and about five percent are Hispanic and Asian. Most conspicuously, nearly ninety percent of our adult student population are female. And almost all of these women ask themselves whether this is really the "right" time for their return to school.

When is the "Right" Time?
The Returning Woman's Dilemma

All the nurturing I expertly gave to others for so many years, I'm now giving back to me. I'm taking this time for myself, not necessarily taking it away from them. I've earned this me-focused time, and I intend to really enjoy it.

Forty-eight year-old first-year college student, Journal entry

The single greatest source of strain for both prospective and matriculated adult women students is finding the courage to "take time" for themselves, usually after years of deferring their interests to others' needs and goals. Despite social progress toward equalizing women's educational opportunities, many women continue to feel undeserving of self-determined time for pursuing their own intellectual potential. Reluctance to commit ourselves to activities emphasizing self-interest stems, of course, from female social training. As girls and women, we learn to channel our resources into boosting others' chosen paths; we excel in drawing out the potential of children or spouses, for example, people whose achievements are supposed to tacitly reflect our hidden talents. Taking time for ourselves does indeed, as my student says, raise concern about taking time away from others whom we somehow still consider more deserving.

Women typically return to college when their families' and their own lives dramatically change. These changes are often referred to as "adult life transitions," and they include such commonly experienced events as divorce, children leaving home, marriage, remarriage, new employment, unemployment, retirement, and widowhood. Often, in response to these periods of transition and readjustment, women find themselves re-evaluating their rôles as wives, mothers and daughters. Thus, in terms of both the timing of their decision to enroll and the time required for college study, women's participation in higher education seriously tests their willingness to challenge age-old mythologies about what is appropriate for whom and when.

To support these emerging women students in their newly-found orientation to self, I have developed "Women in Transition," an interdisciplinary, introductory-level seminar which uses feminist studies to discuss theories of adult development. By focusing on periods of transition, my students and I learn together about temporal issues from the perspective of women's experiences and expectations throughout the life cycle. This course has become an effective feminist tool for teaching about time, age, change, choice, self-image and the related implications of women's changing roles.

Disillusioned with the "equal" employment opportunities that elude them, or with the narrowness of traditionally prescribed behavior for women and men, women today, more than ever before, aspire to self-improvement through beginning or returning to their college education. As a result of sheer numbers, it has become increasingly common for adult learners to find themselves in classes with other older women whose thinking is similarly engaged. Recognizing strong, unexpected ideological connections among new peers, many returning students embrace the opportunity to verbalize their individual discoveries. When such disclosures are supported by feminist learning processes and contextualized by feminist theory, these women risk making public assertions about gender bias for the first time. Close affinity with their classmates, a woman-centered curriculum and age-related incentive to seize the present moment, can all fuel older students' eagerness to accelerate their personal growth by openly examining sexism in theory and in their own lives. In a women's studies course about adult development, returning students enthusiastically reflect on how the timing of transitional events and gender bias have influenced their personal evolution. I have thus discovered rich avenues for feminist education in teaching a course for returning women that focuses on their temporal experiences, across the life span.

In reflecting on this course as a feminist pedagogical tool specifically geared toward returning women, I am first struck by my students' consistent need to have their personal sense of timing validated. Predominantly, adult women in college feel very much as if their lives—characterized most recently by their "delayed" return to school—are, in Bernice Neugarten's terminology, "off-time."[1] They nod with assent at Neugarten's identification of the "social clock," a term she uses to conceptualize norms which constitute the dominant cultural sense of age-appropriate behavior.[2] Sometimes these women feel self-conscious about beginning their undergraduate studies at the same time that their children enter college. Even when they are as young as their mid-twenties, my students come convinced that their return to school is significantly belated; that they will forever suffer the consequences of being "off-time", as if earlier, relational choices set in motion a pattern of life which actively opposes their intellectual achievement.

As women become aware of the male slant in temporal standards for gauging adult development, they begin to reassess the "rightness" of past and present life decisions. In a woman-centered course about time, returning students learn to assign new value to socially devalued choices typical of their life patterns. Women accept and understand their own lives better once they recognize the sexist fictions in writings based on men's adulthood. This recognition often ignites gradual change in their attitudes and ideas about gender; these changed perceptions then pave the way for women to begin identifying different, individualized barometers for measuring time and maturation across the life span.

Self-transformation and Perceptions of Time

I began to feel old at age thirty-six, before I decided to return to college. I had lost whatever I had of myself in intense personal relationships, and I had no sense of control over understanding the past or redirecting the future. The past felt like quicksand; the future felt like a tunnel that I was about to enter into, and for a while it was very dark. I began to question everything in my life, and to make it worse, I had a strong sense of time running out. I panicked. With encouragement from a friend in school I somewhat spontaneously chose to attend college to help me cope, not even sure after the first semester whether I was making things better or worse. But now that I have learned to value my intelligence ... time has opened up for me again, finally without my feeling that the past was a waste. I can see that who I will be now and next, for however many years I will be productive, depends heavily on who I have been and was. I am a new woman.

Thirty-nine year-old college student, Journal entry

Since a personal re-evaluation of prior life decisions strongly bolsters returning women's self-esteem, I begin the course with Carol Gilligan's *In A Different Voice*, which provides a feminist framework for understanding divergent moral choices typically made by men and women.[3] We enlarge the scope of Gilligan's pathbreaking work on moral development, using her insights to explore, more generally, different gender-based criteria for making significant *life* decisions, decisions which cast the structure of our adult lives. We begin to see why women, trained to view adult responsibility from within the caring mode, have often made life choices in favor of commitment to others, almost always at the expense of individual achievement. Chronologically mature women who (still) struggle with separation and autonomy, are relieved to learn that, according to Gilligan's research, failure to achieve these "masculine" developmental tasks does not represent their failure to progress psychologically. Exposed to Gilligan's corrective, these students see that assessments of adult development based on male markers of maturity inevitably lead women, like themselves, to imagining that they have fallen short or stagnated.

Internalized oppression resides deep inside. For most women, the process of uprooting long-held, self-confining fallacies about being female is both personally turbulent, and intellectually demanding. For the adult learner, consciousness-raising easily becomes enmeshed with intensive life review. Additionally, another factor presents itself, emerging as a further complication to this process: women unlearning patriarchy's lessons often start questioning other, previously unarguable "truths" which they have relied on to draw philosophical, religious, historical or political conclusions. In their influential book, *Women's Ways of Knowing*, the four authors reveal dramatic and progressive shifts in women's thinking about truth.[4] Testimony from those interviewed in the book corroborates my students' experience that such extensive shifts in knowing necessarily converge with intense personal disorientation. It seems inevitably true that when an adult, whose world views are deeply-set in many ways, makes a significant cognitive leap from seeing truth as absolute to seeing truth as a reconstruction, and does so concomitantly with feminist re-evaluations of her significant past and present life decisions, she is likely to suffer a double or triple blow.

In *Women's Ways of Knowing*, the authors organize their interviewees' responses by placing them in one of seven epistemological categories. These women's cognitive perspectives range from the voiceless position of "silence," in which women see themselves as passive learners entirely dependent on acquiring knowledge from external authorities, to the self-confident position of "constructed knowledge" in which women describe themselves as active thinkers generating their own contextual and integrated ways of knowing.

Predictably, women in this latest position seem to rebound most strongly from the throes of acute intellectual transformation. When these "constructivist" women experience the shake-up of self-scrutiny, they talk about reaching a turning point during which they reclaim themselves by moving "outside the given."[5] One hand-rail they use when stepping onto new thresholds of awareness is extended self-analysis, when they "intentionally take time out to get to know the self and to reflect on the contexts that confined and defined them."[6] This transition into deeper self-knowledge sparks confronting personal questions, questions inevitably followed by the challenge of re-direction.

I find that students struggle most gainfully with the complex, simultaneous task of recasting both their ideology and gender-based identity, when they participate in rigorous consciousness-raising-groups as part of their classroom experience. Small groups assigned to explore, for example, the possible impact of gender on each adult's major life decisions, help the older woman cope with the multiple effort of developmental, cognitive and feminist transition. Structured exchange which weaves together academic and personal learning, offers adults a welcomed, uncommon opportunity to learn about and with their college peers. Students in my class consistently describe the small group discussions of *In a Different Voice* as "invaluable;" they say that struggling together with both self-help and theory-probing allows them to profoundly understand, then shed, stultifying social myths about women's life patterns and sexual difference.

Supported by Gilligan's analysis and its resonance with their own, shared experiences, adult women are ready to recognize the far-reaching, liberating implications about time that come from acknowledging women's maturity as "a maturity realized through interdependence and taking care." Having discovered the power of this particular challenge to established beliefs, these women now describe time past with personal affirmation; those early years were not, they decide, spent "simply" in the service of others; the centrality of continuous, evolving attachments characterizes a different, and equally progressive developmental path.

Once they no longer measure time past against male standards for adult achievement, women express optimism about time to come. In their new visions, they imagine themselves proudly building their futures on a rich foundation of "care." When returning students review significant life decisions with feminist yardsticks, I have found that their perceptions of time change; they exude fresh confidence about living the rest of their years strengthened by reconstructed, feminist values. For these newly enlightened women, time can take on the novel appearance of a life-long companion, rather than the dreaded opponent it once seemed. Then, growing older naturally promotes their evolution into the self-assured, capable, authentic adult selves they may have unknowingly subdued in response to male-derived "adult" expectations.

Women's Life Transition

I feel as if I have always been in transition. I went through every stage myself, and then again with my husband. My life feels bound up in his.

Fifty-one year-old undergraduate

In recent years, life transitions and their impact have been researched, defined and predicted by a growing number of theorists interested in understanding the complex unfolding of adult development. The literature alternately refers to transitions as rites of passage, movement through life stages, bridges connecting the old and new, crisis events and, more generically, major life change.[8] While the study of adult transitions has been carried out by various scholars and writers representing wide-ranging views, most research on the subject seems to have incorporated the developmental perspective on adult maturation. This perspective outlines a linear, mostly chronological sequence of tasks and changes, and assumes a series of life cycle events, which implicitly ignore the possibility of distinctiveness in women's transitional experiences. Since many of my students have read or have heard about mass-market publications of developmental analyses, such as *Passages, Transformations* and *Seasons of a Man's Life*,[9] I use their familiarity with these books as a springboard for assessing differences between women's adult life changes and the "male" transitional model these popularized theories reinforce.

After examining cultural assumptions about gender underlying the developmental schema, my students usually decide that this approach is largely inadequate as a basis for describing the rhythm of female adult life. Our major point of departure from books like Levinson's and Sheehy's, for example, emanates from returning women's insistence, on the whole, that if they apply these writers' descriptions of transitional periods to themselves, they would conclude that they have been psychologically "in transit" almost all their adult lives.

We use these students' responses to examine unique threads in the fabric of women's and men's transitional experiences. Are women in particular susceptible to "transition" because their lives are interwoven with so many others' transitions, creating a boomerang effect? Or is this feeling of continuous redirection a natural consequence of most returning students' current lives, a temporary response to their life-altering decision to study? The student quoted above prompts the former interpretation; another student echoes her point in a different way: "In order to get what I needed, I knew I couldn't rock the boat. If I rocked his boat, I rocked my own. If his inner or outer life changed, it's as if I would have to change mine too." It seems logical that both the influence of others' life changes, and the adult college students' lifestyle may together induce this feeling of constant flux among returning women. To give some theoretical framework to this hypothesis, we call to mind *In a Different Voice*, recognizing that any discussion of change in women's lives must be seen in the context of women's relational and situational commitments.

In fact, Carol Gilligan suggests in her book's final chapter, that gender differences lead to different transitional experiences for women and men. She speculates that since women's interpretation of social reality concentates on "experiences of attachment and separation, life transitions that invariably engage these experiences can be expected to involve women in a distinctive way ..." Thus, she continues, "... the major transitions in women's lives would seem to involve changes in the understanding and activities of care."[10] From my students' intuitive responses and Gilligan's learned speculations, it is clear that we need new research singularly focused on the timing and nature of women's life transitions.

Nancy Schlossberg's work on adult life transitions offers a starting point for such research and discovery. In "The Adult Experience,"[11] she briefly lists and discusses "coping resources," our personal and environmental "assets and liabilities" that determine how well we manage either anticipated or unexpected transitions. Schlossberg identifies three sets of factors that influence one's adaptation to change: the characteristics of the transition itself; the characteristics of environment, such as social or institutional support; and the personal, demographic and psychological characteristics of the individual herself. If one could identify these factors, one could begin to anticipate and assess the degree to which a particular significant event has had or will have intense personal impact. Stressing the individual's characteristics, along with both the circumstances and the nature of the event itself, Nancy Schlossberg contextualizes the transition, as Carol Gilligan might, and in so doing she cuts through prevailing, generic norms about timing of and response to major life change. Her work thus provides students with a practical schema for analyzing personal transitional events, giving them conceptual frameworks to explain the dynamics of their own, particular transitions. This approach departs from the developmental perspective by its insistence that each person's transitional experiences be considered uniquely, given the complicated variety of factors surrounding any one life or any one life event.[12] Thus, her discussion of the transitional perspective both implies the importance of and directly accounts for socialized gender differences as a significant factor in determining adults' response to change.

The class applies this learning about unique response to change by looking into others' lives as well as their own. For a more objective experience in analyzing transitions, I assign two fictional works: *Ella Price's Journal*, by Dorothy Bryant,[13] a sixties' novel about a returning community college student whose intellectual strides impel personal rebellion against her traditional, dependent rôles; and Henrik Ibsen's *A Doll's House*, starring Nora, the well-known proponent of women's rights, whose impassioned desire to "find herself" gives her courage to leave a secure, protected, patriarchal home.[14] I assign the novel and the play as literary representations of women in transition: both stories portray women whose rejection of their female rôles occurs in tandem with major life change. Through the fiction, we see that, for women, transitional events often involve changed priorities which, before long, affect the gendered roles they play. As we contextually interpret Ella's and Nora's transitions, we consider the impact of conditions within each character's marriage on her leap from male-dependency to self-definition. A contextual perspective on transitions helps highlight wide variation between actual, chronological age and the expected, "staged" order of life events promulgated by most adult development theory.

Women's Age and Life Stages: Recognizing Context Before Chronology

Q: How old do you feel and how old do you wish you were?

A: Most of the time I feel much older than my age, maybe as much as ten years older. I've gone through so much and I have so many older friends. I like how old I am, but that's because this is a good year. I am growing a lot and feeling happy.

Twenty-six year-old student, In-class writing

A: My body feels its biological, middle-age, and my mind feels half that. (Which is the right answer to your first question?) I don't mind being my "real" age or any other, as long as I can do the things I really want to.

Forty-nine year-old student, In-class writing

For most women, chronological age does not reveal the major tasks and resolutions characterizing their adult lives: marriage expectations, career planning, and the family life cycle seem to most profoundly and directly affect women's sense of age and timing. While it may, as Alice Rossi says in her discussion of the menopausal transition, be "premature to conclude that chronological age does not matter ...,"[15] we can certainly see the extent to which age-related expectations are becoming increasingly elastic. Contrasting fluid, contemporary age norms with the "series of events" approaches to development, Rosalind Barnett and Grace Baruch rightly suggest that age would probably seem unimportant if life cycle theories were based on women's experiences. They speculate: "... if one begins not with a consideration of the male experience but with the reality and variations of women's lives, it is unlikely that chronological age would be seen as the central variable."[16]

Instead of concentrating on age, my students and I recognize the centrality of women's relationships through time. As a result, we have difficulty imagining an all-inclusive adult development theory that does not place in the foreground the following, partial list of women's life circumstances and relational commitments: if or when they become divorced, married, widowed or single; what their sexual preference is; whether women have or choose not to have children, and at what age; the effects of racism on the adult experiences of women of color; whether women work inside or outside the home; the effects of low income on female heads of household as they age; what involvement women now have with children or dependent parents; and, what are the major developmental issues facing the partners with whom women share their lives. Compiling this incomplete, yet thought-provoking list crystallizes for us how crucial it is to interpret women's lives in the context of their webs of attachment.

To further understand the tenuous relationship between chronological age and life transitions, we focus on the so-called mid-life period, partly because students' curiosity about this time of life has been stirred by media reports and best sellers, and partly because most of my students are between thirty-five and sixty, that wide chronological "middle-age" bracket. Those women who have already experienced the kind of extensive personal re-evaluation associated with an adult's middle years, insist that only when they were relatively free from caretaking responsibilities (of children, spouse and/or parents), did they have the time for a "mid-life crisis." The fiction we read bears out their experience: In *A Doll's House*, Nora's ability to belatedly grow out of a prolonged adolescence, depends on her ability to pull away from Helmer, her husband-father; her transition to adulthood would not be possible, it seems, if she were to continue masquerading in her pseudo-adult rôles of irresponsible mother and childish wife. Likewise, Ella Price can redirect her life only when she grants herself time to study, a decision which, in her conventional home, necessitates her distancing herself from a traditional, stagnating relationship with her husband. We thus decide that for many women successful engagement in life review happens only when they are either physically separate or ideologically free from dependent others who demand that they remain just as they have always been.

Continuing our study, through fictional portraits, of limiting assumptions about age and life stage, we make an interesting observation fitting both Ella Price and Nora Torvald: the two characters seem to conform most closely with the developmental theories' presentation of the mid-life stage, or "crisis." Each goes through a major re-evaluation of youthful dreams, goals and values; each comes to terms with deep-lying polarities within herself, and tests radically new life choices. Yet, chronologically, these women are somewhere in their mid-thirties and twenties, respectively; neither is especially entrenched in "middle-age." Symbolically, Nora's and Ella's transitional experiences represent their forging autonomous, adult identities for the first time, rather than signalling their lives' mid-point. In fact, each book ends with the protagonist taking off on her first "adult" quest for self-discovery; ironically, she must leave behind her previous, "grown-up" rôles as wife and mother in order to tackle the basic adult task of initiating a life path that is both psychologically and economically self-sustaining.

If mid-life is a time for deep self-evaluation leading to new possibilities for living, we can say that at whatever age a woman significantly transforms stunted, female dependency rôles, and instead develops an autonomous, self-shaped identity, she experiences the equivalent of "mid-life crisis." Interestingly, most of the returning women I teach, whether they be in their late twenties or over fifty, see themselves as going through "mid-life" in their return to school. When we discuss mid-life as described by current theory, everyone is sure she is going through "it" now. What convinces them is their extensive personal reflection and re-appraisal, a new orientation to understanding the self and spending time, both in the present and in the future. This new orientation dramatically changes their priorities. Following discussion of our common perceptions, students see that "mid-life" for women, as it is popularly portrayed and perceived, is a social construct, not intrinsically related to an individual's chronological age at all.

Personal Authenticity and Women's Aging

After the throes of mid-life change, I can let go of the feeling that time is running out ... I finally know what I need, what satisfies me and I have not time to spare to compare myself to others ... I feel excited about my future because it is being planned with conscious choice. Functioning out of my own authority makes time seem more real.

Sixty year-old undergraduate, Journal entry

Personally, at this point in my life, I am long on past experience and short on time to come. I no longer have much tolerance for illusion or superficial nonsense. As an older woman, an elder, really, believe me I have had to struggle hard to arrive at self-acceptance. Imagine that just now I am learning to applaud my own progress, toward achievements I set for myself! ... The most important thing is for me to live each day honestly and to the fullest.

Seventy-two year-old undergraduate, Taped class session

For some women, going to college to pursue a degree gives lifesaving purpose to their so-called "declining years" by tapping earlier, unfulfilled dreams of their creative and intellectual potential. Herein lies one explanation for my students' positive claim on time: setting and working toward goals inspires motivation for making each moment that remains more meaningful, more deliberate. As my class discussed women's feelings about aging, a student told us that her fear of death had actually diminished during her adjustment to college: "With each new goal I set, I re-evaluate my life expectancy. Today I'm full of determination, and a feeling that I have something to offer. What will happen in two years, at age sixty, when I receive my BA? I'll probably worry about death again until I reformulate a new, achievable goal and begin working on that one. If I hadn't awakened as an aging feminist, I wouldn't feel entitled to so much goal-oriented pleasure." This student, like so many of her peers, now sees the aging process as a developmental period in which her task is to confidently take time for herself; she is over women's "guilt-hump," she says, and intends from now on to savour each day, not "wasting" time, as she says she did previously, by participating in other people's valued experiences. She at once solidifies her true identity and reconsiders time as propitious.

From my students' responses I hypothesize that adult women's temporal orientation brightens at any age when they carve new identities as emerging women. This premise is supported, of course, by common sense, as well as psychologial theories which show the importance of self-acceptance, particularly among well-adjusted elders.[17] Sustained by positive retrospective images of themselves through time, images unscathed by "social clock" indictments of inferiority, adult women acknowledge both loss and gain in years already past, and communicate adventurous, realistic attitudes toward the future. In a recently published interview about being an old woman, Cynthia Rich, co-author of *Look Me in the Eye*, weaves together feelings of personal authenticity with positive associations about aging: "Now more and more I feel connected to the woman I'll be in my eighties and nineties if I'm lucky enough to live that long. I feel much closer to her than I do to that woman I used to be in my twenties and thirties. I didn't come out to myself as a lesbian until I was in my late thirties. I feel the same excitement about growing old that I've felt about being a lesbian ..."[18]

Women's relationships with other women become increasingly central as they age, most obviously because we find many more women than men actually living longer. Additionally, women's history of having nurtured female friendship works to our later advantage by making social and sexual intimacy with other women a promising avenue for achieving personal support and self-fulfillment. In fact, studies indicate that aging woman-identified women, more focused on interpersonal behavior and social change than on physical changes, seem less concerned with growing old than their male-identified peers. By continuing to work actively in political and social groups, these venerable women sustain their own lives' meaning as they contribute appreciably to social and political progress.[19]

During these last years, women's interpersonal skills serve as excellent preparation for a world in which communication, in general, becomes a lifeline to remaining family and friends. Looking at examples from "real life," we can easily see how vital the ability to communicate verbally and through caring can be, in fortifying women against the potential loneliness so difficult for many elders. Barbara Myerhoff, in her inspiring study of The Aliyah Senior Citizens' Center, describes aging women as "experts in human relationships,"[20] and she vividly demonstrates various ways in which special-izing in expressive and nurturant roles gives women at the Center enormous advantage over the men.[21] Another female voice, this one from a sixty-seven year-old graduating "senior" in my class, reports similar findings from her own experience: "What's most important is to keep moving, to keep involved with people and in worthwhile, satisfying projects. Women are good at this; staying connected is exactly what keeps my ninety-year-old mother alive today. The need to contribute to other people's lives doesn't change over the life cycle. But other people's assessments of our contributions change when we get old. Actually, there is only one thing that makes me nervous about my seventies: that is the extent to which other people's crazy ideas about seventy-year-old women will affect me."

Discovering Women's Own,
Developing Patterns

Certainly, women's unique temporal experiences would be best understood if we were able to hear the beat of those drums which sound out a distinctively female rhythm. From our earliest years on, parents, teachers and others in institutional authority have assigned us demarcations of time and maturity. Almost always women are told, and we believe, that these determinations and limits prepare us for the other, "adult," side of life, that only a strongly internalized, man-made sense of appropriate time will keep us in the mainstream, and well-adjusted.

The most clearly recognizable markers identified for women as maturational signposts are those processes or events considered emblematic of age and aging: menarche, engagement/marriage, motherhood, graying hair, menopause. But the temporal meaning of these processes and events would undoubtedly change if women were to take full charge of defining their unique rites of passage. First, we must untangle our lived experiences from their current, cultural associations; then, we can set about the pressing, rigorous task of stripping primitive physiological benchmarks of their exclusive power to designate women's coming and being "of age." Revisioning further, we need to fully examine the more subtle and equally forceful social messages women internalize about time and development.

To begin this revolutionary process of revision, women's bodily changes, the social attitudes we encounter as we change, and male-constructed parameters of maturity must each be identified separately so that we can create for ourselves the meanings of and appropriate rituals for marking female development.

The point(s) at which a woman feels "adult" or "old," is an important discussion topic requiring deep thought about gender differences across the life span: We women need to take the time to reflect on and describe those qualities which make us feel, individually and together, that we have reached the many stations of "adulthood." Why does the beginning of menstruation signal the pre-adolescent's entry into womanhood? Posing the question differently, is maternal viability a feminist indicator of "adult" status? On the other chronological extreme, does cessation of this monthly flow connect in any meaningful way with a particular state of mind, or with life's later decades? Not only must we freely and creatively observe our internal rhythms, but we must also, first, sift through the various assumptions which still bind us to conventional beliefs about maturity, development and aging.

A story follows illustrating one "mature" woman's recent enactment of her adult status: the same student who earlier spoke excitedly about finally controlling her own time, told the class about her need to proclaim to family and friends her changed, more autonomous self-image. Although she said she felt quite silly at first, she decided to leave the house each night for a full week, going anywhere she could imagine, determined to stay out well beyond her usual hours. By the end of the week, she was coming home as the sun rose, and feeling more "adult" than the day she learned to drive, or got her first paycheck. For this forty-two year-old woman, curfew defiance was the most symbolic expression of her lifelong struggle to define her own limitations and values. While this particular assertion of authority might be considered superficial or "childish," staying out late at night helped her to move on to other, adult tasks which were more ostensibly rewarding.

We have other, worn assumptions about time and timing which are now ripe for questioning and challenge. Most research is based on the supposition that men and women live together; that men and women experience life stages or transitional events in a heterosexually-partnered family setting. But if women's life transitions are less related to chronology or stage, and more responsive, instead, to relationships, then we can imagine that women living without men might well establish a distinctive rhythm of women's development over the life span. In a world which respected their family choices, women living with other women, or women living alone, or women on their own with children, would potentially be disengaged enough from patriarchal norms to discover and sustain unique, female-affirming responses to adult life changes and "grown-up" expectations. Perhaps we can even begin looking to women in these living situations for leadership in describing new temporal dimensions, processes or categories specifically drawn from women's proclivities and experiences.

Personal observation and preliminary research both point to the likelihood that men and women face different kinds of adult life transition, and also react differently to change.[22] In my view, we urgently need to explore our own sense of timing and progress to free ourselves from the unnecessary burden of guilt, self-consciousness and frustration that women, like my students and myself, often feel before we have found a framework and the words to adequately express our journey's special patterns.

NOTES

1. B. L. Neugarten, J. W. More and J. C. Lowe, "Age Norms, Age Constraints and Adult Socializiation," *American Journal of Sociology*, Vol. 70 (1965), pp. 710-717.
2. Ibid., pp. 710-717.
3. C. Gilligan, *In a Different Voice* (Cambridge: Harvard University Press, 1982).
4. M. F. Belenky, B. M. Clinchy, N. R. Goldberger and J. M. Tarule, *Women's Ways of Knowing* (New York: Basic Books, 1986).
5. Ibid., p. 135.
6. Ibid., p. 135.
7. Gilligan, op. cit., p. 172.
8. For a range of terms used to define life "transition," see, for example: W. Bridges, *Transitions: Making Sense of Life's Changes* (Reading, Mass.: Addison-Wesley, 1980); T. K. Hareven and K. J. Adams, ed., *Aging and Life Course Transitions: An Interdisciplinary Perspective* (New York: Guilford Presss, 1982); D. Levinson, *Seasons of a Man's Life* (New York: Ballantine Books, 1978); M. F. Lowenthal, M. Thurnher, D. Chiriboga,

Four Stages of Life: A Comparative Study of Men and Women Facing Transitions (San Francisco: Jossey-Bass, 1975); N. K. Schlossberg, *Counseling Adults in Transition* (New York: Springer Press, 1984).

9. G. Sheehy, *Passages: Predictable Crisis of Adult Life* (New York: E. P. Dutton ,1977); R. Gould, *Transformations: Growth and Change in Adult Life* (New York: Simon and Schuster, 1978); D. Levinson, *The Seasons of a Man's Life* (New York: Ballantine Books, 1978).

10. Gilligan, op. cit., p. 171.

11. N. K. Schlossberg, "The Adult Experience," in *Beyond Sex Roles*, 2nd Edition, ed. A. G. Sargent (St. Paul: West Publishing Company, 1985), pp. 387-403.

12. To support this perspective on individualized interpretations of adult development, Schlossberg quotes Pearlin whose ideas have, apparently, significantly influenced her own: "All in all it seems untenable to speak of either ages or life stages as though they are made up of undifferentiated people following a uniform life course" ("The Adult Experience," p. 393). For additional reading from L. Pearlin's own work promoting the individual perspective on development, see: "Discontinuities in the Study of Aging," in T. K. Hareven and K. J. Adams, pp. 55-74.

13. Dorothy Bryant, *Ella Price's Journal* (Berkeley: Ata Books, 1972).

14. Henrik Ibsen, *A Doll's House* in *An Introduction to Literature*, 7th edition, ed. S. Barnett, M. Berman and W. Burton (Boston: Little, Brown and Co., 1981), pp. 821-887.

15. A. S. Rossi, "Life-Span Theories and Women's Lives," in *Signs: Journal of Women in Culture and Society*, Vol. 6, No. 1 (Autumn 1980), p. 21.

16. R. C. Barnett and G. K. Baruch, "Women in the Middle Years: A Critique of Research and Theory," in *Female Psychology*, 2nd edition, ed. S. Cox (New York: St. Martin's Press, 1981), p. 286.

17. Almost every book on the subject of the psychology of aging mentions self-acceptance as fundamental to a healthy adjustment to old age changes. See, for a sample: B. Neugarten, R. Havighurst and S. Tobin, "Personality and Patterns of Aging," in *Middle Age and Aging*, ed. B. Neugarten (Chicago: University of Chicago Press, 1968); P. B. Walsh, *Growing Through Time: An Introduction to Adult Development* (Monterey, California: Brooks/Cole, 1983); M. Block, J. Davidson, J. Grambs, *Women over Forty* (New York: Springer Publishing Company, 1981); J. Williams, "Middle Age and Aging," *Psychology of Women* (New York: Norton, 1987), pp. 476-503.

18. Jean Swallow, from "Both Feet in Life: Interviews with Barbara Macdonald and Cynthia Rich," in *Women and Aging*, ed. J. Alexander, D. Berrow, L. Domitrovich, M. Donnely and C. McLean (Corvallis, Oregon: Calyx Books, 1986), p. 203.

19. M. R. Laner, "Growing Older Female: Heterosexual and Homosexual," in *Journal of Homosexuality*, Vol. 4 (1979), pp. 267-275.

20. B. Myerhoff, *Number Our Days* (New York: Simon and Schuster, 1978), p. 262.

21. Ibid., pp. 262-268.

22. M. Lowenthal, et al., "Summary and Implications," in *Four Stages of Life*, pp. 223-245.

* I am grateful to Wendy Goulston for the creative suggestions, enthusiastic support and helpful criticism she generously contributed to this paper.

THE COLD SPRING*

Denise Levertov

i

Twenty years, forty years, it's nothing.
Not a mirage; the blink
of an eyelid.

Life is nibbling us with little
lips, circling our knees, our
shoulders.
        What's the difference,
a kiss or a fin-caress. Only sometimes
the water reddens,
we ebb.

Birth, marriage, death, we've had them,
checked them off on our list,
and still stand here

tiptoe on the mud,
half-afloat,
water up to the neck.

It's a big pond.

ii

What do I know?
        Swing of the
        birch catkins,
        drift of
        watergrass,
        tufts of
        green on the
        trees,
        (flowers, not leaves,
        bearing intricately
        little winged seeds
        to fly in fall)
        and whoever
        I meet now,
        on the path.
It's not enough.

iii

Biology and the computer—
the speaker implies
we're obsolescent

we who grew up
towards utopias.

In this
amnesia of the heart
I'm wondering,

I almost believe him.
What do I know?
A poem, turn of the head,

some certainty
of mordant delight—
five notes, the return
of the All Day Bird—:

truces, for the new moon
or the spring solstice,
and at midnight the firing resumes,

far away.
It's not real.

We wanted
more of our life to live in us.
To imagine each other.

iv
Twenty years, forty years,
'to live in the present' was a utopia
moved towards

in tears, stumbling, falling,
getting up, going on—
and now the arrival,

the place of pilgrimage curiously
open, not, it turns out,
a circle of holy stones,

no altar, no
high peak,
no deep valley, the world's navel,

but a plain
only green tree-flowers
thinly screening the dayglare

and without silence—
we hear the traffic, the highway's
only a stonesthrow away.
Is this the place?

v

This is not the place.
The spirit's left it.

Back to that mud my feet felt
when as a child I fell off a bridge
and almost drowned, but rising

found myself dreamily upright,
water sustaining me,
my hair watergrass.

vi

Fishes bare their teeth to our flesh.
The sky's drifting toward our mouths.
Forty years redden the spreading circles.
Blink of an eyelid,
nothing,
obsolete future—

vii

If I should find my poem is deathsongs.
If I find it has ended, when
I looked for the next step.

Not Spring is unreal to me,
I have the tree-flowers by heart.
Love, twenty years, forty years, my life,
        is unreal to me.

I love only the stranger
coming to meet me now
up the path that's pinpricked with
yellow fallen crumbs of pollen.

I who am not about to die,
I who carry my life about with me openly,
health excellent, step light, cheerful, hungry,

my starwheel rolls. Stops
on the point of sight.
Reduced to an eye
I forget what
        I
was.

Asking the cold spring
what if my poem is deathsongs.

13

From "Corpus"

Mary Kelly

Mary Kelly's illustrations are excerpts from *Corpus*, Part 1 of her major work, *Interim*. Concerned with the representation of women in middle-age, the entire project is based on over one hundred conversations documented by the artist. These, embodied in texts and images, form the work. *Corpus* consists of thirty large silk-screened panels, which are divided into five sections with three pairs in each. The sections refer to the five passionate attitudes described by Dr. Charcot, the nineteenth century French physician who influenced aspects of Freud's theories. Mary Kelly herself describes *Corpus* as "A glossy parody of contemporary feminine stereotypes, using conventions of popular medicine, fashion and romantic fiction."

Supplication

Phone rings. go's on her way. Glad she's coming, though I met her only once before at the museum. Winter, ground covered in ice, everything about to crack, fragile, intense—her performance, my ordeal with the director, our conversation over breakfast. Wonder if she still remembers, if she's changed. Lovely **dancer's body** in baggy pants, huge leather jacket, lace-up boots, all carefully **battered** like her **face**, small features more defined with some success, **emblazoned**: live alone, a loft downtown of course, no nonsense baby, if you want to be an artist **you must pay**. I am in debt, no doubt about it, overdressed and uncommitted, wishing I could seek asylum in her duffle bag. Stunned by the '**rightness**' of **that image** first, then intrigued by every detail, but especially by the **boots**. They had **a presence much like hers**, older but not dated and attractive without trying too hard. They haunted me. I **had to have them**, kept on looking for months after, finally **found some** that were similar, not soulfully worn out but stylishly distressed at least. In these I could do anything, **wore them all the time**, have them on now in fact. Will she be wearing hers? The door. I let her in, look down—the boots are different, lighter, higher heels and polished. Then look up—astonishing, a dress, small flowers, forties, second-hand, cut on the bias, screaming: what the hell, feels good to be a woman sometimes, give me credit I'll pay later. And the jacket, padded shoulders, Persian lamb, not black but very much like mine, the one that I was wearing when we met. She senses this and says that's why she bought it, tried to look smart, stylish even, just to please me. Can't help smiling," See these boots," I ask," **have I succeeded**?" "Well, **almost**", she laughs.

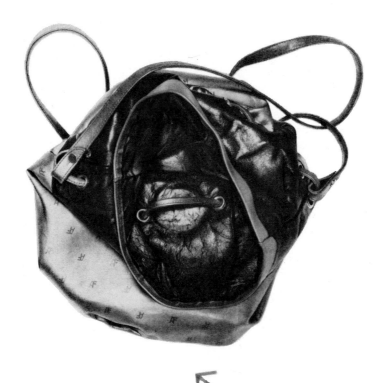

Appel

Fig. 2

It's late and I'm looking up an emergency treatment for cystitis in a self-help manual called "Woman's Body." The index directs me to L 23. En route I catch a glimpse of a **hideous diagram**, keep going, then turn back, M4: The Process of Aging. What do I find so compelling about this graphic destruction of the **female figure** from age 0 to 80. I resist. She looks much too old for 50, obviously based on the down-to-earth-had-a-hard-life-and-glad-it's-over type. I will never look like that, or will I? Brutal, statistical fact, there it is. I am reducible to example d) **middle age** muscle strength and mental capabilities past their prime. So my son had a point asking me if I would still be able to play with him when I was 40. Though it could be worse, e) **fertility** ceases, and then f) **old age:** spine drops, hearing impaired, character changes and brain disorders possible. God, why go on. It's **already started**. Is it irreversible? Anne told me she could remember the exact day, hour even, when she became an older woman. One morning she woke up, looked down at her breasts and realized they had lost their independence. She was laying on her side, she emphasized the importance of her vantage point since it was in that very position she had previously observed two perfectly autonomous hemispheres defying the laws of gravity. That day, they sloped, no, she said slithered to the right as they surrendered to some imperious genetic signal saying "take a break." I asked how old she was, and had to laugh when **she said** 25. But now, reading in reverse I notice c) continuous loss of nerve cells from the age of 25, then b) peak of physical energy over at 12. Finally their optimistic introduction, "The **aging process** begins suprisingly early and efforts to slow it down are simply guesswork." **Organic, inevitable**, yet we are obsessed with avoiding it. Anne is right, women are not at one with nature, they are **at war with it**. The victor becomes a legend like so many aging film stars, forever "Fabulous and Forty-two"; meanwhile, the vanquished who refuse to dye their hair or just don't give a damn **become old bags**, or possibly old ladies if they smile.

Extase

The white dress is part of a plot to escape. From what I'm not quite sure, but all through the cold, dark and indifferent winter I have been planning it. Learned academic by day, and by night, secret reader of holiday brochures and eater of maple sugar candy, planning how the three of us would meet in Miami, happy family reunited - father, mother, child, against a backdrop of blue sky and pounding surf of course. I have told no one. Finally, the day arrives. I **pack** the suitcase **with devotion**, the way a bride would do her trousseau: no jeans, no boots, no leather jacket or coat of any kind and nothing black, only brightly colored blouses, loosely fitting trousers, shorts, halters, high-heeled shoes and all the jewelry I ever wanted to wear and didn't have a chance to. And the dress. I refuse to wear a coat even to the airport in **anticipation** of the happy **metamorphosis** that will inevitably take place when I emerge eight hours later. And it does. The air is hot and thick. I feel it soldering the bits and pieces of **my body** into something **tangible**, entire. I can be **seen**, imagine men are looking at me, even look at them sometimes. Soon, they arrive, seem much shorter, fatter, whiter than I had remembered, but it doesn't matter. **We are together**, I am glad. What's more, today is **Easter Sunday**. Naturally, I'm wearing the **white dress** - simple, silk, embroidered bodice, gathered at the waist, full skirt falling just below my knee, and thinking, thank god no one will see me, (I mean everyone is in New York), and wonder who am I wearing this for anyway. Not him, he doesn't notice and the prospect of negotiating Disneyland has already given him a headache. Then my angelic son tells everyone, "Look at my **Mommy**." The riddle solved. I am transported in a halo of fluorescent light to the land of "good-enough-mothers." The motel manager waves his magic wand and says, "Please come with me into the dining room where you will feast on champagne, strawberries and cream, the Seven Dwarfs will play the Brandenburg Concertos and I'm quite sure you will **live happily ever after**." And we do.

SUMMER 1984

Somer Brodribb

it's two years
the seagulls are circling today
and i will die with this desire
unmet
that's something i never counted on
deep hopes of reconciliation
awakened
and to die still wanting it
nice thought

14

Femalear Explorations: Temporality in Women's Writing*

Irma Garcia
translated by Eva Goliger Reisman

You confound the times with the times and the times remain confounded.[1]

The idea of time occupies a prominent place in literary works. The meaning attributed to it, however, varies greatly depending upon the frame of reference. Michel Butor writes:

> We must superimpose at least three kinds of time upon entering the territory of the novel; the time-frame assigned to the characters' adventures; the time of the creative act; and the time of the reading.[2]

This definition gives rise to the following question: what happens to the three temporal dimensions in works written by women? Do they follow this outline? Even though it seems evident at first that these three very distinct phases apply to any kind of reading, regardless of which literary account it happens to be, we soon arrive at the conclusion that the nature of feminine writing does not lend itself to such a formulation. Butor's temporal complex does nothing to enrich our understanding, nor does it bring to light any basic factor of truth. The time assigned to the adventures taking place in a literary work is closely linked to the creative act because writing is in itself an adventure. As for the readers, we shall be discussing what happens when the challenge of reading makes them actually forget their time. Our intertextual method points in this direction as well.

On the whole, women's time is purely affective time, disrupting pre-established schemas and structures.

> A curious truth: outside time, with neither past nor future, neither true or false; suspended in empty space, it neither postulates nor judges. It refuses, displaces, breaks the symbolic order before it can re-establish itself all over again.[3]

* From *Proménade Femmilière: Recherches sur l'ecriture féminine* by Irma Garcia. Editions des Femmes, 1981 Paris. Excerpted and translated by Eva Goliger Reisman.

This dislocation of the order is especially noticeable on the temporal level. It is only by dismissing time that the heroine can assume an attitude of complete detachment. We must also note the emphasis on the notion of hollowness, which is achieved by negating the linear order. We shall see how this theme is extended and how it gets translated in woman's approach to time.

However, before beginning this study, we must ask ourselves a few preliminary questions: why does woman experience this need to readjust time? What is the reason for her attempt to confer new temporal dimensions on her writing? It seems that woman cannot be induced to accept the time structure imposed upon her when not a single free moment is left at her disposal. Time does not appear to be very favorable to women. Thus, we must take this antagonistic relationship as a starting point, and go on from there to analyze how woman represents time in her works.

We shall first examine feminine time in general, focusing on how the notions of past/present/future are interdependent and blend into each other. This will lead into a more specific examination of the everyday, the quotidian, with its fragmentation into separate, detached moments, which flow directly into the times outside of time. We are thus tracing a circular course: woman steps outside of time and in her writing creates the outside of time.

This perception, which permeates the novels, influencing even the syntax, gradually finds its way into the narrative as we shall attempt to point out subsequently.

Time the enemy

Not one of the women's works studied here gives a positive picture of time. In the social context, the interval between a woman's childhood and her accession to motherhood is very brief. This is one reason why she experiences the negative aspect of time so intensely. Only her childhood will have given her a taste of freedom. It is not long before she experiences the narrow confines of continuity imposed upon her by life in society. Woman quickly comes to understand that the temporal structure, congealed as it is in the realization of certain goals cannot be of any benefit to her, and that she runs the risk of being harmed by it.

Thus a number of the works will concern themselves primarily with time's negativity: in George Sand's *Lelia*, "the hour of freedom never sounds for her." Time does not bring about any improvement in the heroine's fortunes. Its passage erodes the characters, separates them from one another, drains them (cf. Virginia Woolf's *The Waves*). It stagnates listlessly as an inescapable old age draws near (cf. Marguerite Duras' *The Afternoon of Mr. Andesmas*); it disfigures woman's body with its blemishes, condemning her to finding herself gradually ignored, despised, and vulnerable as her beauty, the only token of recognition and integration, vanishes (cf. *Cheri* and *La fin de Cheri* by Colette).

Woman identifies time as a relentless enemy who offers her no way out. This is why she keeps denouncing it by assailing it directly, by putting up a dull resistance against it, or by assuming a totally detached attitude towards it, to the point of seeming to ignore it completely, often tinging this ignorance with humor. Time is an enemy who can hurt without one's being aware of it:

> It was the restless sleep of the night watchman continuously aware of the dangers and of the treacheries of time seeking to cheat her by permitting clocks to strike the passing hours when she was not awake to grasp their contents.[4]

It is a very violent attack as shown by the forcefulness of the words used, (*trahisons, tricheries*). Woman accuses time of not playing fair game with her life; she keeps herself on the defensive and constantly remains on her guard. The notion of chronological time is put into question. It is the living content of time that matters, not its measurement. Anais Nin emphasizes the total absurdity of measuring time.

This mistrust directed against time is based on its readiness to play tricks— (play tricks with a woman's body, with her life). We find this image again in another citation from Anais Nin's work:

> The hours were passing like ivory chess figures, hammering piano notes, and the minutes raced on wires mounted like puppets.[5]

The use of the word "hammer," and the reference to playing games makes time appear as a force which is both threatening and playful, a force which is also subject to being duped. She establishes the analogy by using the word "puppets," which suggests the manipulative action of marionette strings.

We might note how one of the ways to fight against time's clutches is to represent it in visual terms, to put it in concrete form. Woman makes use of all the chronological/temporal divisions in order to better be able to measure the distance between those guide marks and her own life. She refuses to accept these totally arbitrary divisions which keep her from living her life and which restrain her movements like a yoke around her neck. Woman asserts her total unwillingness to adapt to such structures:

> I do not know how to run minute to minute and hour to hour, solving them by some natural force until they make the whole and indivisible mass that you call life.[6]

Woman assails the very symbolism of the calendar which signifies to her the mutilation of her existence—an example of this struggle being what Julia Kristeva speaks of as the shattering of the symbolic order. Or note Virginia Woolf's passage below:

> "I have torn off the whole of May and June," said Susan, "and twenty days of July. I have torn them off and screwed them up so that they no longer exist, save as a weight in my side. They have been crippled days, like moths with shrivelled wings unable to fly."[7]

Woman thus affirms her refusal to accept time's linearity. She experiences herself as a stranger unable to follow this road which has been all mapped out for her. By denouncing the trespasses of objective time, she acquires a different sense of it, which is all her own. We shall see later how her awareness of the threat posed to her by this external reality, leads her to resist it by creating an interior time.

She continuously displays her mistrust when confronted with time-measuring instruments.

> Oh, do not attack me with your watch.
> A watch is always too fast or too slow.[8]

She seems to have a need for concrete, tactile objects that will make her feel more suited to this struggle against time. This is an important idea in that it will help us to better understand how she relates to objects and eventually to words. She needs physical, hand-to-hand combat.

This resistance woman puts up to time by means of the written word, is a laborious, difficult process for her. Her effort to bring time back within the framework of her interior dimensions frequently turns out to be a strenuous one. Nothing is given to women: they have to conquer everything, they have to learn everything. A number of passages illustrate this will to overcome the hostility inherent in time:

> My mother climbed too, mounting ceaselessly up the ladder of the hours, trying to possess the beginning of the beginning. ...[9]

The overlapping quest for the origin and that for identity represent a protracted struggle which is confirmed by what truly defines all feminine experience—the constant turning back to the point of inception.

Time never ceases to glide forward, ceases to retreat, always elusive, always tyrannical, as language can be. This return to the sources seems to be an endeavour enabling woman to undo the links in the temporal chain.

The redundancy and the repetitions in this quotation serve to underscore this patient, obstinate progress of time. As she climbs this feminine ladder, could a woman writer aim any higher than toward that region which she must explore "unceasingly," and which lies within the deepest recesses of her being? How can she possess time, how can she deceive its laws, if not by trying to bamboozle it, so that she can keep her stakes in the game?

Once in a while, however, time succeeds in imposing its law, by dramatically obstructing the narrative, and hindering its progress.

> Yes, but suddenly one hears a clock tick. We who had been immersed in this world become aware of another. It is painful. It was Neville who changed our time.[10]

Woman's interior rhythm which is under her personal control is set over against the rhythm of the universe, of the clock. It is a moment when both the author and the reader experience nothing but this crack, this shift. There is a feeling of defeat and frustration in this reminder as indicated by the little phrase, "It is painful," which expresses the author's displeasure in the face of the oppressive presence of a clock marking time so inexorably.

Sometimes, however, it can be a victorious struggle. Woman succeeds in imposing her own rhythm, in breaking through the course of time. She does not try to "play the game," she does not try to be conciliatory. To the hostility of Time she can only respond with an emphatic refusal:

> Just in front of me there was a splendid nettle in flower. Time seemed to be passing unendurably slowly. I leaned forward and on a sudden impulse broke off the nettle and crushed it in my hand. Why? To wring the neck as it were, of this endless stretch of time. It worked. I held it in my hand and it hurt very much.[11]

This passage established an analogy between time and the nettle .... The struggle which is based entirely on this correspondence obscures the metaphor; we no longer know whether it is the act of smothering the passage of time which is painful or the act of crushing the nettle. The association time/nettle comes quite naturally, the reaction is almost automatic, mechanical; reflection comes after the "why?." The use of pronouns in the last sentence upholds the analogy beyond the rules of co-reference. There is no doubt at all as to the victory shown in the use of the past definite, "it worked." The assertion is peremptory. Everything happens as if the sensation of pain caused by the nettle actually kept time suspended: "I broke off the nettle." The wish to make time into something concrete which can be grasped is brought into relief by the repetition of the phrase, "in my hand."

In the face of the hostility shown to her by time, woman can also adopt an attitude of total detachment which does not stop short of resignation.

> This event was taking root painfully in the arid stretch of the present, but it was necessary nevertheless that it should happen, and that the time it took should pass as well.[12]

In spite of the strength and the subterranean resistance contained in the root of that instant, time in the end imposes its law and pursues its inexorable course. The structure of the sentence accentuates this fateful progress by the heaviness of the noun clauses it uses. This pessismistic statement, however, appears in a very specific context: that of old age, which is a period of stagnation, of virtual immobility—a period when the scope of an individual's activities grows extremely narrow and when time's supremacy is beyond denial. It is a time of sterility as emphasized by the adjective, "arid."

We must attend to the special significance of this barrenness for woman. She can no longer try to be productive, try to enhance this time and bring life into it, for nothing is left. All endeavour fails. Old age leaves one nothing to grasp onto. Barrenness is the opposite of women's essential characteristic which is fecundity, woman's distinctive mark, and it stands in the way of the burgeoning of the written word.

Woman, however, can also display a total detachment, a profound unawareness when faced with the wrinkles of time. The following statement illustrates this attitude:

> Eleven o'clock ... There's no meaning in that. Eleven o'clock is full of eleven o'clock up to the rim of the glass.[13]

This somewhat tautological comment points to the absurdity of chronological time. Great precision involves a certain superficiality. The author uses the image of the glass, a quantifiable object, to bring into relief, through the idea of a glass filled with emptiness, her inability to put up with such a scenario, in response to which she can only think of making this simple, absurd statement.

Such indifference, which is a basic reaction to time's malevolence is even more pronounced in some works. In Virginia Woolf's *Orlando*, this detachment is apparent in the very construction of the narrative. The author does not pay attention to the temporal dimension of the events taking place in the novel. She jumps over different epochs, ignores temporality and passes over the temporal limits of human existence. The attitude, which is tinged with humor, sometimes gives occasion to phrases like the following:

> ... "Time passed" (here the exact amount could be indicated in brackets) and nothing whatever happened.[14]

On the one hand, the author does not deem it necessary to specify the length of time, just an allusion to it is enough. On the other hand, however, she intimates parenthetically that this time could be accounted for, even though she does not take the trouble of doing so. The only clue she gives are the quotation marks, signifying that woman does not take time into account and that she holds herself aloof from it. Thus she negates time twice, by her refusal to measure it and the hollow use of typographical marks.

This attitude does not mean, however, that woman rejects the reality of time; it is only the manner in which its priorities are marked out that she is unwilling to accept. It is as if she were making a feint at the inimical aspect of it, attempting meanwhile to give it new dimensions more suitable to her existence as a woman.

> An hour, once it lodges in the queer element of the human spirit, may be stretched to fifty or a hundred times its clock length; on the other hand, an hour may be accurately represented on the timepiece of the mind by one second.[15]

It is a matter of calling attention to her estrangement from the temporal laws and of giving voice to the incompatibility which exists between clock-time, and time as a living inner space. Another author, Colette, gives expression to this idea in more physical terms:

> Two or three hours are for me mere instants provided I remain relatively idle. At work however, time is as hard to chew as if it were made of coarse hunks of bread one might attempt to eat without anything to drink to help them go down—not even a drop of saliva.[16]

Woman's mistrust of time translates itself into a return to time as lived day by day which is an affective time providing fertile ground for the awakening of memories, for moments, islets of silence, expectation, times-outside-time. All these moments which women refuse to forget encrust themselves in memory which plays an essential role in the life and literature of women.

The Chronology of Memory

She lowers her eyelid and memories rise up into her face, which shapes itself into a rectangular smile.[17]

Generally speaking, woman uses her memory in order to break up the linearity of time. In the various narratives studied here, we find woman remembering, or more exactly, we follow her as she lets herself be carried on the current of the countless unruly and confused memories which inhabit her mind, and whose unfolding abides by the wayward and irregular rhythm of her memory. She constantly summons up the past in her writing, while her innermost self challenges time's passage.

Women's memory is like those antique sewing tables of long ago. They were equipped with secret drawers some of which have been shut for such a long time that there is no way to get them to open. They contain tangled skeins of yarn, hairpins sometimes, and dried flowers which are now no more than rose dust.[18]

As she rummages through these drawers woman acquires a sense of her existence and grasps the totality of her experience. Giving free rein to her stream of memories, she puts no pressure either upon herself or on her writing, and ignores the relentless past/present/future trilogy. Her ability to remember allows her to escape the constrictions of external time. In her attempt not to stifle her inner flow of time, she gives herself up freely to the workings of her memory which she maintains readily accessible as if it were some painstaking labor of her hands, allowing her being to expand in the intimacy of her own universe.

Among all her memories, woman gives preference to her childhood, a happy, free innocent period. George Sand devotes the greatest part of her autobiography to recalling this part of her life. Colette also summons up her earliest memories with great pleasure:

... that pet name of my earliest childhood reopened fountains of youth in me; I listened to bright fleeting memories plashing drop by drop.[19]

We find again the image which opened this section: the drawers, the springs of youth need to be rediscovered in order to seize time where it has been hidden, for it ensconces itself so deeply in woman's memory that it is never completely lost. This memory pervades the texts, occupying all the nooks and corners of the written page. The memory of impressions and sensations lends an airiness and an amplitude to the novels which outstrip the cramped reality of woman's actual temporal experience. Charged with the weight of memory, the narratives are constructed piece by piece, fragment by fragment. The stories of these narratives are made up of a succession of layers, making a jumble of chronological facts and clinging to every detail:

He began to search among the infinite series of impressions which time had laid down, leaf upon leaf, fold upon fold softly, incessantly upon his brain; among scents, sounds; voices, harsh, hollow, sweet; and light passing, and brooms tapping; and the wash and hush of the sea ...[20]

Remembered impressions burst forth in woman's universe, nestling everywhere, ready to spurt out at the sightest gesture. The subtle accumulation of nouns and adjectives which is found in the writings, and the various images invoked in them all serve to emphasize the glow of memory.

This intricate work, patiently executed "pleat by pleat and leaf by leaf," is illustrated to perfection by Virginia Woolf's novel, *The Waves*. The narrative which consists of long monologues projects the lives of six characters, whom we find so completely merged into one another at the outset that they seem as one. Their emergence as distinct individuals with their respective share of memory and experience will be accomplished by time—that dimension of it which, while being connected to affect and memory, is as remote from dream as it is from reality. The fact that past and present blend into one another indicates woman's refusal to yield to one in preference to the other. This attitude, as we shall find eventually, keeps the present moment from being crushed by the burden of the past and future, and allows her to derive more enjoyment from it.

But memory can also manifest itself as failure to remember, as Marguerite Duras puts it: "Oblivion is the true memory."[21] For woman can function as well without remembering. She leaves room for oblivion in the thicket of her memories, and remaining open to the existence of this blank space, she lets it stand. Too attentive to her subjectivity, too sincere, she is unable to divert the flow of her interior time from its course or to dam up the gaps in her memory; these are the secret drawers which don't open. It is a process in which everything flows spontaneously and without any constraints. The following passage from one of Colette's works might be entitled Remembering Oblivion:

> The sequel of her narrative is missing from memory. The blank is as complete as though I had at that moment been smitten with deafness. The fact was that, indifferent to "My Father's Daughter," I left my mother to draw forth from oblivion her beloved dead, while I remained dreaming of a scent and a picture she had evoked: the smell of the soft bricks of chocolate and the hollow flowers that bloomed beneath the paws of the vagrant cat.[22]

The grown woman's memory goes zigzagging along the drift-path of the child's attention as it wanders off into some familiar landcape of images and scents. Colette makes use of the same device as Virginia Woolf. She works with units of evocative words placed side by side with no apparent connection between them, and brushes them on with light strokes. Thus, the half-forgotten scene is conveyed by evoking this failure of the child's memory. It is interesting to note that when the child forgets, it is the mother—woman—who is charged with attending to the task of "rescuing from oblivion." The discourse is completely disrupted, deflected from its course by this "violent break," which splits memory into two.

Oblivion generates a certain kind of freedom which liberates the act of writing. As in the case of most of Marguerite Duras' characters, it can reach the point where they put themselves out of touch with time and cut themselves off from it completely.

"It's been two years since she arrived at my house, one night. Alissa was eighteen," Max Thor said. "In this room," Stein said slowly, "In this room, Alissa is ageless."[23]

But memories may sometimes emerge without warning; they rise up slowly like an awakening, a sudden awareness. States of mind which are a prelude to specific recollections unfold in a domain fluctuating between consciousness and the unconscious:

Michel awoke with his mind a blank, light-hearted except for some vague, un-defined worry which was flying toward him from a great distance.[24]

For memory can also be like a bed of needles, where a preoccupation has the effect on a protagonist of so many pin pricks. Colette excels at depicting the action of memory—its fluidity, its imprecision; characteristics which surface as the text develops.

Before I wake up, before the lucid moment of remembering, there is a confused whirl in my mind, in which shreds of dreams mingle with a hazy reality; my whole being defends itself to *know* Jean is gone. This very struggle and the pitiful unconscious movement I make to huddle myself together and hide in the hollow of the bed, only bring back more clearly the memory of everything.[25]

By withdrawing into herself, woman summons up the memory graven within the innermost recesses of her being. And even if that memory is painful and distressing, she cannot thrust it aside because it is part of her very essence. Her writing searches the depth of her unconscious with undaunted honesty. Verbs such as "huddle myself together," and "hide in the hollow of the bed," suggest the idea of the hollow. She adopts this attitude in self-defense, but: "A woman is her memory. She has been marked."[26] Her perception of time, which is always linked to her past life, defines and determines woman's circular movement. Not seeking to attain any particular goal, she keeps making a circle and returning to her inner self. This notion of the return to the origins has already been addressed and we find it here as a constant, a characteristic of woman.

Although not establishing any limits, the expanding universe which unfolds in women's fiction nevertheless preserves its own coherence. Women's writing unfolds and develops in a dimension of time which is hazy, has no continuity and is kept open-ended by recourse to memory:

"One writes all the time, one has a sort of room within, a shady place, where the whole of living experience gets stored up, accumulated."[27]

The anonymity of the impersonal pronoun conceals the twofold dynamic of a woman's nature: a vessel that empties and replenishes itself. The more she stores up of life experience, the more richness she can pour forth and impart to us in her writing.

The chronology of memory is thus a journey, a flight. Its random quality is essential to our understanding of how women approach time. Memory supports a whole network of resonances of hollows and of to-and-fro activity, which permeate all feminine works of fiction. It is how woman affirms her existence, how she "takes her time."

I listen to her memory as it sets itself in motion, grasping onto the hollow shapes which it juxtaposes side by side, as if in a game with rules that have been lost.[28]

Light and subtle, memory thus plays a dominant rôle in the creation of a feminine writing. This writing, in its use of recollections, repetitions, echoes and redundancies, which shape its syntax and the construction of the narrative, is like a mirror image of memory. It helps the writer to remember by bringing her memories out of the shadow.

Driven by this desire not to let anything escape her, woman makes her way cautiously, imperceptibly, constantly retracing her steps, while the themes of her works, as they move beyond each author's individual personality, resonate with each other, echo one another, and intermingle. This further validates our intertextual approach to them.

Women progress along a circular path: by always being attuned to themselves, they redefine time as an intimate, affective dimension, which follows the rhythm of memory:

I would have to write backwards, retrace my steps constantly to catch the echoes and the overtones.[29]

Through the prism of memory, the temporal dimension of writing takes form before our eyes, forever revolving around itself, coiled around the lines. It comes forward, spreading into ever-widening circles of memories surfacing in our consciousness. The time of the written word winds itself around the protagonists, creating for them as well as for the reader a new script to follow.

In one of her short stores, Geneviève Serreau traces by means of a skeletal dialogue, the wide gaps between memories. With words that render its sinuousities, she fills out that void of remembrance, where a woman's childhood lies dormant:

It was a long while ago, it was the summer when, a long time ago, having returned, her head spinning, her heart frozen, a clump of formless memories afloat in her, like a surging of murky waters.[30]

Certain phrases suggest the perpetual turning backwards of this slanted progression, whose aim it is to keep out of the way of time's erosion. These sentences seem constructed like a chain whose links are closely set into one another. In order not to leave any room for time's gnawing at the body, the sentence freezes, its texture is condensed. Words reverberate, echo and mirror one another, return each other's meanings.

At her back the window was open, for it was a mild night; a calm night; when the moon seemed muffled.[31]

The sentence stagnates a little, unwinds itself like a scarf that has been folded for too long. It seems to defy the too rapid passage of time during the night. This quotation shows the woman writer hard at work, as she reduces her creation to the smallest possible scale, the smallest unit of meaning. The repetition of the word "night," makes the whole sentence resonate; all echoes become muted by the smothered sound of the verbal adjective, "muffled."

A bit further on, we find the same method being employed to describe a landscape, except that temporal symbols are used. We might note that the writer here is relying on the effect produced by adjectives, especially the adjective, "quiet." This could be because the semantic content of this word is enhanced by its phonic value:

> Quiet at midday, except when the hunt scatters across it; quiet in the afternoon, save for the drifting sheep; at night the moor is perfectly quiet.[32]

We clearly see the outline of a day in three stages: noon, the end of the day, and evening. This precision is somehow devoid of any animation, because life has been set aside by the dismissive allusion to the hunt and to the sheep. The exclusion of these elements is dryly indicated by the double use of the idea "except." It would seem that the strong emphasis on the notion of quiet contributes to eliminating the existence of time. The adjective, "quiet" is connected to the notion of time, but its repetition breaks the rhythm of the day's forward progress, and lends it a sense of delay, of dawdling, which suggests a return to the origin, as if the adjective made time turn round and round. The sentence finds itself unreeled completely in its last part, while the equilibrium of its syntax is restored by the presence of the present tense. It ends with the same adjective with which it began, and turns on itself, thus closing the loop. This phrase is a good example of the rambling path writing takes, even when it applies itself to express temporal data.

However, it must be firmly kept in mind that when we speak of woman returning to her point of departure, it does not mean that she makes the same journey, only in the opposite direction. Each return is a way of outwitting time. It is not a regression. To look back on oneself involves an inward movement, a process of memory, but it does not imply retreat or breathlessness.

When woman writes, she summons up all her life experience. This is why her time is so slow. Even if she does not move forward, she makes progress nevertheless in her quest for an inner temporal dimension which includes memory. The time of the written word is multifaceted and it radiates in every direction. Memory intervenes and jumbles up the tracks. It dislocates the linear train of thought by interspersing it with myriad recollections and puncturing it with holes of oblivion.

Sometimes, woman calls upon the reader's memory, forcing her to turn back, to retrace her steps along a path that has become too comfortable, and upsetting the routine she has become accustomed to. Thus, Carson McCullers in one of her novels stirs up a memory, without specifying it, but arousing a passing echo in us as we read on. In an early passage, we read:

> Always she had a stuffed hard-boiled egg, and she would hold it in her hand, mashing the yellow with her thumb so that the print of her finger was left there.[33]

It is a minor detail which might escape the reader's attention. But a little further on, she takes up this idea again, causing us to reread in an attempt to locate and isolate the earlier lines:

> Harry held his stuffed egg and mashed the yellow with his thumb. What did that make her remember? She heard herself breathe.[34]

Recall takes place as we see a previously made gesture being repeated, and as we recognize the same signifiers, but without knowing too clearly what it is that we are being reminded of. The reader's memory hangs on a question; the author registers a pause. The heroine's listening to herself as she breathes invites us to return to an inner temporal dimension, a biological rhythm. This tiny and seemingly insignificant observation isolated in the narrative suggests the presence of time and stirs our memory. All our impressions blend in this fusion between the time of the reader and the time of the writer. As the thumb leaves its mark on the egg, it also leaves an imprint on our memory. It is through this kind of detail that woman succeeds in challenging the reader.

The very construction of certain novels is characterized by this circularity of memory. When this is the case, the reader finds herself forcibly thrown back to the beginning of the narrative, as the outset of the time of reading becomes merged with the outset of the time of writing, which itself originates in the body of the woman writer in quest of her identity.

For example, a novel by Marguerite Duras opens with a murder of a woman by a man. It is a common crime of passion and constitutes nothing more than a vulgar newspaper item, except that it brings about the meeting of another man and another woman, and the beginning of a love affair between them. This is how the narrative ends:

> "What a minute," he said, "and we'll be able to." Anne Desbaresdes waited a minute, then she tried to stand up. She succeeded in getting to her feet .... She stood there. "I wish you were dead," Chauvin said. "I am," Anne Desbaresdes said .... She found herself moving forward again into the fiery red rays, which signified the end of that particular day.[35]

Two levels of reading this novel must command our attention. On the one hand, it is the level given to us by the narrative itself: in this passage, the tense of the verbs indicates recognition of the minute requested by Anne Desbaresdes: "... She tried to stand up. She succeeded in getting to her feet."* The minute passes in the interval of time indicated by these two phrases. Also, the temporal setting is very precise, very exact: "the end of that particular day." On the other hand, however, the remarks exchanged by the protagonists within these limits open up another temporal space which displaces reality. Why does she reply that she is dead already? The beginning scenes of the novel, which show a dead woman, surface at this point in a new light. We hear the entire novel reverberating as we become aware of this correspondence. It is necessary to point out, however, that we are not dealing here with a

---

* The original is in the *passé simple* which denotes an action in the past which has been terminated.

murder mystery: the ending does not offer us a final clue, there is no further elucidation. No resolution takes place, but just the opposite.

It is a fusion, a blending of all these facts, which establishes a closer correspondence among them. We are dealing with an echo which makes the narrative vibrate as it cleverly breaks up the passage of time through the agency of an amalgam of memories which flow over the bounds of the story proper. It is as if all this "were telling us something," something very difficult to communicate regardless of how much is said.

Thus, memory is for woman a subversive element which constantly upsets and overthrows the givens. It makes it possible to divert time from its course and to expand its dimensions. Reading women's works "refreshes our memory." This slightly colloquial expression corresponds to, and is well suited to decribing the moist and fluid quality of female imagination.

The time of the writing thus presents itself to us in the form of a perpetual back and forth motion, continuously disjointing the narrative and justifying many different and lengthy readings and re-readings of the same text:

> It happened once, it happens again, it comes back, it also happens in the future I believe.[36]

It is the motion of the hand hesitating on the page, groping, always proceeding to the next line. Writing done on the smallest and on the largest scale is encompassed within the time it takes this hand to move.

> This tiny little back and forth motion of my forearm on the page stretches the velvet, polishes the silk, wears away the wool as well as my being.[37]

This time of the woman writer listening to her inner voice is a time requiring meticulous care and patience; impossible to define or control. The texts which accumulate are endowed with an indisputable unity and cohesion, even if the labor devoted to them is difficult and sometimes suffocating.

The cautious advance carried out to the rhythm of the writer's moving, memory-filled hand results in yet another form of expression: repetition. This means that the resonances tearing down the casing in which time and the narrative itself are enclosed will find themselves translated by the reappearance of the same group of sentences, by the repetition of whole paragraphs, so that we will be under the impression that the narrative does not move forward. And the result of these repetitions will be to constantly force us to turn back to earlier passages of the text in a way that has nothing to do with moving forward.

The play of memory causes such resonances in certain narratives as to completely break up the linear chronology of time as well as that of the story. The memories evoked, the repetitions, the reappearances of the same words all concur in creating a new rhythm, a slow and circular motion which bears resemblance to that of woman. Through the constant use of these references to earlier times, woman dislocates the narrative, thus lending it a new dimension, and spurring us on to read the texts again.

One of the writers to have used this technique extensively was Gertrude Stein, who thus discovered a very personal method of handling the time of writing. Certain of her narratives are constructed in a circle around a central core represented by a sentence. In *Three Lives*, for example, she tells the story of three women. "Brave Anna" is centered around the following statement of failure: "It was the only romance Anna ever knew." And in "Melanctha" everything is organized as a function of an unshakeable obsession: "She thought that she would kill herself, it was best." The whole text reverberates with this sentence, which gives it its rhythm, its voice, its color. These constructions abound in numerous repetitions, even if Stein often denies their existence. When we look closely, however, we can readily see that they are not carbon copies of each other; instead, their content is slightly altered, producing a hardly perceptible semantic displacement. It seems as if the narrative moves forward very slowly, almost as if it did not progress at all. It is important to obliterate all motion, to conceal external time in order to better be able to listen to interior time.

And at last, our eyes fasten on these lines, our memory is permanently involved as we read. This play of repetitions creates the time of writing. With the assistance of memory, time is manipulated, reshaped and profoundly adjusted.

Everything depends on progressive shifts, on slight changes, on the effects of intensity, insistence, and displacement that modulate these "word packets" and these paragraphs for as long as it is necessary for the thing to get itself written. By adopting this technique, Stein lets time come to her, lets it enter her writing. She makes constant use of it as a method of achieving new and greater depth.

It is by this means that the novel achieves an entirely original structure. The author makes her protagonists richly alive by continuously reiterating certain traits of their personalities. In "Brave Anna," the observation: "With Anna when things had to come they came always sharp and short."[38] Is repeated like an echo brought back to memory a bit further on: "As always with Anna when a thing had to come it came very short and sharp."[39]

Nothing seems to have moved. Every word has been faithfully used again. But we notice a slight shift in the syntactic structure; "always" is placed at the beginning of the sentence, indicating a certain insistence and calling upon our memory. The turn of phrase is heavier, more stress is laid on it as if the passage of time had become a bit more oppressive, as if it had surreptitiously become encrusted in the body of the protagonist, who nevertheless preserves a certain coherence. The displacement, the nuances are hardly perceptible, but it is this difference between the two parallel sentences, which illustrates something of the processes of memory and the inner workings of time.

Another example from the novel illustrates equally well this writing device proceeding directly from woman's perception of time. The analysis will bear here not on a single sentence but on a whole paragraph, because when viewed on a somewhat larger scale, the corpus becomes more significant and the techniques are more easily discernible. It is useful to note that the author makes us aware of the presence of time by evoking everyday gestures as well as concerns which are quite feminine.

> Mrs. Lehntmann in her work loved best to deliver young girls who were in trouble. She would take these into her own house and care for them in secret, till they could guiltlessly go home or back to work, and then slowly pay her the money for their care.[40]

> Mrs. Lehntmann always loved best in her work to deliver young girls who were in trouble. She would keep them in her house until they could go to their homes or to their work, and slowly pay her back the money for their care.[41]

When juxtaposing these two passages, we notice the repetition of syntagmatic groups, specifically at the beginning and at the end. In the second case, "in her work" and "for their care" are reinserted into a more compressed syntactic structure. This is also true of "go home or back to work" as compared with "go to their homes or to their work."

However, when observing these passages more closely and comparing them word by word, we notice that two essential elements have been suppressed from the second quote: secrecy and innocence. It would seem that the affective content, the content pertaining to sentiment has vanished, that it has been eradicated and deliberately omitted. This woman's preferred occupation has come little by little to bear the marks of a certain weariness, a certain unforeseen monotony, even if it continues to be the preferred activity. From as far back as we can remember, everything has remained the same. However, a foe begins to make himself felt—a foe who is no other than time itself. The young girls have become older, they have grown to be young women. ... The writing narrows its rings around time in an attempt to hold it captive, but time performs its task. The rings close in and keep a tight grip on the shreds of memory.

For in spite of women's mastery of the craft of writing and their ability to keep their life experience and their memories flowing along the pages, memory also serves to remind us of the passage of time. The wish to include everything within its limits leads sometimes to very compressed sentences:

> Then slowly between them, it began to be all different. Slowly now between them, it was Melanctha Herbert who was stronger. Slowly now they began to drift apart from each other.[42]

The repetition at the beginning of the three sentences of the adverb "slowly" makes them unwind like spirals. The slow recurrence is like a return to the point of departure, similar to what we have already found above. But the rift deepens in spite of this excessive caution. This rift is shown by the contrast between the phrases "between them" and "from each other." The use of the verb "begin," when it is all over between the two women, reveals in addition the ambiguity that woman possesses in her attitude toward the notions of beginning and end. Again everything merges.

We have been discussing these words in order to illustrate how even the form of writing is influenced by the processes of memory (the memory of the writer as well as that of the reader). However, in our wish not to forget our commitment to intertextual study, let us now turn to another narrative by a different author, who achieves a similar effect. In this passage, the words, or more exactly, the metaphor of a house as a living being persists throughout the story. Although the image itself is somewhat flat, the metaphor confers a highly dramatic intensity on the narrative.

By singling out all these sentences which echo one another, we discover the progression, the framework of the narrative. The author makes use of the same words, but she makes them swell with increasing importance as the story unfolds. Thus we perceive the passage of time not through changes wrought by it, but because it is filled, packed with all the elements of a life being lived. The metaphor returns intermittently like an ocean wave, and like the wave, suggests an inner biological rhythm—the rhythm of the heart.

1.   "... the pulse of the house beats softly."
2.   "The doors go shutting far in the distance, gently knocking like the pulse of a heart.
3.   "... the heart of the house beats proudly."
4.   "... the pulse of the house beats wildly."[43]

Between quotation No. 1 and No. 4, how much time has elapsed! How much writing has gone into that interval! Cohesion is maintained, however, by means of the running metaphor—life at the basic level. The heart brings us to "pulse," which brings us to "beat." As we have noted previously, the sentences break off around a central core, which in this example is represented sometimes by the verb "beat," sometimes by the noun "pulse." The sentences are constructed simply with a regular and balanced rhythm, which makes for a smooth transition from one sentence complement to the next ("softly" and "wildly"), except that they are totally opposed in meaning.

The writing breaks off gently like a skein of yarn, while at the same time leisurely allowing each word to fully render the resonance, the subtle nuances, and the circumvolutions of memory.

We can better understand how all the women's texts which overlap and echo each other through time, bring our intertextual method into prominence. Woman is not afraid of repetition, because she knows that repetition reminds her of her history and of her life as she has experienced it. She knows herself to be inexhaustible and knows how to make use of time to her best advantage. It seems that her ability to retrace her steps and to constantly summon up her memories functions equally well at the level of the written word. The idea of a constant return to the past in order to achieve a better understanding of the present seemed of sufficient interest to us to merit lingering on, especially since memory often proves to be a subversive element insofar as it assists woman in expressing herself as woman in her writing:

Going back and forth between a lost past and the present, woman re-examines the images which have made her what she is; little by little, she rids herself of the mirages which have kept her desire captive; she strips herself of all the cheap finery which engulfed her, and which she had been led to believe was her attire.[44]

Thus, what we glimpse in discussing the chronology of memory is all the labor of reappropriation, of remodelling of time. This venture of exploration, the writing of turning back and of resonances is woman's.

However, having analyzed the relationship between woman and her past, we must address ourselves to the way in which she lives daily, how she inhabits time in her writing, what subdivisions she imposes on it, and what the rhythm of time is as she experiences it.

Having analyzed the relationship between woman and her past, Garcia goes on to discuss woman's relationship to the present and the quotidian. She divides this temporarily into four groups: **Journées** *(days);* **Attentes,** *(times of waiting);* **Instants** *(instants, moments);* **Hors-temps,** *(times-outside-time). Garcia's analysis of the last group follows:*

The "times-outside-time" are situated totally on the fringes of time, where silence treads. These moments are distinct from the other categories we have described, because they are timeless and form holes in the narrative. They are more diffuse, more nuanced. They seem more like interludes before time. Woman has a predilection for these blanks and these spaces in her writing. Instead of attempting to stop time in its course, she places it on an intangible borderline where she likes to take refuge. These *hors-temps* correspond to moments of recuperation in the narrative.

Thus in some works, the text is split open as it were, to leave room for the pure space in which breathing can be heard and which calls for a pause in the reading. This is the case in the following passage from Colette's *L'envers du Music-Hall.* The novel is an account of the dissipated lives of some young actresses, and of their world filled with noise, music, and commotion—a world devoted to the amusement and entertainment of other people. However, as if through an imperceptible slit, a lull slips into the center of this squealing universe full of chatter and laughter. Temporality spills out of its bounds like an ink blot. It becomes completely suspended in the course of this description:

> The five of them are seated on their high rush stools, well-behaved and busy with their work, as if they had at last attained the true goal of the day. This half-hour is theirs. And during this half-hour, they allow themselves the candid diversion of being cloistered young women sewing. Suddenly, they are quiet, as if lulled by a spell, and even shrill Anita no longer thinks about her "rights," and smiles mysteriously at a corner of the table-cloth embroidered in red. In spite of their open wraps, of their raised knees, of the insolent rouge blossoming on their cheeks, their backs are bent chastely, in the attitude of diligent seamstresses. And it is from the lips of the little Garcin woman, naked in her underpants, that a childish little song escapes involuntarily to the rhythm of her busy needle.[45]

This passage deserves our attention for more than one reason. These lines depict a world which is in complete contrast with the world dealt with in the rest of the narrative. It is a milieu of well-behaved, cloistered working-class, women—precisely the reverse of the ambience of free-thinking, flighty actresses conjured up by the rest of the story. The pause afforded them generates a fresh breath, a different life. It is a moment which comes directly from their existence as they experience it. How many upheavals in the lives of these women, how many smothered aspirations come into view in the course of this temporal respite!

At first they take possession of this restricted half-hour, they make it their own. Then they fall silent, words fade. The writing lightens, becomes airier. They detach themselves from the narrow limits of the narrative and break adrift. The text follows the thoughts of each of the women and radiates in several directions: one actress forgets, the other remembers. The distinctive marks of their social world, such as the make-up and the beaded underpants, become obliterated, as if they were incongruous in this new setting. A fine thread of continuity is maintained by the color red—the red of the table-cloth, the rouge blossoming on cheeks. The use of the word, "diversion" emphasizes this time as being separate from the rest, as being a moment of freedom detached from everything else and in which all wishes can surface. During this interval on the fringes of time, we may note two elements which hearken back to two aspects of time studied earlier—showing the consistency and cohesiveness of feminine temporality. On the one hand, we have the isotope of enchantment—"spell," "mysteriously," and on the other hand the return of memory suggested by the childhood song of the little Garcin woman. This song, bursting out of the silence, comes from the depth of the actress's being. The *hors-temps* has allowed this little bit of music to come her way. Prompted by the easy-going ambience, she begins to sing with the utmost spontaneity ("involuntarily").

These *hors-temps* can sometimes upset the course of an entire narrative by making it diverge into a different direction and by creating a gap in the story. In a novel by Marguerite Duras, for example, a temporal remark provoked by the behavior of a little boy, breaks up the dialogue between the mother and the piano teacher. Inserted into the conversation between the two women, this detail forces suspension of the reading; surprised by the sharp questioning cutting through the continuity of the exchange, the reader stops:

> "Madame Desbaresdes, what a stubborn little boy you have here," she said. "You don't have to tell me," she said. The child motionless, his eyes lowered, was the only one to remember that dusk had burst upon them. It made him shiver. "I told you the last time, I told you the time before that, I've told you a hundred times, are you sure you don't know what it means?"[46]

The very abrupt pause thus created by the writer goes unnoticed by the protagonists. It is situated outside the narrative and does not fit into its linear progression. The closed attitude of the child invites withdrawal into the inner self. The useless and repetitive nagging of the piano teacher contrasts with the soberness of the observation. Everywhere, time insinuates itself into words and conversations.

The "times-outside-time" are thus an important part of writing in its long period of gestation. They cause circular vibrations to recur throughout the story. It happens sometimes that the very form the writing takes, conforms to this method. Real time as shown in the tenses of the verbs is put in parentheses. Only some neutral words remain and are linked together with a certain monotony. The syntactic structure encourages these variations in time as shown in this passage from a short story by Virginia Woolf, whose title "Monday or Tuesday" indicates the author's indifference to temporal gauge-marks:

> Desiring truth, awaiting it, laboriously distilling a few words, for ever desiring—(a cry starts to the left, another to the right. Wheels strike divergently. Omnibuses conglomerate in conflict)—for ever desiring—(the clock asseverates with twelve distinct strokes that it is midday; light sheds gold scales; children swarm)—for ever desiring truth.[47]

This excerpt illustrates the presence of an *hors-temps* within the body of the writing. Thus, all the elements related to the outside—the town, the time of day, some children—are systematically set aside by the author who puts them in parentheses; the grammatical definition of this punctuation mark being that it "gives a secondary importance to the term thus being enclosed."

The *hors-temps* concur sometimes in lending to the texts the repetitive, cut-out patterns of lace. These temporal cracks often manifest themselves as silence, an important element in women's universe. These times of silence situated outside of the plot, can be found as far back as in the writings of George Sand, a prolific writer, rarely given to silence, usually preferring to bifurcate her narrative in another direction.

> When he saw that Madame Delmare could only listen to him with an effort, he fell silent, and all that could be heard were the thousand little voices chattering inside the burning wood: the plaintive song of the fire-log dilated by heat, the crackling of the tree-bark as it contracts before bursting into fragments, and those light phosphorescent explosions of sapwood shooting up a bluish flame.[48]

The conversation is suspended. The action slows down completely and is set aside for the sake of this empty moment. The contours of this *hors-temps* swell out by the fireside, and the reader pauses. This suspended motion begins with the moment the man has decided to fall silent. The reason, the motive for his silence is the woman, who is the main character. It is interesting to note that silence is represented by the use of syntactic relations referring to all the sounds, some lower, some louder, which are described ("a thousand little voices," "songs," "cracklings," "burst out," "light explosions"). This antinonic device brings into relief the numerous possibilities of expressing silence which suggest themselves to woman. This moment allows us to hear sounds so familiar to us that we no longer hear them. It is the amplification of those sounds and their differentiation through the use of adjectives which makes us aware of the weightiness of silence.

The delight that woman experiences in insisting on these *hors-temps* which she can manipulate at will, is perfectly understandable; she alone can make decisions about how long each of them will last, she can assign to them her own scenario.

> I was in no great hurry to answer, and I protracted the silence somewhat deliberately perhaps, for I moved at ease in it.[49]

They have their own shape and organization and they conform to woman's needs. She sinks into them, and this enables her to find a certain strength. She takes refuge in them, her body curled up in a rounded, almost fetal position: "She straightened, calmly raised herself up out of her silence."[50]

In order to be conveyed successfully, these *hors-temps* require a great deal of attention on the part of the writer. With stubborn honesty, she disassembles, takes apart piece by piece this strenuous encounter with time:

> What I am speaking about are moments where nothing happens, the nothing we have called an interval. But what was this interval like? It was the enormous flower opening up, swelling with its own being, the sight of it all wide and trembling. What I looked at would solidify under my eyes and become mine—but not permanently: if I pressed it between my hands, it would liquify again in my fingers like a clot of blood. And if time did not become completely liquid, it was only because, in order that I might be able to pluck the things with my hands, these things had to congeal like clumps of fruit.[51]

This passage reveals the author's wish to define these moments "where nothing happens," as she does not hesitate to admit at the start. She shares with us, with the help of words, her groping quiet which aims at driving from under cover and out of every corner what she is attempting to convey. Having denounced the emptiness of time and its blank intervals, she tries to clothe them, give them depth, give them life. In order to do that, she gives materiality to time: in the literal meaning of the word, she grasps it, makes it concrete (accumulation of redundancies: "between my hands," "between my fingers," "with my hands"). The worn metaphor of time as liquid finds itself inverted, turned upside down somehow (the notion of reverse motion is already familiar to us). Time no longer flows but becomes sticky in a woman's hands like clumps of fruit. It has been mastered; it is a tactile object; it is in woman's service. We might also note how difficult it is to hold on to these blank spaces. Woman can never make them her own, but she must simply snatch them up when the occasion presents itself, and a sheet of paper is such an occasion.

This boldly executed meditation illustrates woman's struggle on the fringes of temporality—other struggles being the taking apart of the clock, and the upsetting of all temporal conventions. ....

The study of the concept of time advances research on women's writing. These *hors-temps* are moments of great peace and serenity. They are occasions when woman creates fluently and abundantly, in a manner that enables her to acquire an awareness of her inner world. For we must not forget that this is her goal. These moments induce in her a prolonged thrill of pleasure.

> My hands peacefully crossed over my knees, I was experiencing a feeling of timid and tender joy. It was almost nothing, like a wisp of straw quivering under the breeze. It was almost nothing, but I would then succeed in perceiving the infinitesimal stirring of my timidity.[52]

We see here the great richness and usefulness of the *hors-temps* in the woman's ability to gently glide from a "feeling of timid and tender joy" to an awareness of "my timidity." The shift from an adjective to a noun and from the indefinite article to the possessive shows the close connections between the quest for identity and the creation of a new, temporal scenario. All parts of this work are solidly interlaced........

In dotted outline, woman's prolonged quest takes form before our eyes. It is a quest for a literary form of expression that will bear the mark of a purely feminine time. The passages we have isolated could pass unnoticed in the course of a linear reading, but they strike the eye and attract attention upon a second reading, which is crucial in order to be able to grasp and to follow the trail of feminine thought. A rectilinear reading jumbles the tracks, shuts off the open spaces from view, and drowns these instants, keeping the writing from fully achieving its effect. These *hors-temps* are thus essential for gaining greater insight into women's texts. They also enable us to experience women's temporality and to listen to our silence........

An analysis of the novel sketched out by Virginia Woolf in her journal fully conveys the essence of woman's temporality, corroborating our lengthy discussion of the subject.

> Yet I am now and then haunted by some semi-mystic very profound life of a woman which shall all be told on one occasion; and time shall be utterly oblitered; future shall somehow blossom out of the past. One incident—say the fall of a flower—might contain it. My theory being that the actual event practically does not exist—nor time either.[53]

We arrive at the same conclusion when faced with this profusion of instants, this large body of conquered temporality. On the basis of the approach taken by all women, namely the neutralization of temporality and the amalgamation of the temporal linear chain, an approach which brings about the explosion and the valorization of the present instant, we infer and we affirm the total independence of women in the face of temporal constraints, at least on the level of the written word.

NOTES

1. Hélène Cixous, *La* (Paris: Gallimard, 1976), p. 159.
2. Michel Butor, *Essais sur le Roman* (Paris: Gallimard, Coll. "Idées" 1969).
3. Julia Kristeva, *About Chinese Women* trans. Anita Barrows (N. Y.: Urizen Books), p. 35.
4. Anais Nin, *A Spy in the House of Love* (Chicago: Swallow Press, 1959), p. 44.
5. Anais Nin, *The House of Incest*, in *Winter of Artifice, House of Incest* (London, Peter Owen), p. 199.
6. Virginia Woolf, *The Waves* (Harmondsworth: Penguin Books Ltd., 1975), p. 111.
7. Ibid., p. 45.
8. Jane Austen, *Mansfield Park* (New York: New American Library, 1964), p. 77.
9. Colette, *Break of Day*, trans. M. McLeod (N. Y.: Farrar Strauss, 1961), p. 26.
10. Virginia Woolf, *The Waves*, p. 235.
11. Marguerite Duras, *The Sailor from Gibraltar,* trans. Barbara Bray (New York: Grove Press, 1952), p. 216.
12. Marguerite Duras, *The Afternoon of Mr. Andesmas*, in *Four Novels by Marguerite Duras,* trans. Richard Seaver (New York: Grove Press, 1965), p. 274.
13. Clarice Lispector, *La Passion selon G. H.* (Paris: Editions des Femmes, 1978), p. 192.
   * Quotation translated by Eva Goliger Reisman.
14. Virginia Woolf, *Orlando* (New York: Harcourt Brace, 1928), p. 98.
15. Ibid., p. 98.

16. Colette, *L'etoile Vesper, Oeuvres completes*, Tome II (Paris: Flammarion, 1968), p. 856.*

17. Colette, *Nonoche* in *Les Vrilles de la Vigne* (Paris: Ferenczi Editeurs, 1978), p. 42.*

18. Marguerite Yourcenar, *Anexis suivi du Coup de grâce* (Paris: Gallimard, Coll. "Folio," 1978), p. 73.*

19. Colette, *Claudine Married*, trans. Antonia White (New York: Farrar Strauss and Cudahy, 1960), p. 177.

20. Virginia Woolf, *To the Lighthouse* (Harmondsworth: Penguin Books, 1964), p. 192.

21. Marguerite Duras, *Le Camion, Suivi d'entretien avec M. Porte* (Paris: Editions de Minuit, 1977), p. 107.*

22. Colette, "My Father's Daughter," in *My Mother's House* and *The Vagabond*, trans. Una Troubridge and Enid McLeod (Garden City: Farrar Strauss & Giroux, 1985), p. 50.

23. Marguerite Duras, *Détruire, dit-elle* (Paris: Edition de Minuit, 1969), p. 63.*

24. Colette, *Duo and Le toutonnier*, trans. Margaret Crossland (New York: The Bobbs Merill Co., 1974), p. 56.

25. Colette, *The Shackle*, trans. Antonia White (New York: Farrar Strauss & Giroux, 1976), p. 194.

26. Eugénie Lemoine Luccioni, *Partage des femmes* (Paris: Seuil, 1976), p. 159.*

27. Marguerite Duras, *Le camion* (Paris: Editions de Minuit, 1977), p. 107.*

28. Marguerite Duras, *Le ravissement de Lol V. Stein* (Paris: Gallimard, Coll. "Folio,"1976), p. 173.*

29. Anais Nin, *House of Incest* in *Winter of Artifice, House of Incest* (London: Peter Owen, 1974). p. 207.

30. Geneviève Serreau, *Ricerare, Rencontres* Paris: Denoël, 1973), p. 150.*

31. Virginia Woolf, *Jacob's Room* (Harmondsworth: Penguin Books, 1978), p. 124.

32. Ibid., p. 124.

33. Carson McCullers, *The Heart is a Lonely Hunter* (Boston: Houghton Mifflin, 1940), p. 185.

34. Ibid., p. 208.

35. Marguerite Duras, *Moderato cantabile* in *Four Novels by Marguerite Duras*, trans. Richard Seaver (New York: Grove Press, 1965), p. 140.

36. Marguerite Duras, *Les parleuses* (Paris: Editions de Minuit, 1974), p. 130.*

37. Colette, *L'etoile Vesper, Oeuvres completes* Tome III, (Paris: Flammarion, 1960), p. 892.*

38. Gertrude Stein, *Three Lives* (New York: Random House, 1969), p. 35.

39. Ibid., p. 43.

40. Ibid., p. 31.

41. Ibid., p. 52.

42. Ibid., pp. 106-107.

43. Virginia Woolf, "A Haunted House," in *A Haunted House and Other Stories* (Harmondsworth: Penguin Books, 1973), p. 11.

44. Marcelle Marini, *Territoires du feminin* (Paris: Editions de Minuit, 1971), p. 25.*

45. Colette, *L'envers du Music Hall, Oeuvres completes* Tome III (Paris: Flammarion, 1960), p. 19.*

46. Marguerite Duras, *Moderato Cantabile* (Paris: Editions de Minuit, Coll. "10/18," 1974), p. 10.*

47. Virginia Woolf, "Monday or Tuesday," in *A Haunted House*, p. 12.

48. George Sand, *Indiana* (Paris: Classique Garnier, 1969) p. 35.*

49. Colette, *La Naissance du Jour, Oeuvres Completes*, Tome II (Paris: Flammarion, 1960), p. 353.*

50. Marguerite Duras, *L'après-midi de M. Andesmas* (Paris: Gallimard, 1962), p. 83.*

51. Clarice Lispector, *La Passion selon G. H.* (Paris: Editions des Femmes, 1978), p. 134.*

52. Ibid., p. 198.

53. Virginia Woolf, *A Writer's Diary*, ed. Leonard Woolf (New York: Harcourt Brace Jovanovich, 1954), p. 101.

* Excerpt translated by Eva Goliger Reisman.

fore(e)telling

janice williamson

tea cups   rose budded   tip toward these lips   like ladies'
auxillary   local colour dreaming   back   through different
mothers   somewhere   a focal point   where memory upside down
deserves a reading   attentive   and tender   listen

(I)

in the year king george visited the brandon tarmac there is a
photograph   a woman wearing a diamond ring shaking his hand
remember   the ring prisms glitter at this late hour in front
of   these pages filled with the warmth of the king's glance
at my paternal grandmother   a woman of means and certain
ambition   at the right hand of my grandfather   lean   and
perhaps she finds him   too accommodating   his smile at the
king   not quite reverent   his bow   careful though
unconvinced   but it appears we embellish the record   the
photograph of my grandmother's   faye dunaway suit   feathered
hat   blowing in the flat out wind   nodding toward a floral
excess on the head of the squat woman beside the king   oh
the queen   though she remembers nothing of her garden
advising the grandaughter   without fail   marry a rich man

(II)

an identical prairie low flying through blue shattered
everywhere   and cloudless   where another grandmother's buggy
a half century before the breaking stroke   gathers speed
wraps body against the startling chill   this spinster
thirtiesh   turns toward a schoolhouse   lonely elevator
with some relief from an orphaned childhood   of housework
(motherless at birth)   of servile gratitude to foster home
of pubescent amnesia at the death of her sister   at fifteen
in childbirth   her sister   now nameless   (did she ever know
the love of her christian name?)   impregnated in her room
walls not even paper thin   blankets between her and the hired
hand   or   was it the step brother?   the foster father?   or
some animal come rippin into the loft   tearing through walls
the wool nightie   the thin membranes of my grandmother's mind
when she remembers to tell me this story   at 94   white hair
brilliant   claims not to remember the rest of her childhood
"did i do housework to put myself through normal school the
only thing i knew how to do?"   as though between that
midnight violation   and the turn toward the schoolhouse
burning in bitter cold   my grandmother's body stretches taut
in forgetting

15

Women's Time/Women and Time: Papers from the Agape Feminist Conference, Prali, Italy, July 1984

Translated by Caoran Sowton

The following are excerpts from the published proceedings of the Agape feminist conference in Italy in the summer of 1984. The theme of that year's gathering was Women's Time/Women and Time. The introduction to the material states:

"But why time? ... Which time and meaning what? Not enough simply to say that it was a suggestion made but not made explicit and not pursued at last year's conference; neither does it suffice simply to say that time, women's time, is part of the common ground and feeling reappearing so often in the female archipelago as object of research or the echo of an uneasiness in our concrete, living relation to very real times (bodily times, or the kind of time entailed in preserving life ...).

"These are reasons for the choice, but one must add that the subject of time is closely tied to many things we must deal with: excesses on our part, our tendency to deviate from our course, the communication of needs, the recovery of the traces of a mute daily reality, of signs of those desires which act in individual and collective imagination.

"Reflection on moments between women reveals how silence, or appeal to the incommunicability of experience, appeal to other forms of language, could be veiling something else, something deeper and less visible: possibly a fantasy in every woman regarding her own time; a fantasy of changing or annulling the past, resorting to 'a way out,' 'a secret road.'

"An intimate form of time, into which to retreat 'until one reaches a place not to be reached by others ... an internal time ... an enchanted time (therefore mythical, not historical) ... wrapped in silence, a time as unitary as the external time of women is splintered, as immobile as our external time is restless .... Intended solely for ourselves'. And if this were the case, why not try to voice this fantasy, render it visible and circulate it among ourselves?

"The contradiction between its being internal time, 'a way out' (silent by nature) and the breaking of this silence in order to recognize and abandon the intimate mechanisms of oppression—could we manage it together?

"A problematic conjecture, a risky choice."

Women's Fantasies of Time

The title of this report—proposed by the group—suggests that it is characteristic of women to establish a relationship with time which occurs on the plane of the "imagination" and not on that of reality. Reflecting on this, I asked myself whether there are and what are the ways of speaking about time—in the masculine or in the feminine voice—in an objective manner, one, that is, that does not involve the use of some form of fantasy.

The first image coming to mind is of measured time. Time of the clock and the calendar. A measurement of which, in the distant past, women were the instruments: the physical attribute, woman's cycle, analogous to the moon's action or the cycle of the earth with its natural phases of fertility and barrenness. Is it objective, this time proceeding from the measurement of cycles and seasons? Is a measurement of this sort imaginable unless accompanied by distinctions between "good" times and "bad" times, unless, in other words, one superimposes on quantitatively equal and indifferent segments of time images which besides being measurements of quantity are also evaluations of quality? Good times (of fertility, of the past) are times more full than others. In fact they are celebrated. It is imagined that they can be "forced" to return. A painting on the wall of the cave depicts a hunting scene. Why? It contains a memory of the past and a desire bearing on the future. Apparently it is only a record; in reality it is perhaps a propitiatory magic ritual saying, may this day return, not lost forever as might be believed from the objective movement of time away from that day towards death.

Side by side with measured time, time in quantities, there always exists a time in the mind: a representation, an invention which stops, reverses, reroutes that direction of time experienced by our bodies. To speak of time means to speak of these "desires" concerning it. We may think of the stories of Cronus and of Persephone as two ways in which this has occurred.

A particularly powerful fantasy exists, one we cannot escape measuring ourselves against: historical time. The myth meant to confer a form on the passing of decades and centuries in such a way as to convey homogeneity of meaning in the lives of millions of individual men who lived and died before us. A discussion that would lead us too far afield. But I do hope that during these days of our work here we will not forget that men's "fantasies" of time have included the possibility of thinking of collective past as history; that we will not let ourselves be deceived by the official idea that history is simply there with all the weight of facts (and, for women, with all the weight of the fact of their exclusion); that we remember that if history is visible, in whatever way, it is because the net of a "time fantasy" has been thrown over facts.

While on the subject, we might remind ourselves here of (at least) two myths of history which we will necessarily have encountered at some time in our lives. The idea that in historical time a plan or design is being fulfilled which will mark the end of time and liberate us from its tyranny; and the other idea, closer to us and more recent (not more than three centuries old), that historical time moves forward towards the better. The idea that the progression of time *is* the progress of man, that time can be made to yield profit and hence that the elapsing of time summons everyone to incessant activity, struggle and production. Men also began modelling personal *biography* on this fantasy. The chronology of the natural life cycle—development, maturation, decline—is replaced by the image of indefinite *growth*. Here is another keyword on which to reflect. Since the imposition of this image within our culture, there has been behind the question, "Who, what am I?", another: "Who, what am I becoming?". In the background are images of maturation (that is, of "good" growth) which call up concepts like *autonomy* which, in turn, signifies separation, power to "do without." To become adult in the masculine and in the feminine: how has this life experience of us all been imagined?

I know of no women who have fantasized history on a grand scale. They may appear, and before too long. I may be mistaken, but certainly I do not suggest limitation on our part, in saying that it has been and is a female quality to be more connected with, more knowledgeable in experiential time. Another great vein among "fantasies" of time: the idea that there is, let us say, an "interior," subjective way of experiencing time which belies "objective" images of time, historical and natural. Time exists, it is said, but it is a dimension of our subjectivity. To quote a famous passage: "The past is the present of our spirit turning toward what no longer is, the future is the present of our spirit turning toward what is not yet" (Augustine).

"Private" time comprises duration, quality and the impossibility of spacing past, present and future; "public" time is measurable, irreversible, has a direction and, according to many, proceeds by cause and effect.

In the present-day world this distinction is no longer as sharp. There is less certainty as to the way in which objective time can be represented and, since the days of Freud and Proust, more acknowledgement of interior time. Above all, perhaps, is the recognition that confidence in historical time has been shattered, whether confidence in historical time as completion, as progress, or as revolution. We catch sight of history as destruction, and it leaves us at a loss for possible myths; we discover how little accustomed we are to work with the idea of an end that is not a goal.

It is of "private" time that women have begun to speak. Writers, feminists, but also silent women who have spent (but not lost) their own time in transitory labors. Not able to make one time bear fruit in another, they have worked with hours and with days, defending the span of their lives—as *human* time—against the threat of its disappearance in a cycle of nature (fertility, sterility, which, as Lea Melandri says, have had "to render pain fruitful").

Women have produced a great deal in the first person. They have worked, especially in these last ten years, to make their own memories bear fruit. In this immense mass of discussion, with which many of us have come in contact, there is much speculation about time, fantasies which are critical modes of considering one's own life and therefore (why not?) conceiving also of history.

I have, with some dismay, dug back down into my years of work with women, retrieving fragments of speech which were in each case also exchanges in a dialogue pursued in the presence of other women. Fragments of personal history *entrusted* to the group sooner than to a plot of first ... then ..., a plot which was never wholly taking place. I was searching for "forms" that could unite faces and situations strewn along a time arc of only ten years—but with ten years being an immensity from such a point of view.

I propose four images, perhaps issuing principally from my present, but which I put side by side with four figures of women because they so present themselves to me today, proceeding from experience that assuredly is not mine alone.

The first regards the verb "to grow." It is a woman—in a workers' education program for the completion of elementary school—who says: "My mother saw me getting different from her, little by little—that's how the separation happened that makes you *different* and *against*."

The themes evoked by these words are: if to grow is to become autonomous and if to become autonomous means to separate, to close doors behind one, to abandon oneself and others, in what different ways do men and women do this? This woman would have liked to affirm her own difference *without* being in opposition. To experience a separation without struggle; a distance, a departure from the prior without its cancellation. A difficult undertaking. But is it true that it is impossible? Has it ever been seriously endeavored?

The second image concerns the permanence of the past in the present. Another woman says: "When I found myself speaking of my family I had to make a great effort of memory. Things I had in me and which I had regarded as put aside, I was suddenly still immersed in. The very situations—and feelings the same as I had when I was living those situations." Why can it seem that the past returns resembling the present? Perhaps because one cannot be said to have *chosen*. But to choose means, among other things, to abandon one thing for another. It is an act of separation based on negatives as well as on affirmatives. What, for women, is the experience of non-choice? An objective condition of coercion or, in addition, a reluctance to say "no?" Perhaps women know, from their contact with men, how limited is the truth of the heroic image of the man who "grows" by leaving behind him a past ordered according to the stages of his choice-making? Have not women themselves always paid the price of this image of history, individual or otherwise?

The third image is that of change as rebirth or awakening. Here the voices and faces become a crowd. I choose an archetypal character, the Sleeping Beauty of the fairytale, and an Englishwoman who, writing in 1653 the story of her own religious conversion, and having described a long series of "rebirths," concludes: "life, in short, is all a conversion." It seems as much an image of omnipotence ("one can be born again") as the last image was of impotence ("we cannot separate ourselves from our past"). In reality perhaps they are two consistent feelings. In the image of the awakening a person prefers losing the past altogether to having to consciously reject it or to effecting a struggle. Here, to change is not the result of a victorious effort which allows us to escape, but of the prodigal gesture with which one throws oneself away (I do not mean "sacrifices oneself," perhaps it is not precisely that) in order to receive the new. Certainly, to be reborn or to "awaken" seems a sign of passivity. The merit would seem to be the Prince's. But will it always be (certainly it has been and is) anathema to imagine change within, and perhaps only within relationship to others? Does becoming adult necessarily mean an always greater power to do without the other, the particular, actual other?

"When I think of the past I think not so much of what I have been, as of what I could have become and did not." This final image too is a kind of theory of history, and one to which I would apply a question: is it really inevitable that we read this remark as an expression of regret, resignation, defeat? To think of the past as a knot of possibilities unactualized—is that really so much more mortifying than to think of it as necessary cause, irreversible, logical premise of the present?

Gabriella Rossetti

Time and Women—Notes Towards a Discussion

My starting point is the contradiction which I live, between otherness and the will to thrive, between the reality of having a sex which is not the one represented and recognized in the world and the fact that I want to be present and to count in the world.*

I have noted about women that we often act as if time were endless before us. Thinking we will sooner or later attain to doing and being everything important to us.

In the end I saw that this delaying of things, especially things truly important, is a way of not confronting ourselves with reality. A way to want and not to want. Inside is terrible hesitation. There is, however, also its remedy through imagination: in a limitless time there is room for everything—understanding, creating, reading, traveling, loving, enjoying, seeing, meeting ... to the point where we find what we really want. What? We do not know, we do not say.

* This contradiction has been articulated in the green issue of *Sottosopra* (an Italian feminist journal); my starting point is therefore that issue.

At times the remedy abruptly ceases to work and we end in depression. Things become foreign and indifferent.

In working with women I have often noted their aversion to deadlines. The aversion to deadlines and, in general, to a reasonable position relative to time, is usually justified by saying that society imposes deadlines and times which do not answer to what a woman is. Appeal is made, therefore, to a female otherness. Women's deep and widespread experience. I think a "true" experience—as true as an experience can be, of course. An experience, that is, calling for meaning.

But here there is a problem, the manifestation of meaning. It is true that when a woman searches for social existence she finds herself placed in difficulties by ways and meanings which do not, or not completely, accord with her. This happens where time is concerned. The problem thus presents itself of inventing and affirming a different time. And this takes shape far from easily. Some women invoke slow rhythms and extendible deadlines of maximum elasticity; possibly appealing to such things as maternal production, nature, etc., without acknowledging that nature has deadlines entirely hard-and-fast—like the nine months of pregnancy, like eating, drinking, sleep.

But it does not seem that women are refractory to the deadlines imposed on them from outside, by nature, by children or by a husband's timetable. Rather, they rebel against, or I might say, obdurately resist being the ones to give themselves time limits. Resist, that is, rendering time significant in light of what *they* are and want.

It is the problem of taking on meaning. We remain in the obscure, hesitant to move from our hearts into the world of signs. It is a world hostile to the female sex's manifesting itself and starting to speak without disguise. In fact in that world we go disguised as "women" (women as women are imagined by men) or concealed behind our imitation of men. Often without really knowing what we want, and continually changing our plans.

We speak readily in commonplace circumstances and become almost mute when the question is of something touching us profoundly. We willingly allude to experiences of extraordinary richness, with respect to which language would be absolutely inadequate. We let ourselves be transported by the grandest fantasies and then, in practice, we content ourselves with little or nothing.

The facts, certain facts, seem to indicate that we prefer to guard our sex in silence. In this world there is only one sex present and represented, the male. Humankind is, in actuality, the male race.

Women, when they realize this, rebel against men. But sometimes they do so in a way that is rather a turning towards men, so that men may say and do what they, women, do not know how to say or do. For their recognition of themselves they ask of men.

But signs, as far as I know, are produced by the things themselves to which they appertain and can have no other source. Everything desiring to be present and represented must find in itself the strength and the reason to be so.

If I want something and I want to bring it about, this something must find a place in time and I must therefore reckon with time. The deadline is one confirmation, and there are others, of my being at the desired place.

Certainly the solution is not to be found in a time totally regulated by the human subject. That would be an obsessive time, a pure instrument of control, frequently destined to failure. Being connected with the world requires knowing how to harmonize different kinds of time. Things too have their times of being and not being.

Time is a sign of finitude; as such it is a negative which can become a positive. Whoever denies the negative, dreams or is deluded. Whoever keeps before her the negative only, is overwhelmed by depression or is sheltering in mediocrity (non-committalism). To live in contradiction is inevitably human and is humanly difficult.

I think of some women once full of life who are as if struck down now time has changed their bodies. At one stroke, fallen. Touched by a negative never converted into a positive.

I am aware that the measurement of time in our society does not correspond to our sensibility; suffice it to mention, as an example, the so-called free time of many housewives, and what it really is. I ask what to do to create correspondence and I see the obstacle of hesitancy, of a withdrawal into fantasies, of a fear perhaps. Many of our criticisms of male society are of small worth—they are actually eclipsing an internal contradiction which it is for us to resolve. Not individually—I do not believe that possible in general—but collectively, in relation to other women, to give ourselves strength, ideas and determination.

Luisa Muraro

Fragments from the Discussion

Gianna: In the green issue of *Sottosopra* strict alternatives are outlined: either pathetic losers or mutilated winners. That understanding of the choices is too narrow; in women's reality there is something else, there is more.

Luisa: I would very much like to believe that not all women find themselves bound to those alternatives. But the choice described does not classify women, it represents an interpretation of our present condition, arising from theoretical thinking: that we live an opposition between our otherness and our desire to win out. In our times, in this age of female liberation, there is powerful external and internal pressure upon women: to advance in freedom on the one hand, on the other to maintain a traditional female position. Women oscillate; this is seen in our lives. They waver because liberation gives and it also takes away—it is crippling and one returns to the traditional feminine, which, however, cannot satisfy.

If you say, but there is something else ... that to me seems reticence, retreat; an attempt to believe that female identity resides somewhere else, removed from the contradiction which we in the meanwhile experience. In short, a way of not confronting that contradiction, of not surmounting it. And to continue dreaming, for as long as possible, is to be always imagining a womanhood that exists elsewhere, imagining a time when we will possess such an identity. This means, then, projecting onto something that is in fact an evasion—the proof being the imminence of depression; women are seriously threatened with depression: as long as they believe that there is plenty of time, that there are many possibilities, as long as they have a small child, as long as ... as long as there is some kind of mobilization, some kind of exemption, all goes well. But then we have this thing ... our depression on the score of everything unrealized, everything displaced onto the imaginary and finally onto the night when we will no longer be able to imagine ourselves or to dream. The terrible danger is of our being crushed by a reality which does not belong to us, which has never engaged us.

Antonietta: The mistake has been made in the past of assigning all blame to the outside world; I hope we will not counter that mistake with another error, also typical of us, that of assuming all the fault ourselves. We should instead pursue, between these two poles—myself and the world—a rigorous analysis, for the attainment of a balance. Let us bear in mind how much responsibility rests with a world, the world of men, which has not simply expressed its own point of view, but has presented it as the only one, in a process of annihilation that weighs us down immeasurably.

As long as women said nothing, men did this unconsciously perhaps, not having interlocutors; but even now when women have begun to speak, men in reply still confer on us a meagre, often false image. In my own life I am continually constrained to re-explain myself, reiterate, reassert. It is a continual waste of my energies, this lack of real dialogue. They pretend to say yes, they are actually saying no, they say no and it is actually yes. These are constant traps.

In the *Notes*, as in *Sottosopra*, we find only denunciation of our own limitations: that discourse is impoverished, I feel ... a simplification.

Chiara: There is a part in the *Notes* which I would like to take up again: towards the end, where "obsessive" time is spoken of, we say that things for their part have a time. In speaking of time, we always have the contrast between an objective social time and a subjective invented time related to pleasure, and a clash of the two, or negotiation in defence of subjective time.

There are two ways of seeing time, I think. One is to see it as a huge reservoir where you put everything. Basing oneself on a subjective type of time, seen as a great reservoir where you place your desires, but also seen as the way to organize time, you run the risk of slipping into an obsessive time, into a compulsion to repeat time, a time organized systematically, even if in a personal way. The other possibility is to think of things as being there and of time as elastic and surrounding these things. As things exist, so exists the time

which surrounds them. And I would argue for this elastic time. A time of
things that are born and that die, not a time which I bestow, but one which I
always rediscover beyond the opposition between objective and subjective time.

Tina: In the *Notes* it is said that only one sex is present and represented,
and that humankind, according to representation, is male. I think this is
absolutely true. The female sex is an absence. This is confirmed by women
themselves. Also in our use of time. Women have always acted by using their
time for someone else. In a discussion a woman might say: I like writing
letters. And then she adds: because I know that they give pleasure to the
people receiving them.

For me too the need has arisen to harmonize different times, the internal
and the external, and to arrive at this new thing which Chiara has defined as
time belonging to things, "elastic" time. I don't know whether it can be
realized in practice but it could certainly be a starting point. I need to feel
that I am whole; fragmented time doesn't suit me.

For myself and for other women this is a question of our being at ease. So
this new effort will not mean representing myself in comparison with the
male. *I* do not want to demonstrate to men that we exist, that we know how
to adapt ourselves thoroughly to their times. And I am clear on another
thing: that in assuming this vision I am assuming a transformative outlook,
of continuous development, the changing of my point of view in the course
of time. This does not mean that every day I change: precisely because I am
able to change in the course of the day, I can also choose to change after
years. Today I said, a little laughingly, that if we adopt this point of view our
strength will be enormous, we could overcome death ... because it is an
organic time, time in which death is included.

Group papers

*Groups met to develop papers for the plenary; particular passages dealing
summarily with the question of time were chosen by each group as a starting-
point for discussion.*

Summary of the First Group

> On the train I thought of how the fields flying by, the curtains of trees, the houses, all the
> nooks, would serve to create memory, would make the past. As banal as the hour was, and
> it was boring, coming across it again one day would not be banal.

It seemed to us that we had chosen this passage because it contained implicitly
the two essential concepts of time: *time as space* (bound up with space,
representable only in space) and *time as history* or historicization, the valorization of a certain moment of being constituting part of the past. Moreover,
and not least important, the poetry of the passage suggests the concept of
time as affect, as the affective, having nothing to do with the time of the
calendar, of which it is the opposite. Our *history* and our *emotion* were

represented in *space* by a *design* which each of us made in her own way and with her own colours. Time: a master we endure; a spiral; a straight line laid out in the direction of progress; a line that declines and dies; time which defines us and in which our identities are inscribed, as unique persons and as human species, over the span of one life or over centuries. *Time-identity* is given by our body/mind which passes through time, somewhat active, somewhat passive, composed of a profusion of coexistent selves (in continuous transformation one into another, or stratified, never superseded or obliterated), selves determined through *choices* which do not signify loss or exclusion, but the journey towards a project, even if a mutable one. To make choices is to invest oneself with meaning in a way universally communicable, even if individually we are also defined, also represented by everything unchosen, by the non-chronological moments, the fragments, the possibilities never realized. To invest oneself with meaning is to represent oneself *as a woman*, giving other women authority as interlocutors; without this, every meaning of ours is personal and incomplete, has no historical "force." To have meaning in time, in the *present, immediately*, accepting deadlines, agreeing to divide one's entirety into parts, expressing them in turn, somewhat truncated, loving the substance which moves towards expression. Proposing to assume our meaning *in the future* puts reality at a distance, makes us dubious as to what we have in us, diminishes us. Deadlines are verification for us, they are empty form; not an obstacle when we love the matter to be expressed. It is because of its content, not because of its calendar that the external/male world is hard to endure. *Daily time*, then, shows the traces of our capacity to give ourselves meaning in the present: it will be a friend or an enemy, too expansive or quite possibly too restrictive, according to how we succeed at self-signification. For many of us demands still exist, the trap of doing things *for others*. For some women in the group, time of their own is time of solitude-freedom, or of *solitude-productivity*, useful time; for some women their own time is time *with others*. Varying requirements for self-determination in daily life, but with the common characteristic of demand for harmony, rhythm more than elasticity, and above all a space which we find favourable, in which to evince and express our desires and the threads which constitute our lives, because we have chosen them.

Reported by *Enrica Pessione*

Summary of the Second Group

> I explained to her that the present is understood from the past. That the past serves for this and the present serves for invention of the future as we wait for the present to end.
> She asked: "And the future?"
> I answered: "The future never comes."

We tried to open our way by talking about our perceptions of the future. Differences emerged immediately: some live as if the future were not there, some perceive it as the time to which to defer whatever has no place in the present, some construct future for themselves piece by piece, live in function of it, and some, conversely, feel it to be utopian time, when everything will be possible.

"You live as if the future were not there, because you're so young," one of us said to another. Explanation of the difference was sought in age.

Difficult to form comparisons among positions so dissimilar. The greatest danger was of abstraction. At this point we put some concrete questions to ourselves: "Have we ever experienced a time genuinely ours?", "Which time of the day do we feel is really ours?" The answers ranged: time on one's own, time devoted to oneself; time for reading or writing not for productivity's sake or with social motives, but to follow the thread leading one back to the deepest part of oneself; or the time of bodily love ....

By degrees, as we progressed in discussion, we grew aware that the contrast—proposed throughout the conference—between internal/immobile time in the imagination and external/active time was disappearing; we were confirming that it did not express reality for us, since in none of our answers concerning "our" time did we speak of immobility and fantasy only, but of actions too, journeys of search, "realities" to which we had given practical scope. Thus we felt this observation on the part of one of us to be conclusive: "My time is when I experience identification with what I am doing, when I am wholly in it ... when nightfall seems right."

Why, then, do we women produce these theories of dichotomy (internal/external time, nature/reason, silence/speech ...) or rather—men constructed them before us—why do we so often accept them and perpetuate them?

This question was not posed explicitly but it was there in the proceedings, and probably present in our pasts. In fact the points successively added to the discussion by various women—without much linearity perhaps but with the effect of remarkable enrichment—indicate that we were reaching down to the problem:

● "Women, when they tell of themselves, bestow fragments on each other; if this helps us to escape flatness it also impedes linearity of movement; we tend to replace linearity with what might be called stable assets (our internal time, for instance)."

● "There is risk that this inner/immobile time may be an alibi we construct to justify our incapacity to organize 'our' time."

● "'Incapacity' but also isolation, the isolation in which the women's movement has been left, the lack or ambiguity of answers to its demands for profound transformation."

● "Yes, but to project oneself, to come out of oneself, means to make history and to make history one must sever ties, 'separate from', and for women this is extremely difficult to do."

● "When I reconstitute my history, I am able to identify the stages of my journey, am able to sever moorings, and I have an idea of where I want to go; I can do the same when I reflect on the women's movement...."

Reported by *Antonietta Lelario*

PRO FEMINA: ONE, TWO, THREE*

Carolyn Kizer

One

From Sappho to myself, consider the fate of women.
How unwomanly to discuss it? Like a noose or an albatross
    necktie
The clinical sobriquet hangs us: cod-piece coveters.
Never mind these epithets; I myself have collected some
    honeys.
Juvenal set us apart in denouncing our vices
Which had grown, in part, from having been set apart:
Women abused their spouses, cuckolded them, even
    plotted
To poison them. Sensing, behind the violence of his
    manner—
"Think I'm crazy or drunk?"—his emotional stake in us,
As we forgive Strindberg and Nietzsche, we forgive all
    those
Who cannot forget us. We *are* hyenas. Yes, we admit it.

While men have politely debated free will, we have
    howled for it,
Howl still, pacing the centuries, tragedy heroines.
Some who sat quietly in the corner with their embroidery
Were Defarges, stabbing the wool with the names of their
    ancient
Oppressors, who ruled by the divine right of the male—
I'm impatient of interruptions! I'm aware there were
    millions
Of mutes for every Saint Joan or sainted Jane Austen,
Who, vague-eyed and acquiescent, worshipped God as a
    man.
I'm not concerned with those cabbageheads, not truly
    feminine
But neutered by labor. I mean real women, like *you*
    and like *me*.

Freed in fact, not in custom, lifted from furrow and
    scullery,
Not obliged, now, to be the pot for the annual chicken,
Have we begun to arrive in time? With our well-known
Respect for life because it hurts so much to come out
    with it;
Disdainful of "sovereignty," "national honor" and other
    abstractions;

We can say, like the ancient Chinese to successive waves of
 invaders,
"Relax, and let us absorb you. You can learn temperance
In a more temperate climate." Give us just a few decades
Of grace, to encourage the fine art of acquiescence
And we might save the race. Meanwhile, observe our
 creative chaos,
Flux, efflorescence—whatever you care to call it!

Two
I take as my theme, "The Independent Woman,"
Independent but maimed: observe the exigent neckties
Choking violet writers; the sad slacks of stipple-faced
 matrons;
Indigo intellectuals, crop-haired and callous-toed,
Cute spectacles, chewed cuticles, aced out by full-time
 beauties
In the race for a male. Retreating to drabness, bad manners
And sleeping with manuscripts. Forgive our transgressions
Of old gallantries as we hitch in chairs, light our own
 cigarettes,
Not expecting your care, having forfeited it by trying to
 get even.

But we need dependency, cosseting and well-treatment.
So do men sometimes. Why don't they admit it?
We will be cows for a while, because babies howl for us,
Be kittens or bitches, who want to eat grass now and then
For the sake of our health. But the role of pastoral heroine
Is not permanent, Jack. We want to get back to the meeting.

Knitting booties and brows, tartars or termagants, ancient
Fertility symbols, chained to our cycle, released
Only in part by devices of hygiene and personal daintiness,
Strapped into our girdles, held down, yet uplifted by man's
Ingenious constructions, holding coiffures in a breeze,
Hobbled and swathed in whimsey, tripping on feminine
Shoes with fool heels, losing our lipsticks, you, me,
In ephemeral stockings, clutching our handbags and
 packages.

Our masks, always in peril of smearing or cracking,
In need of continuous check in the mirror or silverware,
Keep us in thrall to ourselves, concerned with our surfaces.
Look at man's uniform drabness, his impersonal envelope!
Over chicken wrists or meek shoulders, a formal,
 hard-fibered assurance
The drape of the male is designed to achieve self-
 forgetfulness.

So, sister, forget yourself a few times and see where it gets
 you:
Up the creek, alone with your talent, sans everything else.
You can wait for the menopause, and catch up on your
 reading.
So primp, preen, prink, pluck and prize your flesh,
All posturings! All ravishment! All sensibility!
Meanwhile, have you used your mind today?
What pomegranate raised you from the dead,
Springing, full-grown, from your own head, Athena?

Three
I will speak about women of letters, for I'm in the racket.
Our biggest successes to date? Old maids to a woman.
And our saddest conspicuous failures? The married
 spinsters
On loan to the husbands they treated like surrogate fathers.
Think of that crew of self-pitiers, not-very-distant,
Who carried the torch for themselves and got first-degree
 burns
Or the sad sonneteers, toast-and-teasdales we loved at
 thirteen;
Middle-aged virgins seducing the puerile anthologists
Through lust-of-the-mind; barbiturate-drenched Camilles
With continuous periods, murmuring softly on sofas
When poetry wasn't a craft but a sickly effluvium,
The air thick with incense, musk, and emotional blackmail.

I suppose they reacted from an earlier womanly modesty
When too many girls were scabs to their stricken
 sisterhood,
Impugning our sex to stay in good with the men,
Commencing their insecure bluster. How they must have
 swaggered
When women themselves indorsed their own inferiority!
Vestals, vassals and vessels, rolled into several,
They took notes in rolling syllabics, in careful journals,
Aiming to please a posterity that despises them.
But we'll always have traitors who swear that a woman
 surrenders
Her Supreme Function, by equating Art with aggression
And failure with Femininity. Still, it's just as unfair
To equate Art with Femininity, like a prettily-packaged
 commodity
When we are the custodians of the world's best-kept
 secret:
Merely the private lives of one-half of humanity.

But even with masculine dominance, we mares and
    mistresses
Produced some sleek saboteuses, making their cracks
Which the porridge-brained males of the day were too
    thick to perceive,
Mistaking young hornets for perfectly harmless
    bumblebees.
Being thought innocuous rouses some women to frenzy;
They try to be ugly by aping the ways of the men
And succeed. Swearing, sucking cigars and scorching the
    bedspread,
Slopping straight shots, eyes blotted, vanity-blown
In the expectation of glory: *she writes like a man!*
This drives other women mad in a mist of chiffon
(one poetess draped her gauze over red flannels, a
    practical feminist).

But we're emerging from all that, more or less,
Except for some lady-like laggards and Quarterly
    priestesses
Who flog men for fun, and kick women to maim
    competition.
Now, if we struggle abnormally, we may almost seem
    normal;
If we submerge our self-pity in disciplined industry;
If we stand up and be hated, and swear not to sleep with
    editors;
If we regard ourselves formally, respecting our true
    limitations
Without making an unseemly show of trying to unfreeze
    our assets;
Keeping our heads and our pride while remaining
    unmarried;
And if wedded, kill guilt in its tracks when we stack up the
    dishes
And defect to the typewriter. And if mothers, believe in the
    luck of our children,
Whom we forbid to devour us, whom we shall not devour,
And the luck of our husbands and lovers, who keep
    free women.

About the Editor
and Contributors

THE EDITOR

Frieda Forman has been the Coordinator of the Women's Educational Resources Centre at The Ontario Institute for Studies in Education since 1976. Before that she taught Women's Studies and Philosophy at the Ontario College of Art. She is an activist in the peace movement, New Jewish Agenda and was a founding member of the Feminist Party of Canada.

THE CONTRIBUTORS

Caoran Sowton is a writer, editor and translator. She is associate editor of this volume and translator of the Proceedings from the Agape Women's Conference. She has worked on *La Pluma*, a multilingual journal of women's writing published in England.

Mary O'Brien is Professor of Sociology in Education at the Ontario Institute for Studies in Education. For over 20 years she was engaged in nursing, including the practice of midwifery in Scotland. She took her BA as a part-time student at Atkinson College and completed her graduate work in political science at York University. She was a founding member of the Feminist Party of Canada in 1979. Her publications include *The Politics of Reproduction* (Routledge & Kegan Paul, 1981) and *Reproducing the World* (Westview Press, forthcoming).

Robbie Pfeufer Kahn writes and teaches in sociology, women's studies and the humanities at Brandeis University. She was an activist in the childbirth movement for a number of years and a contributing author to the 1976 edition of *Our Bodies, Ourselves*. She has a chapter, "Taking our Maternal Bodies Back: *Our Bodies, Ourselves* and the Boston Women's Health Book Collective," appearing in *Women and Educational Change*, edited by Joyce Antler and Sari Biklen (Albany: State University of New York Press, forthcoming). She is the mother of a 15-year-old son.

Elizabeth Deeds Ermarth works on theoretical issues having to do with literary language and narrative; she has published a book on narrative temporality in English novels of the eighteenth and nineteenth centuries (*Realism*

199

and Consensus in the English Novel, Princeton, 1983) and is currently writing a book on contemporary anti-realist fiction and its anti-historical versions of temporality. She is also the author of *George Eliot* (G. K. Hall, 1985) and of articles on feminist issues, narrative theory, and George Eliot in *Nineteenth-Century Literature, Critical Inquiry, Novel, Studies in English Literature,* and in edited volumes, *Representation and Women* (English Institute Essays for 1981), and *Narrative* (Stratford-Upon-Avon Series). She is concurrently writing a volume for the Routledge (London) five-volume *Novel in History* under the general editorship of Gillian Beer. She has lectured on narrative and on feminist and narrative theory at various universities in this country and abroad.

Cheryl Walker is the author of *The Nightingale's Burden: Women Poets and American Culture Before 1900* (Indiana University Press, 1983). Her new book, *Masks Outrageous and Austere: The Intersection of Culture and Persona in Modern Women Poets*, investigates theoretical questions (such as women and time) as they emerge from the work of specific women poets like H. D.

Patricia Jagentowicz Mills is Assistant Professor of Philosophy, University of Massachusetts, Amherst. Her teaching and research are in the fields of social and political philosophy, and feminist theory. Her recent book, *Woman, Nature, and Psyche* (New Haven: Yale University Press, 1987) is a feminist analysis of the relationship between the domination of nature and the domination of woman rooted in the critical theory of Horkheimer, Marcuse, and Adorno. This description of her academic life is, however, only a palimpsest on which the goals and promises of the early women's liberation movement remain inscribed.

Marie-Luise Gaettens was born in Hamburg in the Federal Republic of Germany, where she studied History, English and Education. She then studied at Indiana University and at the University of Texas at Austin where she received her PhD in Comparative Literature. Her dissertation dealt with contemporary German women authors' reconstructions of Nationalsocialism. She currently teaches German and women's studies at Southern Methodist University in Dallas and researches issues relating to women and history.

Maïr Verthuy was born in Wales into a very left-wing family and educated, up to and including her undergraduate degree, in "segregated", i.e. female-only, institutions; she values all these influences very highly. She has studied in Britain, France, Canada and has travelled widely, meeting and working with women and women's groups across the world. She was the first principal of the Simone de Beauvoir Institute at Concordia University, where she teaches women's studies and French women's literature and, more recently, co-founder and director of the Centre de recherche et d'enseignement sur la francophonie des femmes at the same university. Her book on Jeanne Hyvrard (co-authored with Jennifer Waelti-Walters) has just been published.

Heide Göttner-Abendroth taught philosophy at the University of Munich for 10 years and has published numerous philosophical and scientific works. Since 1978 she has been deeply engaged in research on women, and has published many articles on feminist method, mythology, and the history of matriarchy. In 1986, she founded HAGIA—Academy and Coven for Critical Matriarchal Research and Living, a community dedicated to the exploration and practice of matriarchal culture and spirituality, where she now lives and works. She is the author of *The Goddess and Her Hero: Matriarchal Religions in Myths, Fairy-Tales, and Medieval Epics* (1980), *The Dancing Goddess: Principles of a Matriarchal Aesthetic* (1982), and a book of poems: *Landscapes from the Otherworld* (1983).

Lise Weil, editor of *Trivia: A Journal of Ideas* since 1982, spent this past year teaching in the Comparative Literature Department at Hamilton College in New York State. She is currently at work on a book called *Feminist Realism in Modern Fiction*.

Margaret Davis was born in 1951 and grew up in California and Kansas. She is currently living in South Bend, Indiana, having just received a BA in biology, and is planning to go to law school in the fall. As a feminist writer (she has had stories published in *Kalliope, Third Woman, and Analecta*), her goal is to write stories in which the woman does not "resolve" her problems through death, love or insanity.

Meg Fox is a feminist scholar with a doctorate in Renaissance English literature from the University of Toronto. Much of her political work has been directed towards changing the way in which women are viewed and used in the birth practices of our culture. This article grew out of her experiences of hundreds of births as a lay midwife, and from the births of her own three children.

Jerilyn Fisher is Assistant Dean for Adult Learning, Bloomfield College, New Jersey. She has previously published about feminist pedagogy and the returning student and is currently thinking about daughters who tell their mothers' stories in contemporary fiction. Jerilyn has two children, and lives with them and her husband in New Rochelle. She looks forward to the experience of running among 9,000 diverse women in the NYC mini-marathon every spring.

Mary Kelly's work, *Post-Partum Document* (1973-79), was widely shown in Britain, Europe and America and was published in 1983 by Routledge & Kegan Paul. She has been active in the women's movement through her teaching and writing as well as through her art and earlier film-making. She has been Artist-in-Residence at the University of Cambridge and is currently teaching at California Institute of the Arts.

Irma Garcia. Several attempts were made to obtain biographical information about Irma Garcia, without success.

Eva Goliger Reisman was born in Poland and is a survivor of the Holocaust. She is a writer and translator. She has been a reference librarian at Barnard College and is currently on the staff of Fairleigh Dickinson University Library. She has two daughters and lives in New York City.

The Agape Women's Conference was held in Prali, Italy, in 1984. It was organized by Caterina Erni with the participation of other feminists.

Index

THE ATHENE SERIES

An International Collection of Feminist Books

General Editors: Gloria Bowles, Renate Klein and Janice Raymond

Consulting Editor: Dale Spender